## DATE DUE

| | | | |
|---|---|---|---|
| | | | |
| | | | |
| | | | |
| | | | |
| | | | |
| | | | |
| | | | |
| | | | |
| | | | |
| | | | |
| | | | |
| | | | |
| | | | |
| | | | |
| | | | |
| | | | |
| | | | |
| | | | |
| GAYLORD | | | PRINTED IN U.S.A. |

SOUTHERN BIOGRAPHY SERIES

# James Lusk Alcorn

James Lusk Alcorn, about 1879.

# JAMES LUSK ALCORN

## Persistent Whig

✺

## LILLIAN A. PEREYRA

LOUISIANA STATE UNIVERSITY PRESS

1966

973.80924
P41j
57489
Mar. 1967

*To*
SEAT OF WISDOM

# Preface

SEVERAL YEARS AGO, in a seminar on Reconstruction, the late Professor Samuel Telfair of Fordham University, discussed possible research topics with his students. He named a number of Southerners who had been prominent during this period but about whom adequate biographies had never been written. Among them was James Lusk Alcorn, whose feud with Adelbert Ames over control of the Republican party in Mississippi seemed especially confusing to students of United States Reconstruction history.

Attracted by the idea of pioneering in an area where little or no work had been done, I chose to write a seminar paper on Alcorn. Research revealed a colorful and controversial figure who invited investigation if only in the hope of explaining the twists and turns of his career.

In many ways Alcorn proved to be a rich personality for the historian. From the time he migrated from Kentucky into Mississippi in 1844 until his death in his Delta mansion at Eagle's Nest in 1894, his life was part of the most turbulent period in his state's history. Those fifty years saw spectacular changes in every part of the American scene, and, as his sister remarked in 1851, Alcorn was not disposed to be "a silent auditor of the proceedings."

Not only was he an articulate and active participant in those changes, but more often than not he set himself against the prevailing current and thus stands out from his more conforming contemporaries. He joined the Whig party when it was at its apex, participated in its decline and the accompanying sectional strife, and, in common with many other Whigs, searched for a new political home in the 1850's. Yet he had become such a thorough Whig that he continued to personify the party's ideas long after the country as a whole had ceased looking toward it for political expression.

Civil war and Reconstruction presented challenges to which he reacted in his own distinctive manner. He fought for the Union until his state seceded, and then spent most of his time during the war defying both the Confederacy and the invading Federal army without compromising his standing as a loyal Southerner. After Appomattox he made his own capitulation, joined the Republican party, served as Reconstruction governor of his state, and then as United States Senator attempted to speak for both the Republican party and the South. Only in the last act of his career did he seem to move with the current by his participation in the Mississippi constitutional convention of 1890.

Part of Alcorn's attraction comes from a basic internal consistency which underlies the contradictions and ambiguities of his career and reflects a blending of typical nineteenth-century American traits, commendable and otherwise. He was self-reliant, adaptable to his environment and flexible in his methods, a man driving for wealth and status, a believer in white supremacy, and a practitioner of a pragmatic sort of idealism and a deep conservatism. His career is the story of the use of frontier tactics and frontier land to achieve a goal steeped in tradition: that of becoming a manorial lord. It represents a synthesis of the old and the new, the Hamiltonian and Jacksonian, the South and the West. Those common traits, displayed by an unusual personality over such a span of time and period of change, add up to a tale well worth telling.

An examination of Alcorn's activities also helps to deepen and to complicate prevalent historical views on some aspects of the past. In the rough, democratic frontier of the Yazoo-Mississippi Delta, Alcorn quickly became a member of an elite, and its Whiggish view of an aristocratic rule of intellect and wealth colored his entire career. In Alcorn the frontier produced an enterprising yet conservative leader who carried his early nineteenth-century views into the post-war world of Reconstruction and the New South with some degree of success.

No period of Alcorn's long career better qualifies as a vehicle for illuminating and clarifying a portion of the past than that dealing with Reconstruction. In spite of the trend toward reexamination of this period, the disconcerting role he played in Mississippi still raises embarrassing questions, and historians seem to have avoided Alcorn because he cannot be comfortably explained in terms of the generally accepted interpretation of Reconstruction as a regrettable episode in American history. He was an obviously loyal Southerner, a consistent supporter of the national Republican organization, and a good Reconstruction governor. A few years ago a Mississippi historian remarked that Alcorn's career was "still tender for controversy," and no doubt he was right. But it would appear that in line with current historiography the moment has come for this controversy to be faced and if possible resolved.

I am sure that some of the conclusions reached in this study would have brought flashes of anger to the piercing black eyes and a roar of disapproval in the booming voice of its subject. But true to his sense of reality, once mollified, Alcorn would have been willing to consider the new viewpoints and additional historical evidence which have come to light since his time. Perhaps he even could have been persuaded to agree with such historians of our time as C. Vann Woodward, John Hope Franklin, and Vernon Lane Wharton that there is much to be corrected and much more to be learned in connection with historical research on Reconstruction in the South.

# Acknowledgments

EVEN IF THERE were no other incentives to continue to pursue research, the helpful, friendly attitude of the guardians of archives and libraries along the researcher's trail makes one want to return. Among those who helped to lighten and add pleasure to the task of accumulating data I would like especially to mention Miss Charlotte Capers, Mrs. Carl Black, and Mrs. G. L. Grimes of the Mississippi Department of Archives and History at Jackson, Miss Anona Jenkins of the Carnegie Public Library at Clarksdale, Mississippi, and Dr. James W. Patton and Dr. Carolyn Wallace of the Library of the University of North Carolina at Chapel Hill, and also the ever-kindly people who watch over historical collections in the Huntington Library, San Marino, California; the Cossitt Memorial Library, Memphis, Tennessee; the Rutherford B. Hayes Library, Fremont, Ohio; the National Archives; and the Manuscript Division of the Library of Congress.

Others less formally attached to the field of history provided priceless aid in smoothing the path of research, particularly descendants of Governor Alcorn: Mr. and Mrs. James L. Alcorn of Los Angeles, who started me off on my thoroughly rewarding search for other Alcorn relations; Mr. and Mrs. Viet A. Hain of Hot Springs, Arkansas; and Mrs. Amelia Swift Manice of Eagle's Nest plantation, Jonestown, Mississippi, under whose roofs, in addition to obtaining priceless historical information, I experienced gracious hospitality similar to that the Governor once showed visitors at the original Eagle's Nest. Mr. and Mrs. William Swanson of Hot Springs, Mr. Alcorn Russell of Jonestown, and Mr. and

Mrs. Morris G. Heins of Memphis were also generous in help and hospitality. They all contributed toward opening windows on the past which I trust I have used in the same spirit of honesty and sincerity that they displayed.

So many others contributed, often in intangible as well as tangible ways, such as Mrs. Mary Fisher Robinson, Coahoma County's respected historian; my ever-patient typist Mrs. Sally Covert; and the University of Portland which adjusted my teaching load to provide time for revision of this study for publication. Most important, since under his tutelage the bulk of this book took form, has been my doctoral advisor Dr. Harold M. Hyman, who criticized, encouraged, grumbled, and grinned in the right places and at the right times to bring this project to fruition. It is impossible to express fully my gratitude for his assistance.

As must be pointed out, all errors are my responsibility and the conclusions drawn are also my own, mulled over in private, distilled out of research, reading, conversations, and no doubt, the subjective influence of my own background.

# Contents

# List of Illustrations

# James Lusk Alcorn

# 1

# Mississippian by Choice

THE 1840's IN THE United States saw many an ambitious man migrate in search of his fortune. Settlers were moving across the plains into Oregon, California, and Texas, and down the Mississippi River into Arkansas, Louisiana, and Mississippi.

In western Kentucky, twenty-eight-year-old James Lusk Alcorn also decided it was time to move. His state had not yet recovered from the effects of the Panic of 1837, and the western section with its poorer lands was especially hard hit. As a struggling young lawyer with a wife and two small children, he felt his surroundings offered him neither the economic nor the social opportunities he wanted. Ambitious and proud, he sensed that a community which had known him and his family well would be slow to confer social distinction upon him. Many years later his son-in-law Charles J. Swift, Jr., recalled that Alcorn "was fond of illustrating the adolescent disadvantage which surrounds a young man in familiar contact and daily intercourse amongst those with whom he had grown up, in comparison with the greater dignity and deference paid to him by comparative strangers away from his early surroundings and in a new country." [1] Several anecdotes, however apocryphal, make the same point. According to them, an acquaintance entered Alcorn's law office in Salem, Kentucky, one day in the late spring of 1844 and remarked casually and perhaps a bit patronizingly, "Nice place you have here, Jim," whereupon Alcorn closed shop,

1 Charles J. Swift, Jr., "James Lusk Alcorn" (MS in the Mississippi Department of Archives and History, Jackson, written between 1894 and 1900), 4–5.

*3*

returned home, and informed his wife that they were leaving.

He bought a flatboat on which he loaded his household belongings, and together with his wife, older child, and an elderly slave woman, started down the Ohio and Mississippi rivers. A few miles below Memphis he stopped to buy supplies at the tiny river town of Delta in northwestern Mississippi and was met by a group of the local citizens who were trying to attract settlers. In the course of extolling the natural resources and future of the area, they addressed him as "Colonel" Alcorn. He immediately returned to the flatboat and informed his wife that they were settling there, and that henceforth he would no longer be familiarly known as "Jim." [2] "Colonel" was a decided step in the right direction for a young man who had deliberately made up his mind to move upward in the unstable social and economic circumstances of his times.

At this juncture in time, Mississippi offered unusual opportunities for social, economic, and political advancement to a young man like Alcorn, who sensed that society was only temporarily fluid and who wanted to rise to the top before it solidified. Although land had become available through Indian treaties as early as the 1820's, the Panic of 1837 had delayed its occupation. By 1844 settlement of the land had begun, and Mississippi was about to enter upon a brief period of national prominence and prosperity. The state was also attractive for those with political ambitions, for its constitution, ratified in 1832, was a typical example of Jacksonian democracy.[3] It contained no property qualifications, assured universal white manhood suffrage, and provided for the popular election of the governor, boards of supervisors, and judges.

When Alcorn arrived the Yazoo-Mississippi Delta was still frontier country. Coahoma County, where he would live for the balance of his life, had been organized as a political entity only a year or two earlier, but Alcorn's pioneering background and experience helped him adapt to his surroundings. Both his paternal and maternal grandparents had migrated in the 1790's from North Carolina into Kentucky and had settled along the Ohio River. Alcorn, the only son and oldest child of James and Hannah Alcorn,

2  Mary Fisher Robinson, "A Sketch of James Lusk Alcorn," *Journal of Mississippi History* (1950), XII, 30–31.
3  Charles Sydnor, *The Development of Southern Sectionalism, 1819–1848* (Baton Rouge: Louisiana State University Press, 1948), 283; Edwin Arthur Miles, *Jacksonian Democracy in Mississippi* (Chapel Hill: University of North Carolina Press, 1960), 43.

was born in 1816, in Golconda, Illinois. Shortly after his birth
his parents moved across the river to Salem, in Livingston County,
Kentucky, where they acquired a farm, and his father struggled,
somewhat unsuccessfully, to earn a living as a boatman on the
Ohio and Mississippi rivers.

Alcorn's early life was austere but not harsh. He grew up the
center of attention for his mother and seven younger sisters. The
family was poor, and he had to work hard on the farm, but his
mother encouraged him to stay in school as long as possible and
appears to have given him an interest in reading which he never
lost. In 1836 lack of funds and disinclination for a scholarly life
shortened his stay at Cumberland College, Princeton, Kentucky, to
less than a year. He tried teaching for a while at Jackson, Arkansas,
and then returned to Kentucky to become deputy sheriff under
his uncle Randolph W. Alcorn. In this capacity he learned to
cope with the lawlessness of the frontier, and developed the
physical courage necessary for survival in his occupation. He also
studied law, gaining the needed experience by his court attendance.
In 1838 he received his license to practice, and that same year
married Mary Catherine Stewart, who subsequently bore him four
children, three of whom survived infancy; Catherine Mary, Milton
Stewart, and Henry Lusk.

When Alcorn arrived in Mississippi he was a sturdily-built young
man with jet-black, wavy hair and piercing black eyes, which he
used effectively to hold audiences and juries. His black hair and
eyes contrasted well with his fair skin and unusually high color
(he had been nicknamed "Red Lips" in Kentucky). His great
nervous energy and powerful personality drew the attention of
most of his contemporaries. He could radiate geniality, but at the
same time he tended to dominate any group of which he was a
part, as he sought to be the center of attention. This competitive-
ness, which underlay so much of his activity, made for him life-
long friends or enemies, for those who came into contact with
him were often forced either to follow or oppose. He was frequently moody, proud to the point of arrogance, brave, and possessed
of an intelligent, practical, and inquisitive mind. Both his writings
and the anecdotes about him show a good sense of humor, even
at his own expense, which came from a healthy sense of realism.
His library, judging from the extant volumes, leaned to history,
including Macauley's *History of England* and Sir Walter Scott's

*Napoleon,* and to collections of biography (his mother had given him Plutarch's *Lives* when he was a young boy), humor, and miscellaneous facts. A copy of the Koran, dated 1859, survives.

In keeping with his Scotch-Irish background, he was raised a Presbyterian. His maternal grandmother had founded the first Presbyterian church at Golconda, and his mother, with his aid, was instrumental in establishing the first one in the neighborhood of the Yazoo Pass.[4]

He was industrious, scrupulously honest in all his personal dealings, and a devoted and loving, if strict, family man. For him family had a clannish structure, extending to parents, an uncle, sisters, brothers-in-law, cousins, and members of his wife's family. As he achieved success, he began to consider himself chief of these numerous kinsmen, providing for them when necessary but expecting to be listened to when he gave advice. This sense of duty to his relatives expanded into a sense of responsibility for those with whom he identified himself, for "his people," a concept that gradually widened as the conflicts and contacts in which he engaged increased. For Alcorn, as he became increasingly prominent, was slow to claim many as his equals. He felt himself to be a leader in the aristocratic sense, above those whom he would lead rather than one of them. In this role he came to see himself as spokesman for the Delta planters among whom he settled, later for all Mississippians, and eventually, during and after the turbulent days of Reconstruction, for all Southerners.

This identity with the South considerably modified his Presbyterian background. He drank freely, although not excessively for his region and time. He enjoyed gambling, horse racing, the theater, dancing, and other forms of amusement. Social affairs were an important part of his life; he thoroughly enjoyed the company of women, and they apparently found him charming. Part of his attraction may have resulted from his fondness for impeccable, fashionable clothing which went well with his erect, stocky figure and good manners. His fine appearance gave backing to an impressive command of oratory, fed by a quick mind and delivered in a booming but melodious voice.

Alcorn was not an original or deep thinker. He articulated, to the extent to which he assimilated them, many of the ideas of the

4 Hannah L. Alcorn to John Thomas Lusk, February 22, 1847, in possession of Mrs. V. A. Hain, Hot Springs, Ark.

nineteenth century. Among them were a strong sense of personal destiny, deeply ingrained middle-class ideals, and a pervasive class consciousness. In American society everywhere, but more noticeably on the frontier, these ideas produced a middle-class aristocracy, an aristocracy of works which, once it had acquired by its own labor economic security, was expected to engage in politics and self-improvement, thus, according to the ideal, placing its intellect and wealth at the service of its fellow citizens. On the southern frontier its members, in their early careers, were indistinguishable from the poor whites at whose side they struggled to tame the land, but they were the ones who quickly rose above their fellows and, as they prospered economically, began to emulate the ways of the planter aristocracy. The frontier forced them to make great concessions to democracy in order to earn the political support of the humbler folk who in the early period tended to accept their leadership, but this did not greatly modify their sense of class superiority.

The Yazoo-Mississippi Delta, a rich expanse of lowland lying between the Mississippi River on the west and the Yazoo River on the east, extends from just below Memphis to Vicksburg, and during this period was an area where West and South met. The interplay of the interests and influences of these two sections, particularly the class ideals of each, can be seen clearly in Alcorn's attitudes and career. He believed in a society of classes in which an aristocracy of intellect and wealth, not necessarily of high origin, was destined to lead. He was sure he was a member of this aristocracy, having attained membership by his own efforts, and he practiced its ritual all his life—as a rising young frontier lawyer, as a political leader, and as a successful planter. The frontier and a sense of destiny gave men like him their drive, and the Southern myth provided them their goal.[5]

Immediately after his arrival in Mississippi, Alcorn settled a few

5 Descriptions of various aspects of this aristocracy and discussion of its place in American society can be found in Carl Russell Fish, *The Rise of the Common Man* (New York: Macmillan Company, 1927), 17–19; in Vernon L. Parrington, *Main Currents in American Thought* (New York: Harcourt, Brace, 1927), II, 132–33; in Thomas Perkins Abernethy, "The Southern Frontier; An Interpretation," in Walker D. Wyman and Clifton B. Kroeber (eds.), *The Frontier in Perspective* (Madison: University of Wisconsin Press, 1957), 138–40; and in Gerald M. Capers, Jr., *The Biography of a River Town* (Chapel Hill: University of North Carolina Press, 1959), 80.

miles inland on a quarter section of land on the Yazoo Pass, now
a narrow waterway which links Moon Lake, once a channel of
the Mississippi River, through a series of bayous and streams with
the Yazoo River. When Alcorn lived there it served him as a
means of transportation and of gauging the rise and fall of flood
waters each spring. He erected a cabin for his household on his
land facing the pass, and in Delta he opened a law office, catering
to a clientele that ranged from outlaws, bear hunters and lumber-
men, to landholders contesting titles. His fearlessness and mental
ability soon established him in the frontier community, and less
than a year after his arrival the Whig party convention of Coahoma
County selected him as its candidate for the Mississippi House of
Representatives.

Alcorn's first venture into politics had been under the auspices
of the Whig party in Kentucky, where he was elected in 1843
to the state's house of representatives and attended one session.
Several factors could have influenced his choice of party. His
own temperament, beliefs, and ambitions drew him toward the
more aristocratic of the two parties; also the effects of the Panic
of 1837 were still being felt in most of Kentucky, and disillusionment with the Democratic party was widespread. Alcorn never
really lost his political identification with the Whigs, any more
than he did his class identification. In fact, they were intertwined.
The historian Ulrich B. Phillips called the Southern Whigs "a
company of gentlemen politically inclined," [6] a description which
Alcorn would have heartily approved.

The Whigs with whom he allied himself were merchants,
bankers, and wealthy slaveholding planters. In Mississippi after
the Panic of 1837 they opposed the repudiation by a Democratic
legislature of bonds issued by the Planters' Bank and the Union
Bank, bonds which had originally been authorized with Whig
support to encourage the economic development of the state. As
a group, most Whigs believed in a strong national government,
had a liberal attitude toward government-sponsored internal improvements, and favored a national bank. They disapproved of
the Democrats' advocacy of broader suffrage, and endeavored to

6  Ulrich B. Phillips, "The Southern Whigs, 1834–1854," *Essays in American
   History Dedicated to Frederick Jackson Turner* (New York: Henry
   Holt, 1910), 226.

portray themselves as patricians in politics, disinterested patriots rather than office seekers, and as educated men who studied the issues, then acted for the welfare of the entire nation. They were conservative in the Federalist tradition, and considered themselves to be the aristocrats of American society.

Nationally the Whig party in the 1840's was at the height of its power, having been kneaded by Henry Clay from a collection of anti-Jackson factions into a fairly disciplined political organization. It was a good social and political vehicle in which to start upon a career.

When Alcorn moved to Mississippi he easily assumed the posture of a Southern Whig, and he quickly found acceptance in Coahoma County where the vote in the presidential election of 1844 was eighty-one for Clay and none for James K. Polk.[7] In 1845 these voters elected Alcorn to the Mississippi house of representatives, where he came in contact with an exceptionally able group of Whig leaders, including William L. Sharkey, George Poindexter, Seargent S. Prentiss, and J. S. Yerger. Some of the Democratic leaders against whom he sharpened his talent were John A. Quitman, Albert Gallatin Brown, and Jefferson Davis.

The legislature had scarcely assembled when Alcorn, with the sure instinct of a politician, made his presence known. He introduced a resolution that each session be opened with a prayer. When one member objected that the legislators had not come to listen to preaching but rather to legislate, he replied that he had attended many legislative sessions and had never seen any which did not begin with a prayer, but if the house felt that the blessings of God should not be asked upon its deliberations, he would not insist on his resolution. Of course the resolution was adopted, since no politician could afford to vote against such a worthy exercise, and the local newspaper gave a detailed account of his effort on behalf of a higher spiritual tone in the legislature.[8] Alcorn scored on the first round. Both the legislature and the electorate had been made aware of his presence, and his political career was under way.

In 1847 Jefferson Davis, already a Democratic party leader in Mississippi, came back from the Mexican War a hero, at about the time of the death of Jesse Speight, one of Mississippi's Senators

7   Grenada (Miss.) *Harry of the West*, November 16, 1844.
8   Jackson *Southron*, January 14, 1846.

in Washington. In view of Davis' popularity the Whig minority in the legislature suggested to the Democrats that there was no need to nominate competing candidates to succeed Speight, and that they would join the Democrats in electing Davis to the United States Senate. But in the joint session of the legislature convened for that purpose, the first name on the roll call was that of Alcorn, and he "scornfully" voted for "John Smith."

The reporter who wrote of the incident years later felt that Alcorn had done so because he had the courage not only of his convictions but also of his contempt, especially for Davis and the Democratic party.[9] If a political statement by Alcorn's father in 1850 can be applied as his opinion on the situation at this time, Alcorn, along with most of the Whig party, saw the Mexican War as another problem which the Democrats had created for the country.[10] His reaction to the returning hero would be quite understandable, since Davis was a Democrat. His action was also an early indication of a characteristic he would exhibit throughout his career, that of taking a stand independent of his party's leadership; he always found it hard to be a follower.

The feature of the Whig program with which Alcorn became most closely identified was the preservation of the Union. For him, as for most Southern Whigs, this was a practical rather than an idealistic position, because of his corollary conviction that slavery, an important form of property holding, could best be protected under the United States Constitution. He retained this conviction longer than most of his political companions.

Reaction in Mississippi to the repeated introduction of the Wilmot Proviso in Congress during 1849 illustrates well the line of cleavage and unity between the two parties on the subject of preserving the Union. David Wilmot's amendment to a bill to appropriate funds for the purchase of land from Mexico forbade the introduction of slavery into the acquired territory. It was discussed and debated heatedly North and South. Almost all issues of national importance, such as a national bank, the tariff, internal improvements, problems of commercial expansion, could be debated in the South as elsewhere. But with regard to one issue—slavery— only the means to its preservation could be discussed, with the

9   New Orleans *Picayune*, August 18, 1894.
10  James Alcorn to John T. Lusk, September 1, 1850, in possession of Mrs. V. A. Hain.

maintenance of the Union always subordinated to it.[11] In spite of his later apparently liberal attitude toward Negroes, there is nothing to indicate that Alcorn's stand with regard to slavery during this period was other than completely orthodox. Charles Swift suggests a difference in his manuscript biography of his father-in-law, and Alcorn's early association with Kentucky Whigs suggests that he must have been exposed under sympathetic circumstances to Clay's views on gradual emancipation. But Alcorn was not the kind to wrestle with abstract principles when they did not seem to be immediately applicable; both then and later, pragmatic assessments of the situation at hand dominated his thinking on the subject.

In October, 1849, Whig and Democrat leaders met at Jackson to draft a call for the election of delegates to a convention of southern states to consider the worsening relations between North and South. Whig leader William L. Sharkey, then chief justice of the state, presided at the bipartisan meetings out of which came the call for the Nashville Convention of 1850. These leaders asserted the separate sovereignty of the states, although they pledged loyalty to the Union. Significantly, they voiced the first open advocacy of secession, but as a last resort.[12] The people of Mississippi went a step further by electing John A. Quitman, a "fire-eating" Democrat and secessionist, as governor in the fall of 1849.

The basic unity of the state in the face of any apparent threat to its "peculiar institution" is evident in the reaction to the Compromise of 1850, whose resolutions, managed by Stephen A. Douglas as a solution to the growing North-South controversy, were brought before the Senate in late January of that year. In this struggle the Whig party in Mississippi as well as in other southern states, notably North Carolina, Georgia, and Alabama, began to lose the sharp outline it had assumed as part of Clay's disciplined national organization. While Sharkey supported the Nashville Convention, and would the following year preside over its official

---

11 Arthur C. Cole, *The Whig Party in the South* (Washington: American Historical Association, 1913), 343; Percy Lee Rainwater, "An Analysis of the Secession Controversy in Mississippi, 1854–61," *Mississippi Valley Historical Review* (1937–38), XXIV, 35–36.

12 James Wilford Garner, "The First Struggle Over Secession in Mississippi," *Mississippi Historical Society Publications* (1901), IV, 90; Avery O. Craven, *The Growth of Southern Nationalism, 1848–1861* (Baton Rouge: Louisiana State University Press, 1949), 63.

meetings, within the Mississippi legislature in the fall of 1849 a minority group of Whigs and Union Democrats began a tenacious fight against the movement toward secession. They regarded the Nashville convention as a step in the direction of disunion, and they therefore opposed the legislature's naming delegates to it. In the state senate this group was headed by Alcorn, again in opposition to the leadership of his party. He represented the three Delta counties of Panola, Tallahatchie and Coahoma, and among his supporters were A. E. Reynolds of Tishomingo County (Tishomingo, in the northeast corner of Mississippi, on the Tennessee River, was settled largely by Union-minded East Tennesseeans), Walker Brooke of Holmes County, J. E. Sharkey of Warren County, J. M. Tait of DeSoto and Tunica counties, and James J. White of Bolivar County. These other counties were partially or wholly in the Delta region.

Brooke, supported by the others, submitted a minority report from the Committee on Federal Relations urging that Mississippi acquiesce in the admission of California as a free state if her people so wished it. A move to have this report substituted for the majority report condemning the Compromise was lost.[13] When the legislature met in joint session to elect delegates to the Nashville convention, Alcorn was among those who signed a resolution of protest against such action. Yet Sharkey was chosen as one of the delegates.[14]

Outside the legislature another coalition group took shape, including some of the same participants. On February 15, 1850, also in Jackson, a group calling itself the "Friends of General Taylor and the Union" met and elected Sharkey chairman.[15] A committee which included Brooke, Reynolds, and Tait issued a series of resolutions declaring that the people should acquiesce in the admission of California as a free state if her people wanted it, but that they would regard any act of Congress to prevent the entrance of slavery into any territory or state "as dangerous to the public liberty." [16]

In Congress the Mississippi delegation, in accordance with instructions from its legislature, voted solidly against the Compro-

13 *Journal of the Senate of the State of Mississippi, Regular Session* (Jackson: Fall and Marshall, 1850), 7.
14 Natchez *Semi-Weekly Courier*, March 15, 1850.
15 *Ibid.*, February 26, 1850.
16 *Ibid.*, March 5, 1850.

mises, but toward the end of the struggle Senator Henry S. Foote, a Democrat, broke with the radical Southerners and announced his intentions of supporting these measures. Soon after this he wrote Sharkey asking his advice on the course he had taken. Sharkey's reply, published in the Natchez *Weekly Courier* of June 18, 1850, reflected the Whig attitude of the period:

We must take things as they are and not as we would have them and shape our conduct according to exigencies. It would have been folly to have insisted on what you and I regard as strictly Southern rights. Nothing would have been obtained by that course. If the compromise can be adopted, our honor at least is safe. Indeed, it secures the principle for which we have been contending. The mass of the Southern people would be content with it. . . . Ultra men can never be pleased. . . . Take my word for it, conservative men will approve your course. Whigs generally approve it, and moderate men of your own party.

Sharkey's words carried considerable authority, for he had just returned from the Nashville convention where Union Whigs had gained the ascendancy and had elected him president. Declaring the preservation of the Union as its purpose, the convention had added the usual reservations about the rights of slavery in the territories, and had then adjourned to await congressional action on the Compromises. After the passage of the measures, the secessionist delegates attempted to reconvene the convention, but Sharkey refused to preside, and although Mississippi Governor Quitman sent three new secessionist delegates, the rump convention accomplished nothing of significance.

Passage of the Compromises also prompted Quitman to call a special session of the legislature in the fall of 1850. In his message he declared that the admission of California and the attitude of the North constituted a threat to the slave interests of the state. Therefore he recommended the calling of a state convention "to adopt such measures as may best comport with the dignity and safety of the State and effectually correct the evils complained of." [17] Besides providing for a secession convention, Quitman wanted the legislature to pass resolutions praising the anticompromise stand of the Mississippi congressional representatives and censuring Foote.

17 *Journal of the Senate of the State of Mississippi, Called Session* (Jackson Fall and Marshall, 1850), 7.

The Whig–Union Democrat coalition fought to block both parts of his program. In the senate, under Alcorn's leadership, the group offered resolution after resolution maintaining that the admission of California did not offer sufficient grounds for secession. It also tried to prevent passage of resolutions censuring Foote and praising the other members of the congressional delegation.[18] During these unsuccessful battles on behalf of the Union, Alcorn first came into contact with a man who was to become one of his principal political opponents, John J. Pettus, who frequently acted as spokesman for the prosecessionist majority.[19]

As the struggle progressed, the eventual failure of the Unionist group became more and more apparent. "The result of our legislation will be the call of a convention, the question of acquiescing in the adjustment measures of Congress will be canvassed before the people," Alcorn wrote Amelia Glover of Alabama, whom he would marry in a few weeks. Whig-like, he doubted the wisdom of the common folk in political matters. "This will," he continued, "afford a fine field for the little demagogues of the day, and strenuous will be their efforts no doubt, to enlighten the 'dear People' upon their constitutional rights." He told her to inform her father, who warmly favored secession, that "the Mississippi Legislature is with him upon his great question, but that I hope and trust the *people* will be found on the other side, but I even have fear of this. I know the gullibility of the people." [20]

Although the legislature passed an act to call a secession convention, the coalition group succeeded in having Alcorn appointed chairman of the committee which would do this. From this vantage point he supported a resolution by J. E. Sharkey that members elected to the convention take an oath to support the Constitution of the United States; but this was tabled in spite of his group's efforts. He himself then introduced an amendment to the report of his committee that the voters be asked if they wished a convention. This was also tabled over their opposition.[21] In the meantime, excitement in Mississippi and throughout the South over the

18  *Ibid.*, 22–23.
19  *Ibid.*, 39, 45.
20  James Lusk Alcorn to Amelia Glover, November 26, 1850, in Alcorn File, Mississippi Department of Archives and History. Hereinafter cited as Alcorn File.
21  *Journal of the Senate of the State of Mississippi, Called Session* (Jackson: Fall and Marshall, 1850), 45–50.

passage of the Compromises was abating, and sensing a change, a few days later Alcorn abruptly reversed his stand and in the final ballot voted for passage of the act calling for a convention, without the support of his group.[22]

As the legislative battle went on, outside of the Capitol the antisecession movement was tightening its organization. The issue was still the question of whether the passage of the Compromises was sufficient to warrant secession. On the key point, the preservation of slavery, all were in complete accord. At a conclave on November 18, 1850, while the special session of the legislature was meeting, the "Mass Meeting of the Friends of the Union" passed a number of resolutions. These stated that the Compromise measures were constitutional and should be acquiesced in, and that the group was resolved to preserve the Union "because we believe that therein we shall preserve to ourselves the inestimable blessings of civil and religious liberty bequeathed to us by our forefathers." But the members then listed the measures which would be considered intolerable and would lead to resistance: interference with slavery, with the interstate slave trade, or with slavery in the District of Columbia; refusal by Congress to admit a new state because it tolerated slavery; or the passage of any law prohibiting slavery in the territories. They also called for the organization of a Union party and expressed approval of Foote's course in Congress.[23] The repeal of the Missouri Compromise restriction on slavery in the territories north of latitude 36'30° was still four years in the future, but Mississippi's most pro-Union group acted as if it had already taken place.

The party was formed around Mississippi's lone congressional dissenter, Henry Foote. Alcorn, who actively aided in bringing about this new political grouping, nominated Foote for governor, contributed materially to his election, and continued to support him as long as he was involved in Mississippi politics.[24]

Secessionist sentiment continued to fade during the winter of 1850–1851, and enthusiasm for a Union party mounted. Alcorn journeyed home to obtain the endorsement of the local Whig organization and then returned to Jackson in early May as the

22   *Ibid.*, 69.
23   Natchez *Courier*, December 1, 1850.
24   John Livingston (ed.), *American Portrait Gallery, Containing Portraits of Men Now Living* (New York: John W. Amerman, 1854), 6.

delegate from Coahoma County to the new state Union party convention. There he was named to the Committee on Resolutions which merely endorsed *in toto* the resolutions adopted at the "Friends of the Union" meeting of the previous fall.

Immediately after the convention, the Whig paper in Jackson published a declaration "To the People of Mississippi" signed by a committee of six, one of whom was Alcorn. It stated that the committee had been appointed to explain to the people the various topics handled by the convention, and to give a correct explanation of the actions of the convention of October, 1849, the bipartisan one which had called for the Nashville convention. The declaration discussed the "insulting" Wilmot Proviso, passage of which would cause the southern states "to take care of their own safety." It professed devotion to the Union "as it was formed," and declared that slavery was a state institution possessing thereby ineluctable congressional limitations; that slavery antedated the Constitution so that the latter was made to conform to the former; that Congress had a duty to protect property in the territories and possessed no power to abolish slavery in the District of Columbia; and that the admission of California with its present Constitution was "an act of fraud." However, in dealing with the Compromises the announcement stated that people had an inherent right to self-government, just as Texas had the right to give up land if it so wished. The Fugitive Slave Law was constitutional, and with regard to the abolition of slave trade in the District of Columbia, while Congress could not do away with it between the District and a state, the position had never been assumed that the national legislature could not abolish the traffic within the District. As for governments in the territories, Congress had, in earlier acts, recognized the right of slavery and still had the duty to protect that right "where it exists."

The declaration closed with the statement that the committee had endeavored to prove that the Compromise acts were passed in "entire conformity to the requisitions of the principles of both the October Convention and the subsequent acts of the legislature." Therefore, since the Compromises did not violate constitutional rights, the voters should rally behind them and elect pro-Union delegates to Quitman's secession convention.[25] The Union party's position may have been short on logic, but it contained two trump

25 Jackson *Flag of the Union*, May 23, 1851.

cards which assured at least temporary success: it took a vigorous and orthodox stand on slavery and it expressed devotion to the preservation of the Union. The slavery stand, of course, came first.

The conservative platform of the Union party, with its subtle combination of Unionism and pro-slavery sentiment, forced the regular Democratic party into appearing extreme. Realizing the extent of public reaction against the possibility of secession, Quitman refused to run again for governor in 1851, and Jefferson Davis was prevailed upon to resign his seat in the Senate and to oppose his fellow senator, Foote.[26]

Alcorn campaigned in the Delta in the fall of 1851 both for Foote and for reelection as a state senator. As it was throughout the state, the dominant issue between Alcorn and his opponents was secession. At Charleston, in Tallahatchie County, he started an hour-long speech by stating that he had been in Jackson when "this monster secession" was born, that he had seen it before it was dressed or adopted, and that therefore he was familiar with "all its damnable heresies." From that moment he had fought secession and would continue to fight it, and he defended the congressional Compromises at length. A pro-Union reporter who witnessed the speech exulted that "never did, or never will, the fire-eaters wince like they did under Col. A's bitter sarcasm; long will they remember him for he threw into their camp grape, canister, and other combustible material until the room got too warm for some of them." [27]

Alcorn thrived on political campaigning. It provided an outlet for his aggressive energy, an audience for him to hold, and a platform from which to demonstrate that leadership he believed he was destined to exercise. Some of the exhilaration he felt spilled over into a letter he wrote his wife while on his campaign tour. "I see by the returns from Alabama that Smith (Union) has beaten Col. Erwin in the Eutaw district for Congress. The Union Men have carried the state, three cheers for the Union men of Alabama." [28]

The election of delegates to the state secession convention

26 Henry S. Foote, *Casket of Reminiscences* (Washington: Chronicle Publishing Company, 1874), 173. Henry Clay wrote letters on his behalf during the campaign.
27 Jackson *Flag of the Union*, September 12, 1851.
28 James Lusk Alcorn to Amelia Alcorn, September 26, 1851, in Alcorn File.

occurred before the regular gubernatorial election and marked the high point of this pro-Union reaction. When the convention assembled in Jackson in November, 1851, the Union delegates, Alcorn among them, took over the business at hand and executed it in five days, harassed but not seriously hampered by a secession-minded minority. In quick succession on the first day they defeated a motion to omit having the delegates take an oath to support the Constitution, and a motion to adjourn immediately *sine die*. The resolutions of the majority report, which were adopted one by one after vigorous debate, echoed the Union party platform. While not wholly approving of the Compromises, the Unionists stated that Mississippi would abide by them, and by the Constitution and national government "as it is." They further cautioned that the right of secession "is utterly unsanctioned by the Federal Constitution" which was framed to establish, not destroy, the Union, but violation of rights could occur which would justify "measures of resistance." The Unionists then took a slap at the legislature. A resolution passed which stated that the ordering of a convention without submitting the question to popular vote was "an unwarranted assumption of power." [29]

In the gubernatorial election which followed shortly thereafter, Foote won but by only a slight majority, a much smaller one than that by which the Unionists had dominated the would-be secession convention. Excitement was subsiding throughout the state, and indications were that Union Democrats were already returning home.

With Foote lodged precariously in the governor's mansion, the power of the coalition Union party began to wane almost immediately. In the legislature it took a long, hard struggle to get the Democratic-dominated Senate's consent to setting the election of two Senators to replace Davis and Foote who had both resigned, one during and the other after the gubernatorial contest. In the Senate Alcorn led the fight to proceed with the election, charging the Democrats, led by Pettus, with trying to thwart the popular will because they were afraid Foote would be elected. Eventually, two Union men, Walker Brooke, who had been a consistent member of the Senate coalition group, and Stephen Adams were selected. A reporter from the local Democratic newspaper described the last speaker on behalf of Brooke: "Finally, that handsome

29 Jackson *Flag of the Union*, November 14 and 21, 1851.

individual of slow and stately utterance, elegance of whisker, and classic outline of feature, exquisitely gloved hand, and finely polished cane—Alcorn, of Coahoma—came to the rescue. He vindicated right heartily and lustily the whiggery of Walter [sic] Brooke, and proclaimed, in earnest accents, that the green earth kissed the footsteps of no more implacable federalist." [30]

This was the last victory the Union party achieved in Mississippi. When the legislature met in the fall of 1852, its members were unable even to pass a resolution rescinding the motion of censure against Governor Foote which had been enacted two years earlier. Alcorn had obtained a leave of absence and was not present when the motion was made and tabled.[31] But he was politically active that fall, being selected by the Whig convention to be a candidate for elector-at-large pledged to Winfield Scott, and he campaigned for him throughout the state. The state went for Franklin Pierce; Coahoma County voted for Scott.[32]

Unionist citizens were in the minority in the state, and in the South as a whole. The pressure of the opposition finally forced Foote to resign in January of 1854, after warning against secession "fanaticism!" [33] Leadership passed to John J. McRae, who had been appointed by Quitman to serve briefly as interim Senator following Jefferson Davis' resignation in 1851. With him the Democratic party came into power and remained in control for nine years.

Within the space of ten years Alcorn had become a figure of considerable prominence in his adopted state and was deeply involved in a position of leadership in the most widely debated issue of his times. Furthermore, he had successfully used a disintegrating party as a springboard from which to launch what already showed signs of becoming an unorthodox and controversial career.

30 Livingston, *American Portrait Gallery*, 7.
31 *Journal of the Senate of the State of Mississippi, Called Session* (Jackson: Palmer & Pickett, 1852), 59, 133.
32 Eliza Jane Alcorn to John T. Lusk, July 23, 1852, in possession of Mrs. V. A. Hain. That summer the citizens of Coahoma County moved their county seat from Delta to Friar's Point which they attempted to rename "Union."
33 *Journal of the Senate of the State of Mississippi* (Jackson: Barksdale and Jones, 1854), 5.

# 2

# Fight for Levees and the Union

ALCORN'S POLITICAL PROMINENCE and personal fortune increased at about the same rate during the years after his arrival in the Yazoo-Mississippi Delta. Land development in the region had been slow between 1837 and 1847, but when the war with Mexico ended, settlers began to arrive in large numbers. The land records of almost every Delta county showed great increases in sales and transfers beginning about 1846, and reaching a peak in 1849 and 1850. Litigation arising from this activity gave attorney Alcorn priceless knowledge of the region and opportunities to invest in valuable land. One contemporary attributed Alcorn's rapid success to his "natural vigor of intellect, remarkable industry, and thorough knowledge of the law," and added that "his unsurpassed aptitude for speculative operations, very soon opened the way to him for the acquisition of large bodies of valuable land and ultimate affluence." [1]

There is no doubt that his energy and aggressiveness served him well. Within two years after his arrival in Coahoma County he had accumulated enough land to send for his parents and sisters in Kentucky and settle them on a farm of their own near his holdings on the Yazoo Pass.[2] Several cousins and the uncle under whom he had served as deputy sheriff in Kentucky also followed him to Coahoma County during the 1850's. He helped them settle

---

1 Henry S. Foote, *The Bench and Bar of the South and Southwest* (St. Louis: Soule, Thomas and Wentworth, 1876), 249–50.
2 Hannah Lusk Alcorn to John T. Lusk and his wife, May 11, 1846, in possession of Mrs. V. A. Hain.

in the area and in turn they supported him in his political activities.

Alcorn's first wife, Mary Catherine, who accompanied him on his trip from Kentucky, died in childbirth in 1849. She was once described by him as "independent," in contrast to his second and more "dependent" wife. But little more is known of her than is known of the myriad of frontier wives whose short lives were filled with hard work, the struggle to establish new homes, and childbearing. Her death caused him to consider for a time the possibility of migrating to California, and he had even obtained a letter of recommendation attesting to his party loyalty for presentation to President Zachary Taylor in the hopes of obtaining a political office there.[3]

But during the spring legislative session in 1850 he met Amelia Walton Glover, daughter of an affluent and well-established Alabama planter. Presumably Mary Catherine had been a girl of his own neighborhood in Kentucky, poor and his social equal. Amelia, on the other hand, had been raised on a large Alabama plantation, Rosemount, which at one time is said to have comprised over five thousand acres and to have possessed its own steamboat to transport cotton to Mobile. The house, still standing, is an excellent example of a luxurious antebellum plantation home, and must have appeared in sharp contrast to Alcorn's cabin in the Delta.

The match was a great social step upward for Alcorn, and represented the meeting of the new frontier aristocracy with the older established class which had preceded it by a generation. Alcorn himself was very conscious of this social difference. As he realistically described himself to his future wife, he had come from a respectable but exceedingly poor family, and he quite frankly regarded himself as its superior member as he was the only one to acquire what he modestly described as "the means of comfort." While they were all respectable, he was the only one with "energy, perserverance, economy, capacity, and I might say *talent*." He loved them dearly, had provided for his parents, and was idolized by his entire family. Five of his seven sisters were then married, but, because they were uneducated, had not been prepared to make favorable alliances, although he quickly added that all except one had married "gentlemen." In the same letter he reminded her that she could still change her mind, and mentioned the influences

3 Patrick Henry to President Zachary Taylor, March 4, 1850, in possession of Mrs. V. A. Hain.

to which she was subjected from those who wanted her to make
a better match.[4]

In her reply, Amelia told him of her parents' approval and
quieted his misgivings about taking her into the wilds of Coahoma
County by pointing out that her parents had started their married
life in a log cottage in the wilds of Alabama.[5] They had moved
from their cottage into a white-columned, antebellum mansion;
she and Alcorn eventually moved from their cabin on the Yazoo
Pass into a three-story Victorian home. On the frontier the rewards
of prominence went to the able, the energetic, and the acquisitive.

During 1850 Alcorn's energy proved sufficient for the demands
of both his political and social life. While he fought for the Union
at the spring and fall sessions of the legislature, he also courted
Amelia in a series of eloquent, pleading letters. These led to success
when, at the close of the called session which authorized a secession convention, he hurried from Jackson to Alabama to marry
her. But his preoccupation with secessionists and Amelia did not
completely preclude a continued desire for feminine society. That
summer he had written that he hoped she would pardon him, but
he was passing the word around that she had rejected him, because
the girls would not pay any attention to engaged gentlemen, and
he had so few enjoyments.[6] Presumably she did pardon him, but
she was to discover that marriage did not cure this particular
fondness of his.

They were married at Rosemount on December 19, 1850, and
the event is said to have been celebrated in true antebellum style,
with guests from the entire countryside dancing and banqueting.
When Alcorn and his bride left for Coahoma County they took
with them her father's wedding gift of twenty slaves. Tradition
claims that Amelia, in spite of her brave words, found conditions
difficult and frightening during the first years she lived on the
Yazoo Pass, and life with her energetic, ambitious husband was
anything but dull. The following spring, while they were on their
way to Jackson, the steamboat on which they were traveling caught

4 James Lusk Alcorn to Amelia Walton Glover, September 16, 1850, in
   Alcorn File.
5 Amelia Walton Glover to James Lusk Alcorn, October 5, 1850, in Alcorn
   Papers, No. 5 in Southern Historical Collection, University of North
   Carolina. Hereinafter cited as Alcorn Papers.
6 James Lusk Alcorn to Amelia Walton Glover, May 29, 1850, in Alcorn
   File.

fire during the night. Alcorn threw his bride overboard (she could not swim) and jumped after her. He saved her from drowning by catching onto her long brown hair and dragging her to some willows where they remained until they were rescued. Two days after this incident Alcorn was in Jackson at the Union party convention which nominated Foote to be governor.

In many ways Amelia proved to be the ideal wife for him. She helped him with his plantation business, particularly during the Civil War; she knew how to draw him out of his depressed moods; and she shared his love of social life. "Brother and Amelia have just returned from Jackson," Eliza wrote her uncle in 1854. "They say Jackson was unusually gay last winter. They attended a number of elegant parties had their portraits taken and come home heartily tired out." [7] They also made frequent trips to New Orleans and to Rosemount, and often entertained members of the Glover family at their plantation on the pass which Alcorn, sometime after his marriage, named "Mound Place." There six of their nine children were born, three of whom died in infancy.

Mound Place was not only Alcorn's home but tangible proof that he was beginning to acquire that fortune which he had sought in 1844 when he floated down the Mississippi and Ohio rivers. It was to be a fortune expressed in terms idealized in the South—land, slaves, and an aristocratic way of life—but its acquisition presented a challenge. At the time of his arrival serious efforts were only beginning to be made to conquer the tangled jungle of brush, trees, and stagnant water that covered the promising soil. With frontier-bred practicality he realized that only concerted effort to protect that rich land would enable it to serve as the basis of his fortune. Therefore, during the antebellum period a good part of Alcorn's energy was expended on a project that was primarily economic, although it had political overtones—a centralized levee system for the Delta region.

From the beginning of his political career Alcorn identified himself with, and quickly became the leader in, the struggle for such a system—what Mississippi historian Dunbar Rowland called his "great work." [8] However he differed from many of his fellow

7 Eliza Jane Alcorn to John T. Lusk, April 6, 1854, in possession of Mrs. V. A. Hain.

8 Dunbar Rowland, (ed.), *Mississippi* (Atlanta: Southern Historical Publishing Association, 1907), I, 62.

planters in seeking a solution to the problem of flood control
which would be based on a broader entity than the Delta alone
and would include leadership that would transcend local factions.
He may have gotten the nucleus of his idea from the action of
Kentucky which in 1835 had established a Board of Internal Improvements to make its rivers in the eastern part of the state
navigable and to provide flood control. He no doubt drew his
broad concept of government sponsorship from Henry Clay's
advocacy of internal improvements. He considered the reclamation
of Delta lands and their protection as a public improvement of
wide significance, and believed that the state of Mississippi and
the federal government, as coequal entities, should cooperate in
the appropriation of public funds for this purpose.[9]

Since the Delta was strongly Whig in political feeling, no doubt
self-interest and political considerations helped to spur him on.
In addition, the need for protection against floods often transcended
party feeling and gave him a broader basis of support in his locality
than could have been provided by the shifting Whig factions of
the 1850's alone.

In 1844, when Alcorn settled in Coahoma County the county
boards of police (supervisors) and the local landowners, particularly
those along the river front, were responsible by legislative act for
building and maintaining levees in each county. The result was a
disjointed line, varying in quality, and marked by gaps where land
was still in public domain or the owners had failed to act. And
that year brought a flood so devastating that it began to be evident
that the property owners along the river front could no longer
be expected to be responsible for adequate levees.

Almost immediately after Alcorn arrived in Jackson as a member of the state house of representatives he was appointed to the
Committee on Internal Improvements, and appears to have become its chairman since he reported out most of its bills. During
the session of 1846 the two houses passed a joint memorial to
Congress asking for the title to certain overflow lands to be
used as a source of revenue for levee building.[10] The legislature
also passed an act giving the first official instructions on levee
construction and providing a system of levee taxes by which "back

9 Swift, "James Lusk Alcorn," 8.
10 *Journal of the House of Representatives of the State of Mississippi*
(Jackson: Price and Fall, 1846), 658.

lands" were to be taxed to build levees in proportion to the benefit they would receive.[11]

In 1849 and 1850 floods dramatized again the need for greater protection from the river.[12] In 1850 Congress passed the second Swamp Act transferring to the states concerned all the overflow and swamp lands along the Mississippi River which still remained in the federal domain, with the understanding that funds from the sale of these lands would be used to build the levees and drains necessary for their reclamation. Louisiana and Arkansas established state organizations to carry out reclamation, but Mississippi, in the tradition of Jacksonian localism, divided the land scrip representing the value of these lands among the northern river counties to be used as each county saw fit.[13]

Loyalty to the Whig party as well as concern over the problem of building levees no doubt prompted the voters to elect Alcorn in 1848 as a state senator to represent the three Delta counties of Panola, Tallahatchie and Coahoma at Jackson. During his first term as a senator, Delta interests overrode a basic Whig stand when he and a fellow senator, W. A. Lake, protested against an act which would have permitted the sale of 500,000 acres of swamp land donated by Congress in order to pay for the defunct Planters' Bank bonds which the state had underwritten and later repudiated. Although the state should meet its obligations, this would be a violation of the trust placed in it, since the land had been donated "for a declared purpose." [14]

At the beginning of his term Alcorn became a member, and later chairman, of the senate's standing internal improvements committee. During the regular and called sessions of the senate in 1850, the extraordinary session of 1851, and the regular session of 1852, he introduced acts "to provide for the construction of a levee on the Mississippi River in the counties of . . ." covering in differing combinations all the river counties from DeSoto on the Tennessee border down to Warren near Vicksburg, in an apparent attempt to coordinate the line of local levees. During

11  Robert W. Harrison, "Levee Building in Mississippi Before the Civil War," *Journal of Mississippi History* (1950), XII, 66.
12  Robert W. Harrison, *Levee Districts and Levee Building in Mississippi* (Washington: U. S. Department of Agriculture, October, 1951), 8–9.
13  Harrison, "Levee Building in Mississippi," 72.
14  *Journal of the Senate of the State of Mississippi* (Jackson: Price and Fall, 1848), 604.

the special session of 1850 called to consider a secession convention, he diverted the lawmakers' attention from disunion for a time at least with his levee bills.[15] Some of his bills were passed, but the majority were tabled or lost in committee.

In the years during which Alcorn fought for a unified levee system, he developed certain basic arguments. He could inundate his listeners with figures on the flow and fall of the Mississippi River, on the number of bales of cotton per acre grown in the Delta, on the potential yield from reclaimed land, and on the ultimate return to the state in land sales and taxes. He would also threaten his listeners with foreign competition, particularly Britain's attempts to encourage cotton production in its colonies, and he kept a record of the amount and price of British and foreign cotton shipped to England from 1820 to 1833. [16] On behalf of one of his measures he argued that by selling 100,000 acres of submerged land at two dollars an acre the levee could be built and the higher price of the reclaimed land would provide a fund to educate every poor child in the state.[17] According to one Whig newspaper Alcorn's speech was so convincing it silenced the violent opposition of the representatives from the interior counties,[18] and the senate passed his bill on February 21, 1852. [19]

The year 1852 also saw the defeat of Winfield Scott in the presidential election and with it hopes of a national Whig party revival.[20] The Union party likewise was rapidly disintegrating, and Alcorn began to devote more and more of his energy and activity as a legislator to obtaining the type of levee system he wanted. In April, 1853, his name appeared as a member of the new Board of Levee Commissioners of Coahoma County,[21] and the following year he succeeded in obtaining passage of a bill which in theory at least attempted to integrate the levee building pro-

15  *Journal of the Senate of the State of Mississippi, Called Session* (Jackson: Fall and Marshall, 1850), 27, 33, 42.
16  Small notebook in Alcorn Papers.
17  Jackson *Flag of the Union*, January 16, 1852.
18  Natchez *Courier*, February 16 and 17, 1852.
19  *Journal of the Senate of the State of Mississippi, Extraordinary Session, November 1851* (Jackson: Palmer and Pickett, 1852), 461.
20  I use the term "revival" because if the decline of the Whig Party is marked by its entrance into coalitions, then, in Mississippi 1849 must be taken as the beginning, with the call for a Southern convention by leaders of both parties.
21  *Journal of the Senate of the State of Mississippi* (Jackson: Barksdale and Jones, 1854), 478.

grams of the Delta counties by forming a Superior Board of Levee Commissioners with general jurisdiction over all levee construction in the region.

Alcorn assumed personal responsibility for the success of this board by becoming its president when it began operations in June, 1854. But he was unable to surmount the divisiveness of the local factions, as he admitted in his report to the legislature of 1856. He pointed out that the law had fallen short of its objective because it had placed responsibility for the levees with the respective counties which had rendered the board inoperative simply by not cooperating with it. He asked for stronger central authority and defined a good levee system as a "system of agricultural insurance" which would be for the common good of the entire region, not just that of the local interests. His entire report was practical and convincing, containing specific examples of the law's weaknesses and concrete suggestions for a statute that, in his opinion, would be functional.[22]

In spite of the soundness of Alcorn's views, he must have felt that his request for more authority had cost him vital political support in the Delta, for in 1855 he decided to run for election to the state house of representatives rather than the senate. Thus he needed to appeal only to the voters of his home county. The citizens of Coahoma County elected him again, mainly on the basis of his fight for levees,[23] indicating that at least those in his immediate area continued to support him and his concept of strong leadership.

During the same session that saw passage of the act to form the Superior Board of Levee Commissioners, the legislature also passed an act abolishing the boards of levee commissioners for Tunica and Coahoma counties and replacing them with a single commissioner in each county. This commissioner had somewhat more power than his predecessors, being responsible for his own accounts and having the power to sue to force completion of contracts. In addition the act provided for the compulsory use of slaves from neighboring plantations to work on the levees. Alcorn assumed the position of levee commissioner for Coahoma County, and in his report of 1856 used his county as an example of the

---

22 *Journal of the House of Representatives of the State of Mississippi* (Jackson: E. Barksdale, 1856) 256–67.
23 Eliza Jane Alcorn Clark to John T. Lusk, March 20, 1856, in possession of Mrs. V. A. Hain.

advantages of individual management. But his fellow Coahomians did not all agree. A storm of protest arose from both counties against one official having "such dictatorial powers," and against the use of valuable slaves on the levees. The unpopular act was repealed in 1856, [24] and again Alcorn's attempt at strong leadership was repulsed.

In 1856 opponents of the levee system combined to introduce in the house of representatives a committee report recommending that the Yazoo Pass be opened and declared a navigable stream. This would have broken the levee line and subjected large sections of northern Coahoma County to flooding. After a fight Alcorn, Charles Clark, and C. L. Robards succeeded in defeating a motion to accept this report. [25] Possibly his discouragement over legislative opposition, combined with the unfavorable political situation (Mississippi was overwhelmingly Democratic, and the Whigs had been forced to combine with the Know-Nothings), contributed to Alcorn's decision in 1857 not to seek reelection to the Mississippi legislature. He did run for Congress and, as he had foreseen, was defeated, which in effect freed him to devote his time to the actual construction of levees.

A record-breaking spring flood in 1858 broke through the levees which had been built, setting off wholesale criticism of the Superior Board of Levee Commissioners. Apparently Alcorn came under fire, not only as president of the board but as levee commissioner under the repealed act of 1854. Since he was no longer a member of the legislature, he addressed a pamphlet to Governor William McWillie asking that he give his views on levees to that body. In this pamphlet Alcorn denied that he had ever made a cent of profit from the swamp lands, that lands entered in his name had been sold for the benefit of the county. He accused the legislature of pursuing a course that went from bad to worse, isolating the levee interest from the general interests of the state, and breaking it down again into a system of county jurisdictions, because of "stupid and unworthy jealousies."

In more specific terms than ever before he urged a consolidated system, tying it into wasteland reclamation on other rivers so as

24 *Journal of the House of Representatives of the State of Mississippi* (1856) 200–61; Harrison, *Levee Districts*, 12.

25 *Journal of the House of Representatives of the State of Mississippi* (1856) 389, 414.

to generalize interest in it. He wanted "a consolidated interest, a consolidated treasury, a consolidated credit, as in all other great public works; also a directory, a president, a chief engineer and an engineering corps." He pointed to examples of great railroads to show the feasibility of such a plan in spite of the distances involved, and in imitation of them, he suggested creation of a four-year term Board of Directors elected by the actual levee-taxpayers.[26] In July of that year he also published *An Address to the People of Coahoma County* to vindicate himself and to urge reconstruction of the levees. Besides defending himself, he pointed to the dykes of Holland and the levee work in the Po Valley as examples of what could be done. He called for putting the entire system under a head with plenary powers, such a person to be paid an adequate salary so that it would be possible to engage an able man who would devote his full time to the project.[27]

Behind the charges and denial of charges which swirled around Alcorn, as well as behind his proposals for a strong authority, there seemed to be a conflict between him and his fellow planters with personal overtones and a basic difference of opinion on the method of exercising authority. The attractive, aggressive Alcorn may have been too domineering for his Jacksonian neighbors to accept. His driving thirst for power and his forceful exercise of leadership were opposed to their taste for a division of authority and a more democratic, if less efficient, manner of taking action.

Events, however, were forcing action upon them all. As settlers continued to come into the Delta and the region began to develop, it seemed apparent that in it the slave-operated cotton plantation economy of the older states could be successfully continued on a large scale, thus making feasible the acquisition of the slaves and land to which so many of its inhabitants aspired. But effective protection against flooding was needed, and the severe flood of 1858 led to increasing demands, which resulted in the most comprehensive legislation the state would pass to aid the richest section within its borders.

26  James Lusk Alcorn, *An Address to His Excellency, William McWillie, Governor of the State of Mississippi, upon the Subject of Levees, and the Reforms in Legislation; and Administration Necessary to Success* (Memphis: Hutton & Clark's Publishing House, 1858).

27  James Lusk Alcorn, *An Address to the People of Coahoma County, Mississippi upon the Subject of Levees* (Memphis: Bulletin Company, 1858).

Although he was not a member of the legislature, Alcorn claimed that he was responsible for the law passed on December 2, 1858, creating a board of levee commissioners with jurisdiction over the entire Delta region. This board was to elect a president who would have broad powers to enforce its rulings. It had the power to pass ordinances, employ inspectors, let contracts, and in time of emergency assume almost absolute police powers. It was to absorb the activities and, after two years, the debts of the local levee boards.[28] Some members of the legislature found its grant of authority so large they signed a protest that this new board was being given what amounted to dictatorial power.[29]

When it met early in 1859, the new board of levee commissioners elected Alcorn as its president, and the legislature voted him a yearly salary of $6,000, the highest amount paid any official in the state at that time.[30] The position provided him with the type of challenge he particularly liked and one he had obviously sought. He took a characteristically aggressive attitude toward his duties and endeavored to use every means possible to establish the secure levee line he had been advocating. His energy did a great deal to stimulate the board and the engineering forces,[31] and natural and man-made impediments seemed to yield a little. Soon after his election Alcorn started out with parties of surveyors and engineers to chart the line for his projected levee, although water from the spring floods was still standing in the lowlands. While the early summer heat, heavy with humidity from the stagnant water, did not seem to bother him, almost all the members of his Eastern-imported engineering and surveying staffs were stricken with fever.

The $500,000 in land scrip allotted to the board did not sell well, and its inadequate funds were tied up when the Chancery Court of Yazoo and Sunflower counties declared the levee law of 1858 unconstitutional. Alcorn asked the river counties to assess a twenty-five-cent levee tax permitted by law and to allow the board to administer the funds, to which they agreed and which, as he pointed out in one of his reports, amounted to an act of confidence in his personal integrity.

28  Harrison, "Levee Building in Mississippi," 80.
29  *Journal of the Senate of the State of Mississippi* (Jackson: E. Barksdale, 1858), 196.
30  Horace S. Fulkerson, *A Civilian's Recollections of the War Between the States,* ed. Percy L. Rainwater (Baton Rouge: Otto Claitor, 1939), 6.
31  Harrison, *Levee Districts,* 16–17.

Although the High Court of Errors and Appeals reversed the Chancery Court decision, Alcorn continued to experience legal troubles. He was deluged with lawsuits for damages to property over which the levee would go, or which would be left outside its protection because of the decision reached by him and his chief engineer to move the levee line further inland. In his first report to the legislature he said bluntly that he had determined "on my own responsibility" not to pay a cent from the levee funds. He had ample use for those funds over ground where the right of way had been freely given.

His biggest problem, as he pointed out in this report, was revenue. Although he felt that the law of 1858 "laid down the beginning of the true principle for future action," the legislature would have to decide whether to discontinue the project or "place it on a basis of security." He told the legislators he expected to spend every cent under his control that season, and "the future must be left to provide for itself." But he closed his report on a note of Whiggish optimism:

Who can predict the coming wealth of that vast alluvial? To Mississippi it is, if cherished, an inestimable treasure. Wealth is power! The wealth of a State consists in the property and intelligence of her people; every intelligent proposition which has for its object the increase of knowledge, or the enhancement of aggregate wealth, should receive the calm judgment of the Legislature.[32]

The suspicious Democratic house of representatives was unimpressed with his long report and passed a resolution asking for another accounting of the "acts and doings of said Board." [33] While Alcorn was preparing it, the representatives from the hill counties prevented the appropriation of any additional funds for the board. In his supplemental report, Alcorn conceded defeat, and asked only that the board "be allowed to retreat with *our honor*," by which he meant that he wanted the period of taxation by the levee board extended for two years so that it could redeem the land scrip it had sold.[34] The extension was granted, to be repealed a year and a half later.

The board continued to function for another eighteen months,

32 *Journal of the House of Representatives of the State of Mississippi* (Jackson: E. Barksdale, 1858), 310–14.
33 *Ibid.*, 366.
34 *Ibid.*, 366, 451–52.

and Alcorn, in his last report, dated November 25, 1861, was able to boast that the region had sustained no loss from floods during the preceding two years. He protested against the recently passed laws which suspended the levee tax and made the collection of damages too easy, and against the popular opinion that the salary of the president should be reduced. Long years had he struggled for "a proper embankment on the great river shore," he wrote, and then he briefly described the forces opposing him: ". . . the river influence is disposed to the local system, a system which will ever bring ruin in its train. The interior counties think that they should not be taxed, but their neighbors should bear all of the burdens, while the landsharks are ever on the alert to see how the law may be avoided. . . ." [35] Regretting that he had been unable to convince the people that a unified system with an adequately-salaried head was the cheapest way in the long run to build a levee, he resigned his position.

Because of lack of funds and the fact that the Delta was the scene of sporadic military operations during most of the Civil War, the board virtually dissolved following its president's resignation. Living on his plantation during the war years Alcorn saw his work destroyed. Grant dynamited the levees in the Yazoo Pass area in an attempt to float gunboats down to Vicksburg through the Yazoo–Sunflower river system, and the remaining works were ruined by a severe flood in the spring of 1865.

Notwithstanding final defeat, Alcorn and the board made genuine progress in the over-all levee program. By one means or another they managed to keep engineers and laborers in the field during the entire period in which they functioned, even at one point appealing to public-spirited citizens to donate money. In this way they were able to raise about $200,000, with the hope that the legislature would reimburse the contributors, but it never did.[36]

When the war began, the Delta was protected by 310 miles of continuous levee, from the base of the hills near the Tennessee border to Brunswick Landing in Warren County, above Vicksburg.

---

35 *Journal of the Senate of the State of Mississippi* (Jackson: Cooper and Kimball, 1862), 117–24.
36 Harrison, "Levee Building in Mississippi," 90; John William Wade, "Lands of the Liquidating Levee Board Through Litigation and Legislation," *Publications of the Mississippi Historical Society* (1906), IX, 280. Both believe that an excellent job was done. Wade feels that in a short time the entire Delta would have been protected.

Almost half (one hundred forty-two miles) of this levee had been constructed by the 1858 Levee District, and it protected four million acres of rich alluvial soil which in 1860 produced 220,000 bales of cotton and 2,500,000 bushels of corn.[37]

In spite of the charges made against him because of the salary he received and the money and land scrip he handled, Alcorn appears to have come out of the enterprise with clean hands and to have earned the respect of his fellow planters in the Delta, even though they resented his dictatorial methods. His activities brought him lasting fame as the foremost proponent of levees in the state's history, and for thirty years he continued to be a spokesman for the Delta planters whenever the question of levees came up. The support he received from planters on both sides of the political fence cannot be ignored in evaluating his political importance.

His activity on behalf of levees, in addition, sharpened and brought into greater prominence some of the characteristics which distinguished his later career. He continued to believe in the participation of state or federal government in projects whose primary purpose was to benefit a region, as against local or private control and in contrast to the Jacksonian tendency toward unlimited private enterprise and decentralized government. In line with his Hamiltonian-Whig beliefs he attempted to demonstrate how he believed responsible leadership should be exercised, with scrupulous honesty and power sufficient to make such leadership effective. But in an age of expanding democracy his attitude proved to be an irritant of considerable proportions, arousing an opposition among his planter neighbors that contributed to his failure. This was not the only time Alcorn found effective application of the Whig ideal of strong, aristocratic leadership difficult to achieve.

While pursuing his levee work Alcorn continued to sit in the legislature until 1857 representing Delta Whiggery in a predominantly Democratic state, a Whiggery now allied, since the demise of the Union party, with the Know-Nothing movement. In the state elections of 1855 Know-Nothingism absorbed practically all of the Whig party, including its leader William L. Sharkey.[38]

---

37 Harrison, *Levee Districts*, 23; James Wilford Garner, *Reconstruction in Mississippi* (New York: Macmillan, 1901), 126.
38 Percy Lee Rainwater, *Mississippi, Storm Center of Secession, 1856–1861* (Baton Rouge: Otto Claitor, 1938), 126.

During the presidential campaign of 1856 between Democrat James Buchanan, Republican John Frémont, and middle-of-the-roader Millard Fillmore, Alcorn noted with approval a quotation from one of Fillmore's speeches which advocated the application of the golden rule to relations between the states and expressed horror at the idea of disunion.[39] Since both the Know-Nothing and Whig parties had nominated Fillmore at their conventions, Alcorn probably supported him actively.

During the summer of 1857 the Mississippi Know-Nothing party held a convention in Jackson and nominated Alcorn as its candidate for governor, with a platform which was as much an attempt at compromise and coalition as the party itself. Planks included a pledge to maintain the Union "of co-equal sovereign States, and the Constitution as our fathers made it," obedience to the laws and the Constitution, the doctrine of religious liberty and separation of church and state, exclusion of pauper and criminal immigrants, and the revision of immigration laws to protect institutions held in common. The delegates denied the Constitution the power to exclude any property from the territories, and said that states must be admitted to the Union if they had republican constitutions, regardless of their stand on slavery. Also in this regard they called for a cessation of agitation over slavery and pledged themselves to stand by the platform of the Mississippi State Convention of 1850 with regard to the rights of southern states. Robert J. Walker was condemned for giving his inaugural address in Kansas before an "illegal and fraudulent Legislature," and the Democratic party was censured for not removing him.[40] Except for the addition of nativist elements, the stand was that of the earlier coalition Union party brought up to date.

There is no reason to doubt that Alcorn was in accord with this platform. In a notebook compiled during 1856-57 there is an article, or possibly a speech, in his handwriting, which states his arguments against the encouragement of immigration. It is typically Know-Nothing in its fear of foreign inundation of the country, a threat to American institutions, the inability of Europeans to understand popular government, and the tendency of the mass of them to be immoral and incompetent.[41] As a rule, the anti-Catholic bias

39  James Lusk Alcorn notebook, in possession of Mrs. V. A. Hain.
40  Memphis *Daily Appeal*, July 22, 1857.
41  James Lusk Alcorn notebook, in possession of Mrs. V. A. Hain.

of the Northern Know-Nothing movement was missing in the Southern version, and this would seem to be true of Alcorn's views also, but pure nativism was as evident in one as the other. At the line where nativism blended into nationalism, both movements were anxious to preserve the Union, and this characteristic of the groups might have molded them into a conservative nationwide successor to the Whig party, had not the preservation of slavery been stronger in the South than any other interest.

The Know-Nothing movement in Mississippi was weaker than either of its Whiggish predecessors, and possibly because Alcorn could foresee the extent of probable defeat, he refused to accept its nomination as gubernatorial candidate. However, he did decide to run in the First District for Congress against the Democratic party candidate, L. Q. C. Lamar, who was then beginning his political career. Because by 1857 the state was overwhelmingly Democratic, Alcorn knew he could not win, but since he had decided not to seek reelection to the state legislature where defeat might be politically disastrous, he chose this means of remaining politically alive. Also, he was sincerely convinced that the Democratic party, supported by the masses, meant nothing but trouble for the country. As he wrote to his wife: "The democratic legions are not to be moved. They pour out the increase of a blind Idolitary [sic] upon a party powerful for evil impotent for good. I shall be beaten largely, but will reduce the majority. My canvass however will give me reputation, I don't regret it." [42]

In his speeches he blamed the Democrats for all the evils that disturbed the harmony of the nation, condemned the Kansas-Nebraska Bill, which he, more clearly than his opponent, saw benefited the North rather than the South, and predicted worse things to come.[43] During the campaign he denied membership in the Know-Nothing party, but continued in line with the state organization's platform to criticize the administration's support of Robert Walker and its handling of Kansas, and attempted to link the Democratic party and Martin Van Buren to the Freesoilers.[44] The campaign was a colorful one; Lamar and Alcorn were, and remained, personal friends, and the encounters between them were

42  James Lusk Alcorn to Amelia Alcorn, September 9, 1857, in Alcorn File.
43  Vicksburg *Southern Herald*, October 3, 1857.
44  Memphis *Daily Appeal*, September 30, 1857; Vicksburg *Southern Herald*, September 12, 1857.

favorably noted by contemporaries for high-flown oratory in the approved manner and clever but good natured repartee. The latter revolved particularly around the personal appearance of the two candidates—Lamar liked to appear in homespun jeans and a wrinkled shirt, driving a mule and cart, and Alcorn always appeared immaculately dressed in the latest fashion, driven in a carriage. Lightly as this difference in dress was regarded, it is suggestive of a deep difference in attitude toward politicking and the voter on the part of the two men. Democrat Lamar endeavored to create the illusion of equality, of being one of the masses; Whig Alcorn offered the voters the illusion of superiority, of selecting one higher in quality to lead.

As Alcorn had anticipated, he lost, even in his own county of Coahoma. Besides the overwhelming strength of the Democratic party, part of the extent of his failure may have been, as one correspondent indicated, due to the awkwardness of his position in regard to party affiliation. It may also have been partly because Lamar seems to have agreed with him on the need for levees.[45]

Lamar was reelected two years later almost without opposition because the anti-Democratic party coalition had again disintegrated. But during that year, under the pressure of the election, the Whig elements began to congeal into a new grouping. In the spring of 1859 they held a meeting under the chairmanship of William Sharkey to oppose a movement to reopen the African slave trade. The issue was hardly clear-cut because a portion of the Democratic party was also opposed at least to agitation on the subject since it might divide the party. Then in July this new coalition nominated a list of candidates for the Mississippi elections, and adopted a platform which continued opposition to the reopening of the slave trade and called for secession only if a Republican were elected the following year. They were badly beaten, carrying only four Delta counties, not including Coahoma, and do not appear to have had Alcorn's support.[46]

Spurred on by this defeat, the Unionist and Whig groups took steps to tighten their organization, and discovered a national movement with which to identify themselves—the Constitutional Union party. Sharkey called a meeting of the Opposition Central Com-

45 James Lusk Alcorn to L. Q. C. Lamar, August 25, 1858, in Alcorn File.
46 Jack W. Gunn, "Mississippi in 1860 as Reflected in the Activities of the Governor's Office," *Journal of Mississippi History* (1960), XVII, 180.

mittee for March, 1860. Its membership included men who had been identified with the earlier attempt to launch an opposition party, and this time Alcorn's name appeared among them. Plans were laid for a convention and Sharkey, as chairman, called upon all those in favor of "a National Union organization" opposing disunion to send delegates to it. This convention assembled in April and selected delegates to go to the national presidential convention of the Constitutional Union party at Baltimore. Sharkey headed the delegation and was also the state's choice for presidential nominee.[47]

The presidential election campaign of 1860 in Mississippi centered on John C. Breckinridge, the candidate of the Southern wing of the Democratic party, and John Bell, nominated by the Constitutional Union party. The campaign resolved itself into an argument over means, namely, which candidate stood the better chance of defeating Lincoln.[48] Alcorn, still hoping for a compromise, accepted the rather negative Constitutional Union platform of support for the Constitution and its laws, and campaigned actively for Bell. Lincoln's election galvanized the secession movement into almost immediate action, ending the uneasy compromise Alcorn and his fellow planters had worked so hard to maintain for over ten years as a protection for their unprecedented prosperity.

In spite of struggles over levees and politics, Coahoma County in particular had flourished during the 1850's. In that period it more than doubled its population and cotton production.[49] Alcorn prospered as did his county. He built up an extensive law practice and became particularly successful as a criminal lawyer.[50] Soon after his second marriage he took his wife's younger brother Alfred Young Glover into his office, and by 1859 the practice had become so extensive that he made him a partner.[51] In addition to his cabin at Mound Place on the Yazoo Pass, by now enlarged into a comfortable home, he acquired a house in Friar's Point for the use

47  Rainwater, *Mississippi, Storm Center of Secession*, 102, 117.
48  *Ibid.*, 140. Unlike Louisiana, Mississippi does not appear to have had an active Douglas wing of the Democratic party.
49  Herbert Weaver, *Mississippi Farmers, 1850–1860* (Chapel Hill: University of North Carolina Press, 1947), 21, 25.
50  Livingston, *American Portrait Gallery*, 7; James Lusk Alcorn to J. F. H. Claiborne, March 28, 1879, in Claiborne Papers, Box 1, Folder 8, Southern Historical Collection, University of North Carolina.
51  John Livingston, *Livingston's United States Law Register and Official Directory* (New York: John A. Gray, 1859).

of his family when they came to town. In 1850 he valued his estate at $16,625, with seventeen slaves; in 1860 he listed its value at $250,000, with ninety-three slaves.[52] He was well on his way to achieving that cherished goal of every white Southerner—a plantation, slaves, and a way of life, perhaps already half myth, but at least partially attainable.

Alcorn clearly saw that the two necessary ingredients for his prosperity and social standing—a stable economic life and protection for slavery—could best be provided by a strong national government, and he fought for it as long as he dared. Only when the whole fabric into which he had woven his pattern of life pulled definitely the other way did he go along. To have done otherwise would have meant tearing himself away from everything he believed in, including the whole set of personal loyalties to which he was committed, from the welfare of his family and region to the ideal of the aristocratic self-made gentleman. His political beliefs could be expressed in either camp, but the base from which he practiced them could be preserved only by remaining loyal to his region and this, in the long run, was what he did.

52 James Lusk Alcorn notebook, in Alcorn Papers.

# 3

# A Mississippi General

LINCOLN'S ELECTION to the presidency brought the question of secession squarely into the foreground, and in the fall of 1860 the Mississippi legislature occupied itself almost entirely with the subject. Late in November it passed a bill calling for the election on December 20 of delegates to a secession convention to meet in Jackson on January 7, 1861. [1]

Alcorn had a great deal to lose by a Southern adventure in independence, a loss which could be equaled only by the abolition of slavery or his alienation from the region which had provided him with his prosperity and prominence; the same can be said of other members of his class in the South. On the other hand, those for whom the Southern dream had not yet become a reality were strongly opposed to anything which might stand in their way. But to both groups, the haves and the hope-to-haves, slavery was a necessary element, and therefore once again the debate prior to the election of delegates to the convention was only over the best means of protecting the institution.

Many conservative Whigs, Alcorn among them, still felt this could best be done within the Union, but they were capable of modifying their course to secure the desired end. They agreed in substance with Judge Amos R. Johnston, who did not believe the right to secede was inherent in the Constitution. On November 14, 1860, Johnston urged as the strategy of the Unionists that they

1 *Journal of the Senate of the State of Mississippi* (Jackson: E. Barksdale, 1860), 18–20.

*39*

join in the tide of resistance to the national government in order "by calm and conservative action to so direct and steer it as to uphold the Union and at the same time to secure all the rights of our section under the Constitution of our common country." He also argued that should revolt become necessary to gain equality in the Union, the cooperation of all the slaveholding states would be required.[2]

This was a practical position, as well as a typically Whig one. It did not present the issue as the black-or-white one of preserving or dissolving the Union, but left the door open to a great variety and degree of action. The differences of opinion expressed during the campaign were not basic enough to make remarkable the final, almost unanimous, vote for secession. The majority felt this was the best means of protecting slavery, and the minority went along in good, democratic fashion.

The views expressed were those of three groups: the "fire-eating" Southerners who wanted immediate secession; those who wanted to wait for other Southern states to join, or believed that the situation was not as yet grave enough for such a drastic move; and those who believed that disunion would not be a remedy and would not in the long run provide better protection for slavery. Alcorn belonged to this last group, but his final capitulation cannot be seen as a denial of any basic principle, for these differences in viewpoint were only over the means for best preserving the institution of slavery.

As the time for the election of delegates approached, William L. Sharkey promoted pro-Union meetings in the southwestern part of the state, while Alcorn conducted a whirlwind campaign in the Delta. One contemporary felt that it was largely because of his influence and efforts that every county in the river district sent pro-Union delegates to the convention.[3]

Nonetheless, the campaign, coming so soon after the presidential election and raising such an involved issue, did not stimulate voter enthusiasm, and only 60 percent of those who had voted in the previous election took part in selecting the delegates.[4] The term "Cooperationist" was ambiguous and seems to have been applied to anyone not in favor of the immediate and independent secession

2  Rainwater, *Mississippi, Storm Center of Secession*, 165–66.
3  Fulkerson, *A Civilian's Recollections*, 6.
4  Rainwater, *Mississippi, Storm Center of Secession*, 196.

of Mississippi. Alcorn himself was elected as a Cooperationist,[5] although he belonged to the group most clearly opposed to secession.

The membership of the convention was dominated by planters, lawyers, and farmers, a majority of whom were slaveholders, with the cooperationist groups containing a slightly larger percentage of the larger slaveholding planters than the secessionists.[6] Alcorn, with his pro-Union background, seemed especially anxious to prove his orthodoxy. He gave his occupation as lawyer, his religion as Old School Presbyterian, and under "Politics" simply the word "Southern," while many of his colleagues described themselves as "Whigs," "Clay Whigs," "Old Whigs," or "Old Line Whigs." Also he allowed himself to be listed as having been born in Kentucky,[7] a more "Southern" state than Illinois, although Golconda is on the west bank of the Ohio River, just across from Kentucky. That he consciously permitted the error is suggested by the fact that in a letter written a few months later in Kentucky, he spoke of his "return to my native heath [sic]." [8]

The struggle in the convention over whether to secede, and under what circumstances, gave Alcorn an excellent opportunity to serve as a political leader. He was the recognized head of the group which opposed secession, and as such was nominated to be president of the convention. His defeat indicated clearly the minority position of the pro-Union delegates who nevertheless attempted to modify the course of the convention in accordance with Judge Johnston's advice.

While the membership of the Committee of Fifteen appointed to draw up the Ordinance of Secession was divided fairly between Democrats and Whigs, only four pro-Union delegates were appointed: Alcorn of Coahoma County, Walker Brooke of Warren County, E. H. Sanders of Attala County, and John A. Blair of

5 Jackson *Weekly Mississippian*, January 2, 1861.
6 Ralph Wooster, "The Membership of the Mississippi Secession Convention of 1861," *Journal of Mississippi History*, XVI (1954), 255.
7 *Proceedings of the Mississippi State Convention* (Jackson: Power and Cadwallader, 1861), chart bound into front of volume.
8 U. S. War Department, *The War of the Rebellion: A Compilation of the Official Records of the Union and Confederate Armies* (hereinafter referred to as *Official Records*), Ser. I, Vol. IV (Washington: Government Printing Office, 1882), 465, James Lusk Alcorn to Brig. Gen. S. B. Buckner, October 19, 1861.

Tishomingo County.[9] Half of the Whigs at the convention voted consistently with the secessionists. When the ordinance was reported out of committee, J. S. Yerger made a motion for a convention of the slave-holding states before seceding to again seek protection for themselves within the Union, a hope of many cooperationists. Alcorn pointedly voted against the resolution in order to bring moderate secessionists to their side and to give the pro-Unionists a chance to appear to be in favor of ultimate secession. When Yerger's resolution failed, he introduced an amendment delaying secession until Alabama, Georgia, Florida, and Louisiana should secede also, hoping that his previous action would help rally to their side all those opposed to immediate secession. When this second amendment did not pass, Brooks proposed a resolution that the ordinance be ratified by the qualified electors at a special election, but it was likewise defeated.[10]

Immediately after the rejection of these amendments a vote was called for on the Ordinance of Secession itself, and the roll call started with Alcorn's name. Taking full advantage of the drama inherent in the moment, he arose, paused, and then in an emotion-packed voice declared: "Mr. President, the die is cast; the Rubicon is crossed; I follow the army that goes to Rome; I vote for the ordinance." [11] The effect was all he could have desired. He wrote in a letter to his wife ". . . my speech . . . was received by the convention—and in the galleries with long and loud applause, the ladies waved their handkerchefs [sic] and a most profound sensation ensued." [12] Any opposition among the pro-Union delegates crumbled after that, and Walker Brooke also gave a dramatic speech before voting for the ordinance, which was ratified by a large majority.[13]

For a man with Alcorn's political instincts, the setting for his capitulation speech was ideal. He was known as the leader of the minority group. The majority at the convention was strongly in

9 *Proceedings of the Mississippi State Convention* (1861), 7.
10 *Ibid.*, 12.
11 *Ibid.*, 13.
12 James Lusk Alcorn to Amelia Alcorn, January 15, 1861, in Alcorn Papers.
13 John W. Wood, *Union and Secession in Mississippi* (Memphis: Saunders, Parrish, and Whitmore, 1863). Wood, the only delegate to refuse to sign the Ordinance of Secession, published this pamphlet in defense of his position. In contrast to Alcorn and other Whigs, he appears to have had a concept of the Union as a true entity, and he saw an inherent integrity in the national government.

favor of secession, and the graceful gallery, which encircled more than half the chamber, was packed with citizens of Jackson who were enthusiastic proponents of taking Mississippi out of the Union. To have voted against secession in these circumstances would have meant banishment from the political scene, not to mention social ostracism. He was too young, ambitious, and actively involved in the political scene to attempt to retire as Sharkey, older and with an established reputation, would do. He felt strongly that he was destined to lead, and that he had a role to play in the momentous events taking place. But in order to exercise leadership in such a gathering he would have to join it in as public a manner as possible. The opportunity to do this presented itself, and he made the most of it.

Personal considerations and beliefs also had a part in his decision. To have stood in open opposition to secession would have meant risking everything he prized. Since he stood heart and soul with his fellow Mississippians on the need to protect slavery, he had to go along with them, critical though he was of the means they had taken to accomplish this. The significance of his reference to the Rubicon lay in the fact that he believed he was deliberately committing treason. "In this utterance," wrote Swift, "he says he spoke not as a *sophist* after the fashion of Calhoun but as a rebel after the fashion of Caesar." [14]

Early in the convention, when the pro-Union delegates realized that they were outnumbered and were going to be defeated, they met in a series of caucuses to plan strategy. Alcorn presided at the meetings and at one of them sketched a dreary picture of the South "when the northern soldier would tread her cotton fields, when the slave should be made *free* and the proud Southerner stricken to the dust in his presence!" Yet they foresaw that secession would be approved and that they would have to stand up and be counted with the majority. Years later Alcorn described the Whig-inspired reasoning by which the delegates made this move palatable:

The Convention now sitting is a body steeped in treason, maddened in the presence of imaginary wrongs, will listen to no reason. We must appeal to the people! And in appealing to the people we must take upon ourselves, if we would be heard, the crime of secession. Should we fail to commit ourselves, it will be charged that we intend to desert the South. . . . The epithet of coward and submissionist will be every-

14 Swift, "James Lusk Alcorn," 4–5.

where applied to us. . . . But if we shall take upon ourselves the hated
vows, our enemies will not be able to turn the faces of the masses
against our pleadings. Once before them they will turn upon the enemies of the Union and salute the flag of the fathers. . . . I and others
agreeing with me determined to seize the wild and maddened steed by
the mane and run with him *for a time*. We voted for secession and
signed the ordinance.[15]

After thus ingratiating themselves with the voters, the delegates
planned in the fall gubernatorial election to put a state ticket in
the field pledged to return Mississippi to the Union, with Yerger
for Governor, Alcorn for Attorney General, and the watchword,
"Repeal, Repeal!" A true leader would go along with the mob
until a propitious moment when he could assume leadership and
bring the people back to their senses.

No doubt this pro-Union group hoped for the kind of reversal
of feeling that had occurred in 1851, but the outbreak of the Civil
War produced a solidarity within the state which paralyzed their
opposition before it even began. In the midst of enthusiastic preparations for war, Mississippians reelected Pettus as governor almost
without a contest.

Alcorn's actions at the secession convention gained him one of
his objectives, namely, an active part in the proceedings. His
already established position of leadership in the Whig party, the
influence he exerted in the secession convention, and his dramatic
capitulation combined to force the secessionists to include him in
their activities. As he wrote his wife: "I have been my dear Amelia
very busy since my arrival. I am one who is looked to for work,
I have been assigned some very responsible positions, having been
appointed one of the committee of ways and means—whose duty
it is to provide money for the war, the most impossible of all
positions. I think the convention looks to me with great confidence.
My speeches are listened to with great respect."

Even as he was immersed in these activities, another even more
attractive role than that of politician began to beckon him. His
letter to his wife continued: "I have been offered a seat in the
southern congress to assemble in Montgomery Alabama, I have

15 Fulkerson, *A Civilian's Recollections*, 7–8. Fulkerson, who published
   the original of the work in which the account appeared in 1886, cautiously
   added: "The reader must remember that the foregoing are the words of
   Gov. Alcorn."

told my friends that I had rather be placed in the army. To the Battle field my dear wife I must go if war ensues of which I have no doubt. I think I will be elected a Brigadier General." [16] As he desired, the secession convention elected him a brigadier general on the state military board, along with Major General Jefferson Davis, who headed it, Earl Van Dorn, Charles Clark, and C. H. Mott. Alcorn was the only original member who had not had experience in the Mexican War.

A combination of reasons, real and romantic, practical and idealistic, governed his decision to seek a military rather than a political role. He tried to explain them to his wife:

Before this reaches you, you will have learned that I am a Brigadier General. Don't think I have made a misstep. I think not; it will give me prestige; it but paves the way for a civil position. If peace shall come, this will be so. If war comes, with my own good sword I may win the first distinction. Destiny, wife, destiny. I believe in destiny. My mission will be filled. To be called to so high a position from civil life, in the hour of my country's danger, is a compliment to my head as well as nerve.[17]

Long before secession was imminent, Alcorn had predicted that such a step would bring war with it. In the convention he urged military preparedness. "Mr. Alcorn was prepared to go with him who goes fartherest to realize money for the defence of the State," wrote delegate John W. Wood in 1863. "He had no hesitation to vote upon an ordinance *to place the State on a war footing.*" [18] On the military board only he and General Van Dorn seemed to realize that war was likely, and they worked hard to obtain the purchase of arms.[19]

The firing on Fort Sumter confirmed Alcorn's apprehensions and put an end to the political plans he and his group had for opposing Pettus. Left with only the military as an arena for his energy and leadership, he became impatient with the slow progress of the Mississippi military board. Three days after Major Robert Anderson's surrender of Fort Sumter Alcorn wrote to the newly

16 James Lusk Alcorn to Amelia Alcorn, January 15, 1861, in Alcorn Papers.
17 James Lusk Alcorn to Amelia Alcorn, January 26, 1861, copy in Rainwater Collection, Box 2, Folder 26, Mississippi Department of Archives and History.
18 Wood, *Union and Secession in Mississippi*, 24.
19 Fulkerson, *A Civilian's Recollections*, 47.

named President of the Confederacy, Jefferson Davis, that it was apparent the South was on the eve of a desperate struggle and that every man should stand ready to do his duty. "You are aware of my position in the fossal [sic] remains of the 'Army of Mississippi,'" he continued. "You are perhaps likewise acquainted with my position in the State as a business man and civilian. I write to tender my services to your Government. I can do this I hope without being considered an applicant for office." He then indicated he would take any position, military or civilian, high or low, in the service of his country.[20]

It is hard to explain the all-inclusive nature of this offer. At no time did Alcorn indicate any confidence in a Confederate government run by Democrats, and in his later attempts to obtain an appointment in the Confederate army he made it clear he would not accept any position lower than brigadier general. Written when emotional response to the news of Fort Sumter was still strong, it may have been an attempt to take out a little political insurance, or it may have been a highly romanticized gesture—the Southern gentleman chivalrously offering himself to serve a doomed cause because honor required it. Alcorn was capable of either or both gestures. Apparently he never received a reply to his offer. This, together with other subsequent events, no doubt helped erase any feeling of loyalty he may have believed he owed the Confederate government, and added to the bitterness of his attacks on Davis.

Since Richmond remained silent, he had no alternative but to continue to work with the "fossal remains" of the Mississippi army. On July 1 he established his headquarters at Corinth in the northeast corner of Mississippi to process the stream of recruits who volunteered in greater numbers than the board could handle or equip. The extent of the problem became almost immediately apparent: "I have been working day and night for five days my position is most difficult and perplexing, chief in command of five thousand men, *fresh* volunteerd, poorly clad, rather poorly fit, without a sufficient supply of anything, all to be supplied by my orders, orders to issue, Election after Election, to be held, all under my supervision, applications for furloughs."[21]

But military life continued to hold some appeal for Alcorn. The

---

20 James Lusk Alcorn to Jefferson Davis, April 17, 1861, Confederate Records, Secretary of War, Letters Received No. 431, National Archives.
21 James Lusk Alcorn to Amelia Alcorn, June 6, 1861, in Alcorn Papers.

direct exercise of authority which is part of military command proved most congenial. When he became impatient with conditions, he evidently asserted his authority with vigor. "Further, the officers and soldiers stand terrified in my presence, for I have had them arrested, from colonels down," he wrote. In the elections for officers being conducted, one regiment wanted him to run for colonel. He refused but received "upwards" of three hundred votes anyway, which he considered a compliment, especially in view of an anecdote which was making the rounds.

I heard what they call a joke by one of the sentinels, who was sent by the officer in command, to my quarters on business, his business required that he should wait a time. He became restive and I suppose thought it no harm to tell the General he was in a hurry, where upon he was required for this, to stand for one hour in the corner of my quarters without speaking or moving. He went to his quarters, told them they "had better not elect that General Colonel, for he would have 'em all shot before they would git back." [22]

Within another week he had become impatient with the way in which events were moving, and on June 14 he wrote Pettus:

I have heard nothing from you in relation to other suggestions in my last letter. . . . I leave here this evening. Major Davis under the direction of Genl Clark can discharge the small services required. My time is too valuable to be idled away, I am willing, entirely willing to devote it to the service when by doing so I can promote the public interest. Should you desire my services you can command me a dispatch sent to me at 'Helena, Arkansas' care of 'James B. Miles' will reach me from Jackson in about two hours.[23]

This letter could not have increased Alcorn's popularity with Pettus, an old political opponent. With the opening of hostilities between North and South, the top ranking officers on the military board quickly resigned, Jefferson Davis to lead the Confederacy and Van Dorn and Clark to join the Confederate army. This brought Alcorn's name, as the fourth man to have been elected to the board, to the top of the list for promotion to major general and head of the board. But Pettus refused to appoint him, naming

22  *Ibid.*
23  James Lusk Alcorn to J. J. Pettus, June 14, 1861, in Governors' Correspondence, May–September 1861, Series E, No. 52, Mississippi Department of Archives and History.

instead Reuben Davis, a Democrat and ex-colonel from the Mexican War. According to Davis, it was only with difficulty that he persuaded Alcorn not to resign, by pointing out to him the exposed position of the Mississippi Valley, the lack of action by the central government, and the need for Mississippi to provide for its own defense, a view in line with Alcorn's own ideas. Then Davis, A. M. West, another recent appointee to the board, and Alcorn joined together to persuade Pettus to adopt more vigorous measures, independent of the Confederate army.[24]

Alcorn also continued to try to get into the larger arena of the Confederate army. Early in August a long list of prominent Mississippi citizens, including Pettus, sent Jefferson Davis a letter informing him that Alcorn wanted authority to raise a brigade and would furnish half the arms, the balance to be supplied by the government. They added that the granting of this request would greatly facilitate the recruitment of troops and would be highly gratifying to the people of Mississippi. A penciled note on the back of the letter states briefly: "Mr. Joynes No brigades are authorized.— L. P. W." (L. P. Walker, Confederate Secretary of War).[25]

A few days later Alcorn offered, through another prominent citizen, Wiley P. Harris, to raise and arm a regiment.[26] The Confederate secretary of war agreed to accept such a regiment with its field officers elected, and Alcorn next sought permission from Pettus to go ahead, assuring him that thus he could do his state valuable service. "We are, my dear Sir, notwithstanding our recent victories in a perilous condition. Every arms that we can command, should be brought into service. The way to defend the soil of Mississippi is to send her sons out to meet the enemy as he organizes, and contest with him every foot of ground between his place of rondyvous [sic], and our own soil. Thus send me out and I will promise results worthy of sons of the South." [27]

24 Reuben Davis, *Recollections of Mississippi and Mississippians* (New York: Houghton, Mifflin, 1891), 405–406.
25 W. H. Brown, *et al* (21 signatures) to Jefferson Davis, August 3, 1861, in Confederate Records, Secretary of War, Letters Received No. 3219, National Archives.
26 W. P. Harris to L. P. Walker, August 16, 1861, in Confederate Records, Secretary of War, Letters Received No. 3189, National Archives.
27 James Lusk Alcorn to J. J. Pettus, August 26, 1861, in Governors' Correspondence, May-September 1861, Series E, No. 53, Mississippi Department of Archives and History.

The regiment failed to materialize, apparently because Pettus, between Alcorn's first and second offers, began to doubt the wisdom of releasing that many officers and men to serve under other than state control. Anticipating this change in attitude, Alcorn had written in his request: "I think I could make the agreement, or you could do so, that if at any subsequent period you should regard it as necessary for the protection of the state that my Regiment should return thereto—that the secretary of war will formally agree to return me to you at once. Now will you agree to let me equip a regiment on this basis?" [28] Even if Pettus had then considered permitting Alcorn to form his regiment, the Confederate army could hardly accept it under such conditions.

On September 3 General Leonidas Polk moved into Kentucky, capturing the town of Columbus, and two days later General Ulysses S. Grant crossed the Ohio River and occupied the towns of Paducah and Smithland. This increased threat to Mississippi sent Alcorn back into active duty with his headquarters at Iuka, where he once more struggled to arm and provision two regiments of raw recruits. He had hardly begun when an aide of General Albert Sidney Johnston who was also marching into western Kentucky arrived at Iuka with instructions for him to take his troops up into that area. Four days later Alcorn was at Russellville, Kentucky, appealing to Pettus to send him additional arms, for he feared he would see action but would be "an encumbrance" to the Confederate army.[29]

After a couple of glimpses of the enemy and a skirmish, Alcorn arrived at Hopkinsville, Kentucky, where General S. B. Buckner gave him full jurisdiction over the area and told him to consider his command as self-sustaining as possible. He took over the town with great zest, treated the "Lincolnites" with courtesy, and was applauded by the ladies who showered him with gifts and bouquets. "One corner of the tent is the depository where the boquets are thrown." From the letters he wrote his wife, he appeared to be thoroughly enjoying his position. "I have made several arrests, have seized the mails, stopped the post office and put in a man of my

28 *Ibid.*
29 James Lusk Alcorn telegrams to J. J. Pettus, September 21 and 23, 1861, in Governors' Correspondence, May–September, 1861, Series E, No. 63, Mississippi Department of Archives and History.

own. Am cutting up some tall shines but wear my authority with great meekness." [30]

Alcorn's enjoyment of his position was brief. His troops came down with the measles, and the possibility of an appointment as a general in the Confederate army came tantalizingly close, but then faded. On October 17 he was ordered by General Buckner to send men to aid in the defense of Fort Donelson and to report on enemy movements to the east of him in the direction of Eddyville, Kentucky.[31] His reply was an attempt at compliance, mixed with frustration and bitterness. Because almost every man in his camp was sick with the measles, he had no ablebodied men to send to Fort Donelson. Then after giving in considerable detail what he had been able to learn of nearby enemy activity, Alcorn came to the point which rankled him most:

My command has been almost completely mustered into service. . . . This being done, the cause for my continuance no longer exists in force sufficient to detain me. I wish to leave for Mississippi, and ask your permission to fix the 27th instant as the day for my departure. This post is an important one, and should not be commanded by one who has not the confidence or is distasteful to the Government at Richmond. My service as brigadier-general of Mississippi is due that State only. If the Confederate Government wished me I would be appointed. This not being done, I am an intruder. My self-respect, my own honor, is dearer to me than country or life itself.[32]

On October 20, 21, and 25 he wrote additional letters to his immediate superior Buckner asking to be relieved, pointing out that he had been ordered back to Mississippi more than a month previously, and emphasizing the need for supplies and someone competent to take command. He also reported that his departure was "having a chilling effect upon even the Kentucky troops— and upon the people around" him, and urged that someone be sent immediately to assume control.[33]

He was relieved on the date he had requested by Brigadier General

---

30  James Lusk Alcorn to Amelia Alcorn, October 2, 8, and 11, 1861; copy of October 2 letter in Rainwater Collection, Box 2, Folder 26; October 8 letter in Alcorn Papers; and October 11 letter in Alcorn File.
31  *Official Records*, Ser. I, Vol. IV, 459, Brig. Gen. S. B. Buckner to James Lusk Alcorn, October 17, 1861.
32  *Ibid.*, 463, James Lusk Alcorn to S. B. Buckner, October 19, 1861.
33  James Lusk Alcorn to S. B. Buckner, October 25, 1861, in James L. Alcorn Jacket, National Archives.

Lloyd Tilghman, who confirmed Alcorn's dismal picture of the conditions in his camp: "I had hoped that the picture sketched to me of matters here might not have been realized, but I am compelled to think it not too highly colored. Under the circumstances, I doubt not General Alcorn has made the best of things, his camp being merely one large hospital, with scarce men enough on duty to care for the sick and maintain a feeble guard around them." [34]

Buckner also felt Alcorn had made the best of things and could have been a valuable addition to the Confederate army. On October 20, in a report to Colonel W. W. Mackall, he said that when he discovered the newly arrived Mississippi troops had not been mustered into the Confederate service, he had asked Alcorn to retain command temporarily.

In making this request I consulted what I am still convinced was the best interests of the service. General Alcorn deservedly holds a high place in the estimation of his soldiers and has rendered me valuable assistance. The manner in which he has discharged the delicate duties which have been assigned him in the district of country west of here, and of which he was formerly a citizen, entitle him to be continued in the command as a brigadier-general after the regiments shall have been received into the Confederate service. Brigadier-General Alcorn has continued in command at Hopkinsville from motives of patriotic duty and as a personal favor to me.[35]

According to one source, Generals Polk and Johnston, and the officers and men of his brigade also petitioned Richmond on his behalf, but without results.[36] Political enmity no doubt played a part, but military considerations may have validly influenced Jefferson Davis also. A month and a half later, in connection with a different request, he wrote Wiley P. Harris of Mississippi that the Confederate States were no longer engaged in the "partisan warfare" of that summer and fall. "The federal troops are not hereafter, as heretofore, to be commanded by 'pathfinders' and holiday soldiers, but by men of military education and experience in war." [37]

34 *Official Records*, Ser. I, Vol. IV, 485, Brig. Gen. Lloyd Tilghman to Assistant Adjutant General Col. W. W. Mackall, October 29, 1861.
35 *Ibid.*, 466, S. B. Buckner to W. W. Mackall, October 20, 1861.
36 Swift, Jr., "James Lusk Alcorn," 14.
37 Dunbar Rowland, (ed.), *Jefferson Davis Constitutionalist, His Letters, Papers and Speeches* (Jackson: printed for the Mississippi Department of Archives and History, 1923), V, 179.

In spite of his inexperience, Alcorn would appear to have been capable of loyal and brave service, and of inspiring the same spirit in his men. He was a strict disciplinarian and did not hesitate to use his authority regardless of its effect on his popularity.[38] In something less than a top command position he might have been an effective military officer.

Relieved of his duties, Alcorn was back in Mississippi by the beginning of November. He arrived just in time to be given command, along with Reuben Davis, of ten thousand sixty-day volunteers, called out by proclamation of Governor Pettus on November 21. This was done in response to an urgent request by General G. J. Pillow, then temporarily in command of the Confederate forces in western Kentucky, who believed that an attack by Union troops at Cairo and Paducah was imminent. However, the recruits mustered into service were state troops. The proclamation called for each man to arm himself and to bring his own clothing, blankets, and cooking utensils. The legislature authorized funds so that the troops would be paid by Mississippi, would ask only for necessary subsistence from the Confederate army, and would be subject only to the orders of their commanding general.[39]

Alcorn gathered together about two thousand men at Grenada, Mississippi, and by the middle of December began to move them up to western Kentucky where, because of the limitations imposed on their service, he found himself in a more ambiguous position than before. He had to appeal directly to General Polk to get the Confederate commissary to subsist his men,[40] and he found his place in the chain of command vague and exasperating.

Together with his regiments, now increased to three, Alcorn was ordered to Columbus, Kentucky, where he enlarged his knowledge of the unglamorous side of war. The winter weather was exceptionally severe, his troops were inadequately clothed and equipped, and once more were stricken with the measles. The war never seemed more distasteful to him than on Christmas Eve, 1861, when in one of his blackest moods he scribbled a short, bitter note to

38  James Lusk Alcorn to Amelia Alcorn, June 6, 1861 and December 5, 1861, in Alcorn Papers; *Official Records*, Ser. I, Vol. IV, 467–68, James Lusk Alcorn to S. B. Buckner, October 21, 1861.
39  *Official Records*, Ser. I, Vol. VII, 782–83, James Lusk Alcorn to Major George Williams, December 21, 1861.
40  *Ibid.*, 771, James Lusk Alcorn to Major General Leonidas Polk, December 16, 1861.

his wife: "I have had for the past few days a dreadful time of it, my men in the cold rain and mud. I sympathize with them deeply —but can't help them. I am well sitting in a smoky cabin with a dozen [wraps] around me wishing this & that [.] I sometimes wish, Lincoln & Jeff Davis were both in hell. When I get through this sixty days I would see some people where the good people go before I would do anything more." [41]

An opportunity to do more almost came, and with it he caught an elusive glimpse of the chivalrous, personalized combat he had imagined war to be. His command was moved from Columbus eastward to Camp Beauregard, along an uncompleted railroad which ran from Paducah to Fulton Station. It was supposed to connect eventually with the Mobile & Ohio line east of Memphis. Union troops controlled the northern end, and Alcorn and his poorly prepared men now held the southern terminal. On December 29 he discovered the enemy advancing down the railroad, about five miles south of Mayfield and realized anew the awkwardness of his position. He had to send a request, rather than an order, to Lieutenant Colonel J. H. Miller: "I have no authority to order you, but would like to have you march in haste to my support. . . ." Miller reported to General Polk that he was complying with Alcorn's request, "supposing it would be all right." [42] Alcorn in the meantime sent out a company of cavalry to intercept the Union troops and began preparations for a possible encounter.

His cavalry made contact with Union cavalry in a brief skirmish and, according to Alcorn, "but for a stupid mistake and too great delay in executing the order we would have made an expensive work of it to them." The following day, as Alcorn described it to his wife: "Genl Wallace came down to Mayfield Town, with 500 cavalry and sent me word he would fight me man to man anywhere between Mayfield & Viola, but as my force was small my cavalry weary and my arms not of a good class, I returned him word to go to hell, but that if he wished a fight to come down." General Polk sent Alcorn fifteen hundred men, but then, to the latter's deep disgust, "Old Mother Polk" changed his mind and ordered him to evacuate Camp Beauregard. From the comparative

41 James Lusk Alcorn to Amelia Alcorn, December 24, 1861, in Alcorn Papers.
42 *Official Records*, Ser. I, Vol. VII, 808–809, Lt. Col. J. H. Miller to Leonidas Polk, December 30, 1861.

safety of Union City, Tennessee, Alcorn "with the blues" looked
back regretfully at his lost chance for glory.[43]

However, Amelia, who joined him there a few days later, gave
her own judgment of the affair in a letter to her stepdaughter:

Well the Yankees started down upon them at Camp B. Your Father
chased them away, but a very large force was preparing to come upon
them. So Gen'l Polk ordered your Father down here, much to regret
& annoyance of your Father. . . . old Gen'l thought it was for the
best & I am quite sure it was for your Father has many sick with the
measles & there might have been too many for his undrilled men.[44]

Polk described Alcorn's men as sixty-day troops armed with every
variety of weapon, sick with measles, raw, and undisciplined, and
added mildly: "This brigade cannot be expected to be very effective." [45]

Nevertheless, Alcorn deeply resented the loss of his one opportunity to see action. He complained to Pettus that although Camp
Beauregard was in an exposed position, he could have held it
had he been given an additional one thousand men. Then he wrote
bitterly:

Should you organize any other troops for sixty days communicate with
Genrl Polk at Columbus in relation to their disposition as I am weary.
I dont understand this war. It is doubtless my obliviousness, but so it
is. I dont wish to be the tail of the kite any longer, an appendage that
drags heavily in the mud, flapping and slashing round, liable at any
moment to have my brains kicked out, without being able to see the
reason of thing[s]. So turn over the sixty days troops hereafter organized to someone else, unless they are troops for Mississippi *only* on
Miss soil, not to be controlled by any Confederate officers, but by
State authority only.[46]

In a letter to his wife he declared emphatically that he would
not "be pulled & hauled by this dambed [sic] stupid government
any longer." The previous fall, near the end of his first and equally

43  James Lusk Alcorn letter with handdrawn map to Amelia Alcorn,
    January 4, 1862, in possession of Mrs. V. A. Hain.
44  Amelia Alcorn to Mary Catherine Alcorn, January 10, 1862, in possession
    of Mrs. V. A. Hain.
45  *Official Records*, Ser. I, Vol. VII, 826, Leonidas Polk to Sidney A.
    Johnston, December 30, 1861.
46  James Lusk Alcorn to J. J. Pettus, January 4, 1862, in Governors' Cor-
    respondence, Series E, No. 56, Mississippi Department of Archives and
    History.

frustrating sortie up into Kentucky, he had made a similar statement in a letter to his wife.[47] This time he meant it.

The Mississippi brigade remained in Union City for the remaining thirty days of its enlistment period, after which it returned to Grenada, the point of assembly, and was discharged. Alcorn also retired from active duty, but his name remained on the Mississippi Register of Commissions as an officer.

His military career, for all practical purposes, thus came to an end. The experiences of that fall and winter had caused the horizons of his loyalty to shrink so that they encompassed at their outer limits the welfare of his state; he was, in fact, concerned primarily with his region and family. This change had begun when he turned from the Union and joined the secessionists. In the short period when Alcorn was influential in Mississippi affairs, his parochial loyalty affected the state's military system, helping to create a policy which gave priority to Mississippi's own defense, at the expense of the Confederate army. This attitude, together with similar ones formulated by many other southern states, contributed materially to the failure of the Confederacy.[48]

Disillusioned by his brief encounter with military life, Alcorn rode back to Mound Place shorn of some of his belief in the Southern myth and of his loyalty to the larger Southern cause. Once at home he returned to the other two roles of a Southern gentleman —planter and politician.

47 James Lusk Alcorn to Amelia Alcorn, October 27, 1861, in possession of Mrs. V. A. Hain.
48 Frank Lawrence Owsley, "Local Defense and the Overthrow of the Confederacy: A Study in States Rights," *The Mississippi Valley Historical Review,* (1924–25), XI, 525.

# 4

# Wartime Activities in the Delta

ALTHOUGH A VARIETY of reasons originally led Alcorn to give some support to a union of Southern states, he quickly lost what little enthusiasm he earlier had as the specific political coloring of this union became apparent. Democrats were in control of the Confederate government and charges were soon made that Davis appointed no one to office who had been a Whig, charges which Alcorn no doubt felt were confirmed by his own experience. As history would reveal, Southern unity was more apparent than real, and the trend beginning in 1861 in North Carolina which saw Southern voters replace Democrats with Whigs suggests that Alcorn was not alone in his growing distaste for the administration of the Confederate government. Davis and the Democratic party were only fulfilling the grim predictions he had made during ten years of combating the secession movement. They had precipitated an unnecessary war and were now proving incapable of successfully finishing what they had started.

The first extant reference to Alcorn's feeling regarding the Confederacy and its president is in a letter he wrote his wife on December 5, 1861, while he was at Grenada organizing the sixty-day troops, a little over a month after his final rejection by the Richmond government. He pictured himself away from home, "fighting a war, brought on the country, by the corruptions of a party, which long since secured my deepest hatred . . . ." He went on to excoriate Davis as "a corrupt tyrant . . . who disgraces the head of government by his low jealouses [sic], and constitutional timidity . . . a cold sickly dyspeptic, forgets the nature of south-

ern[ers], and will loose [sic] the jewel entrusted to his charge."
They needed a man of "southern" will to lead them "as our natures
require, rapidly, fearlessly, boldly, intrepidly." A few days later
in a speech to his troops he "took occasion to give Jeff Davis a
punch under the ribs." [1]

Almost immediately upon his return to Mississippi after the de-
bacle with the sixty-day troops he was invited to address the state
house of representatives at Jackson. To the *Mississippian*, a vocifer-
ously pro-Democratic and secessionist newspaper which reported
his speech, it was one "of the most startling and despotic character."
According to the paper Alcorn wanted to abolish the Confederate
constitution, muzzle the press, and establish a dictatorship. The
reporter who covered the speech wrote in lurid terms of Alcorn's
"dashing Napoleonic ideas" which would replace liberty with the
"depotism of Mexico," and he attributed the whole tirade to his
disappointed ambitions. [2] Exaggerated though the report may have
been, embodied in the address was the old Hamiltonian-Whig ideal
of a strong central government, capable of the kind of decisive
action Alcorn felt was needed.

Throughout the war years he made similar references to Davis
in his letters. A "Soliloquy" written in his diary in the spaces
reserved for the first half of March, 1863, as he watched Federal
gunboats move through the Yazoo Pass and Federal soldiers ransack
his plantation for provisions, developed his views further:

How hard it is to realize the conditions of the country; I sought to
avoid this terrible war, but the wild mania had seized upon the
passions of the southern people. When I would point them to coming
danger, they would laugh in derision. They boasted that one Southern
[er]could whip ten Yankees, and defied their visit to the soil of
Mississippi. Now the Yankees are here, and the Confederates make but
feeble and it appears to me cowardly resistance. They fly panic stricken
at the very name of Yankee. [3]

He went on to tell how much he detested Davis who protected
Richmond while the Union army ravaged the Mississippi Valley,
which he variously described as "the great artery which permeates

---

1 James Lusk Alcorn to Amelia Alcorn, December 17, 1861, in Alcorn
 Papers.
2 Jackson *Mississippian*, January 27, 1862.
3 James Lusk Alcorn diary, in possession of Mrs. V. A. Hain, March 5
 through 13, 1863.

the throat" of the Confederacy and "the great spinal column" of Davis' government. "It is not so much on account of the acts of Secession that I condemn Davis," he wrote. "The South had suffered wrongs, grievous wrongs; I contended and still contend, that Secession was not the remedy, but I excuse the act." But he blamed Davis "for his stupid policy; his egotism, arrogance, & superciliousness. . . . The capacity of his mind may be judged by his surrender of the Mississippi river; his heart insists on holding 'Richmond,' . . ." He concluded wryly that the Yankees now had the Mississippi River, and "Davis has Richmond still!"

Secession was the wrong means to a good end, and in Alcorn's mind Davis came to embody all that was wrong with that means. Later he would interpret his anti-Davis feeling as a pro-Union one, while at all times he considered himself a Southerner in the full meaning of the word, and his loyalty to his region and its way of life was always paramount. None of this was sophistry to Alcorn, and on this rationale he attempted to base his course of action. When in 1863 Mississippi elected an ex-Whig governor, Alcorn returned to the legislature and took an active part in helping his state resist Federal invasion, while never lessening his hostility to the Democrat-controlled Confederate government.

The difficulty of separating Davis from the South and Union army officers from the North has with the passage of time blurred Alcorn's fine distinction between regional and Confederate loyalty, and caused his day-to-day activities in the Delta to be clouded in ambiguity. Yet he consistently refused to take the oath of allegiance to the Union during the war in spite of the pressure placed upon him, and Federal officers with whom he came into contact were never under any illusions as to where his sympathies lay.

Caught in the cross currents of conflicting demands upon his allegiance, Alcorn and many others in similar circumstances simply retreated to the firm ground of immediate, tangible loyalties which they could serve close to home, and which served them. The objects of Alcorn's loyalty were in the South—his family, his lands, the Delta—and so he was right in considering himself a loyal Southerner. His actions during the rest of the war were influenced by the belief that everything he valued was threatened by one side, and had been betrayed by the other.

During the spring of 1862 Federal soldiers moved steadily closer, and by summer the Union army controlled the Mississippi River down to Vicksburg and had established itself across the river with headquarters at Helena, Arkansas. In June, Alcorn wrote Pettus that they were expecting Yankees daily. He listed them among the disasters the area was encountering, along with floods, cotton burnings, and hog cholera.[4]

Early in August he had his first encounter with them when he and two of his neighbors on the Yazoo Pass were arrested and taken to Helena. Within a few days he was released and permitted to go to the home of his cousin James Miles in Helena.[5] In a letter to his wife he spoke of being "paroled," but the term in his case does not appear to have had any military connotations, nor do there appear to have been any terms imposed, except possibly a warning to behave himself. Soon after this he sent his wife and their small children to the greater safety of her father's plantation near Eutaw, in Greene County, Alabama.

Being arrested apparently did not daunt Alcorn, for less than a month later he was back in Helena to file a formal protest against the action of a Union general in issuing emancipation papers to some of his runaway slaves worth $35,000. He protested this assistance given them to escape as "a violation of his rights as a citizen of the State of Mississippi, and also in violation of the laws of the Government of the United States of America."[6] He was arrested again that fall, but according to the account he gave his wife, he made the acquaintance of some of the "higher officers" at Helena, "had quite a pleasant time of it and was released and my horse returned and *I* treated with marked respect."[7]

And he continued, in all his contacts with the Union army, to be treated with respect, although he did not hide his sympathies and acquired the nickname of "old Chef Sesh" among the Federal officers. He maintained friendly relations with the officers in the vicinity and at Helena, and saved his plantation Mound Place from

4  James Lusk Alcorn to J. J. Pettus, June 15, 1862, in Governors' Correspondence, Series E, No. 57, Mississippi Department of Archives and History.
5  James Lusk Alcorn to Amelia Alcorn, August 8, 1862, in possession of Mrs. William Swanson, Hot Springs, Arkansas.
6  "Protest of J. L. Alcorn, Citizen of Mississippi, endorsed and filed in the Archives of the Military Governor of Arkansas, September 6, 1862," copy in Rainwater Collection, Box 2, Folder 28.
7  James Lusk Alcorn to Amelia Alcorn, November 25, 1862, in possession of Mrs. V. A. Hain.

being burned. Several years later General C. C. Washburn was able to pay him a compliment with regard to his relations with the Union troops stationed at his plantation, without casting doubt upon his loyalty to the South.[8]

Early in 1863 General Grant began to pay particular attention to the region of Friar's Point and the Yazoo Pass, through which he hoped to send gunboats into the Coldwater-Yazoo river system, and down to Vicksburg. Before the end of February, Alcorn became involuntary host to Federal army units under Washburn, who used his house as headquarters and his slave quarters for an army camp. The officers admired his plantation and treated him with great consideration, but the soldiers did all the mischief they could. They killed his livestock, rolled his wagons into the Pass, raided his smokehouse, used up his hay and corn, and burned his fences; "but they kept out of the house, were respectful to the family, and deferential to me, although I cursed them and abused them as a mob of thieves in the most public manner; they generally remarked by way of reply one to the other (sometimes so that I could hear it) 'Old Secesh has got his dander up!' " [9] On March 2 they left him to the quiet of his stripped plantation and the writing of his "Soliloquy."

During most of February, March, April, and May, Alcorn watched the struggle for the Yazoo Pass from his doorstep, but not as a completely passive spectator. A Federal report on progress being made in opening the pass quotes Alcorn as saying there would be no difficulty in reaching the Yazoo River with boats of medium size.[10] In his diary he kept a careful account of the types and names of the Union boats that moved past his plantation, and estimates of the number of men they were carrying. At least once, and probably more often, he gave this information to Confederate scouts.[11] He often entertained Captain A. H. Forest and his men who were busy blockading the pass as fast as Federal soldiers

8  Friar's Point (Miss.) *Weekly Delta*, November 3, 1869.
9  James Lusk Alcorn to Amelia Alcorn, February 24 and March 3, 1863, in possession of Mrs. V. A. Hain, and Alcorn File.
10 *Official Records*, Ser. I, Vol. XXIV, part 1, p. 373, Lt. Col. J. H. Wilson, U.S.A., to Lt. Col. John A. Rawlings, Department of the Tennessee, February 4, 1863.
11 *Ibid.*, part 3, p. 763, Lt. Col. Edmund W. Pettus to Maj. J. J. Reeve, April 18, 1863; Ser. I, Vol. XVII, part 2, p. 808, Lt. W. M. M. Connell to Lt. Gen. J. C. Pemberton, December 29, 1862.

cleared it.[12] Whatever the terms of Alcorn's parole, if any, they evidently did not include a clear-cut promise not to aid the enemy. As his consistent refusal to take the oath of allegiance to the Union indicates, he was scrupulous where his personal word was concerned.

However, any lingering romantic illusions about war were now completely gone. Alcorn found the sight of Yankee gunboats in the pass humiliating, yet imposing,[13] and he repeatedly commented derisively on the myth of greater Southern bravery. Apparently the reverse of the old belief that one Southerner could whip ten Yankees was coming true.[14] In August, on his way home from Alabama, he passed through the railroad town of Grenada, Mississippi, just before Federal troops were due to arrive. He described the scene to his wife: "I could see the lurid glare of the flames that night, said to be the conflagration of Grenada set on fire by the Yankees . . . [as] I reached here, many of our soldiers are deserting, a number are before me, and I have passed scores. Our soldiers are thoroughly demoralized and the people panic stricken." [15]

Writing of the same incident ten days later, he added: "I barely made my way through without molestation, nor did I see any of the Yankees, but heard the occasional deep heavy sound of their cannon as it spoke in notes of terror to the fleeing Southerners, 'twas a humiliating spectacle, my blood boiled with indignation at the thought, my countrymen made cowards by the most miserable of all vagabonds [Jefferson Davis] who sits as their ruler. I looked at our officers, what miserable creatures in appearance as evil as pigmies in mind." [16]

In April, 1864, Amelia Alcorn wrote him from Alabama describing a military review and the festivities connected with it. Alcorn responded with a long, bitter letter in which he pointed out the suffering brought on by the war and the defeat foreshadowed by the fact that Louisiana, Arkansas, Missouri, and Tennessee had taken steps to abolish slavery. He asked: "Where oh where, are the

12  James Lusk Alcorn diary (Mrs. V. A. Hain), May 13–14, 1863.
13  James Lusk Alcorn to Amelia Alcorn, February 24, 1863, in possession of Mrs. V. A. Hain.
14  *Ibid.*
15  James Lusk Alcorn to Amelia Alcorn, August 19, 1863, copy in Rainwater Collection, Box 2, Folder 30.
16  Alcorn to Amelia Alcorn, August 29, 1863, in Alcorn Papers.

Southern Soldiers, who in times past we were told could drive
their invaders back, and bid the South be free, with Sword and
Sash and bayonet charger, cursed the Yankees and spoke of Southern Blood? Where did you say? Yes I see! a way over on the
*tom big bee* [Tombigbee River in Green County, Alabama, where
Amelia was] shaking their light fantastic toes." [17]

Interspersed with these activities and reflections, and consuming
far more of his time were his efforts on behalf of his own and
his family's welfare. He remained at Mound Place expressly to
salvage as much as he could from the devastation, planning to use
cotton, the great war contraband, as his means of accomplishing
this. The early capture of Memphis by Federal troops and the
unsettled conditions in the Delta, where neither side was ever able
to gain complete control,[18] produced ideal conditions for illegal
trade, with cotton the most important item in it. The Confederate
government, anxious to use cotton as a bargaining tool, tried hard
to prevent this trade, and issued orders that cotton be burned
rather than allowed to fall into enemy hands. Early in the summer
of 1862 Federal officers appeared in the Delta with orders to seize
all the cotton they could and give the owners claims on the United
States, to be honored after the war if the holders could prove their
loyalty.[19]

Caught between two prospects of certain loss, Alcorn took the
only means available for collecting on his cash crop. Together with
his neighbors he sold his cotton to smugglers. He wrote Amelia
that he felt like Dick Hatterick in Sir Walter Scott's *Guy Man-
nering* as he waited at night on the banks of the Mississippi for the
"muffled oar" or the cautious footsteps of the smuggler as he
approached the appointed meeting place. "The Smuggling business
has now become popular and people are beginning openly to trade.
. . . I was at Delta a few nights since when nearly four hundred
bales of cotton were openly sold and full fifty men on the bank
participating. . . . You remember how they once talked. It would

17  Alcorn to Amelia Alcorn, April 2, 1864, in Alcorn File.
18  Andrew Brown, "Sol Street, Confederate Partisan Leader," *Journal of
    Mississippi History* (1959), XXI, 155–73.
19  Edgar L. Erickson, (ed.), "Hunting for Cotton in Dixie from the Civil
    War Diary of Captain Charles E. Wilcox," *Journal of Southern History*
    (1938), IX, 496; Frank A. Montgomery, *Reminiscences of a Mississippian
    in Peace and War* (Cincinnati: Robert Clarke Company, 1901), 78

astonish you to witness the reaction. The authorities out in the hills, I am told, are furious." [20]

In his next letter he provided her with more details:

I have been very busy, hiding & selling my cotton. I have sold in all one hundred & eleven bales, I have now here ten thousand Dollars in paper (Green Backs) and one thousand dollars in Gold. I have still some fifty bales of old cotton and about forty bales of new cotton picked out and ginned. If I escape the burners I will be able to realize $20,000.00 more. I am busy I assure you and am making my time count. I got back from Helena last night, took in two days since fifteen bales and sold them for $3200.00 over two hundred dollars per bale, I am now selling at 40 cents per pound; in addition to the money I have on hand. I have three thousand dollars coming to me which I may loose [sic] but I think not.[21]

His letters describing these transactions contain a near-defiant note of self-reliance, pride, and optimism concerning his personal future. Alcorn had sent his wife and children to stay in the relative safety of northwestern Alabama, where they were living with her family, the Glovers. The apparent deterioration of his social and economic position in relation to that of his in-laws no doubt strengthened his determination not to let events prevent the achievement of his goal. When he married Amelia he had given assurances that he would attain a station in life comparable to that she was leaving. Yet circumstances seemed to suggest that he had not done this, and in addition that he had betrayed that station in life by his political stand.

Alcorn was being challenged, in most personal terms, to defend not only an economic position but a social and political one as well. The practical details and arrogant tone contained in his letters indicate that he was responding to that challenge with all the resourcefulness and independence of spirit provided by his frontier background. Again and again he told Amelia that he could and would provide for her and the children, that she was not to worry or accept anything from her family, and that once hostilities ceased he would make a larger fortune than ever.

In 1863 and 1864 wagon trains traveled from Coahoma County to Amelia in Alabama under Alcorn's personal direction or that

20 James Lusk Alcorn to Amelia Alcorn, November 25, 1862, in possession of Mrs. V. A. Hain.
21 James Lusk Alcorn to Amelia Alcorn, December 18, 1862, in Alcorn Papers.

of his overseer. They contained precious articles of clothing obtained from Helena or Memphis, grain for her livestock, corn and scarce coffee and sugar—some items earmarked as gifts for her relatives and others to replace anything she may have borrowed from them.

Alcorn's evaluation of the kinds of money which passed through his hands was shrewd, and was probably based, as one contemporary wrote, on the memory people still retained of what had happened to Continental money after the Revolutionary War, which caused fears Confederate money would experience a similar loss in value.[22] Early in 1863 Alcorn sent specific instructions to his wife on how to handle her money:

Minga [his overseer who was taking a wagon train of provisions to her] will hand you a belt with $4 hundred and seventy dollars in Southern and Confederate money. In your expenditures pay Confederate money holding to the interest bearing notes. They are the large notes. He will also hand you a fruit can which contains twenty three hundred and fifty dollars. Hold on to your Gold as you cling to dear life.[23]

Sometime that preceding winter he had used some of his Confederate money (in November he wrote her that he could get it by the sackful in Memphis at from thirty to forty cents on the dollar) to buy a piece of land in Greene County. He placed this land under his wife's management with advice that went contrary to that issuing from Richmond where Confederate officials were trying to encourage the production of food: "In relation to your farming you had best put in as much cotton as possible you need not listen to what others say, plant corn to do you, and the balance in cotton. Don't try to raise any stock. The war can't last over twelve months longer and cotton at the close of the war will be worth a dollar per pound in good money." [24]

Although he was too optimistic about how soon the war would end, he managed to emerge at its end with Mound Place intact, if largely uncultivated, and with sufficient capital to start again and to prevent his father-in-law's plantation from being sold for taxes. He accomplished this in spite of guerilla warfare, raiding parties from both sides, and the fact that an important part of his

22  Fulkerson, *A Civilian's Recollections,* 111.
23  James Lusk Alcorn to Amelia Alcorn, February 11, 1863, copy in Rainwater Collection, Box 2, Folder 30.
24  *Ibid.*

estate—his property in slaves—steadily dwindled due to the lure of nearby Federal lines and freedom.

In the arena of politics he was able also to retain if not strengthen his position. The year 1863 saw the fall of Vicksburg and the failure of Lee's invasion of the North at Gettysburg. In Mississippi, as in other Southern states, disillusionment brought dissatisfaction with the incumbent Democratic party, and gave the Whigs, as the loyal opposition, the opening they needed to increase their political power.[25] Alcorn was in a position to exploit this change. As he had foreseen, his vote in the secession convention placed him on record as renouncing his allegiance to the Federal government, but at the same time he was critical of, and unpopular with, the Confederate government, and was a long-time political opponent of Pettus. As Swift pointed out, he was in a sense a man without a country, and any distinction given him would have to come from his own county, but the confidence of his fellow Coahomians in him did not abate.[26] Although he was solicited to reenter politics, his diary entries and letters indicate he was far from enthusiastic. "I delivered a speech by invitation on the Sunflower at Shufortsville to attentive listeners on this 15th inst. The effort was very respectable, the audience (for the times) large. You may imagine that I said some harsh things. I will be voted for by many for the legislature, though I hope will not be elected. . . ."[27] On October 5 he noted in his diary that it was election day and that he was not a candidate, but four days later he wrote that he had been elected and for the seventh time the people of Coahoma County had sent him to the state capital.

Since Jackson was occupied by Federal troops, the legislature convened at Columbus, in eastern Mississippi. There they witnessed the inauguration of Governor-elect Charles Clark, ex-Confederate general and secessionist Whig, who delivered a fiery speech denouncing the dream of a reconstructed Union as a delusion and calling for an all-out effort for victory.[28] Alcorn ran unsuccessfully for speaker of the house, but he was appointed to several commit-

25 Daniel M. Robison, "Whigs and the Politics of the Confederacy," *East Tennessee Historical Society Publications* (1939), XI, 7–8, 10.
26 Swift, "James Lusk Alcorn," 16.
27 James Lusk Alcorn to Amelia Alcorn, September 23, 1863, in possession of Mrs. V. A. Hain.
28 *Journal of the House of Representatives of the State of Mississippi, November, 1863,* pp. 158–60.

tees, the most important being that on ways and means. His name also appeared briefly in the legislative struggle to keep Democrat James Phelan from being reelected to the Confederate senate. After a prolonged battle in which Phelan always led in the balloting but could never get a majority of the votes, he withdrew his name and J. W. C. Watson, a Whig, was elected.[29] The Whigs appeared to have returned to power as an unorganized party, and committed to continuing the war.

As an indication of the evident esteem in which Alcorn was held and that his views of Jefferson Davis and his prosecution of the war were not unpopular, he was invited by the house of representatives to address it "and the public on the state of the country."[30] His speech, he observed in his diary on November 19, was well received, and he was "much complimented for his ability." He also served for part of the short session (it adjourned on December 9) as speaker pro tem in the absence of the elected speaker.

When the legislature met the following fall for a brief special session during the first part of August, Alcorn participated actively. In his message Governor Clark asked for changes in the military laws so that more men would be available for the defense of the state. In line with this, Alcorn offered a resolution for a joint special committee to draw up a bill to provide for the abolition of all state, corporate, or judicial offices that could be dispensed with, "as may be conducive to the military service of the State and not in conflict with the Constitution of the State of Mississippi." He was appointed to the committee which then drew up a bill that passed both houses over the veto of Governor Clark who felt too many offices were exempt under it.[31]

While in session the legislature again invited Alcorn to address it,[32] and he responded with a full-dress presentation of his views of the current situation. While secession had been purely a matter of principle at the beginning of the struggle, its success was now

29 David H. Donald, "The Scalawag in Mississippi Reconstruction," *Journal of Southern History* (1944), X, 448; *Journal of the House of Representatives of the State of Mississippi, November,* 1863, pp. 142–71.
30 *Journal of the House of Representatives of the State of Mississippi, November,* 1863, p. 166.
31 *Journal of the House of Representatives of the State of Mississippi, August,* 1864, pp. 15–20, 95.
32 *Ibid.,* 41.

a question of life and death since Lincoln would only allow its supporters to return to the Union as "crouching menials, divested of property, honor, and hope for the future." He accused the administration of blundering, and said that Lincoln had completely out-generaled Davis in the field of diplomacy. The South had done wrong to insist the war was over slavery, this had prejudiced its cause in Europe, and Lincoln had been able to exploit this with his Emancipation Proclamation. Alcorn felt that Southerners had placed their cause on a "false ground." It was not slavery exclusively but a higher purpose, states rights, for which they were fighting. He then suggested that they might still be able to make use of diplomacy. The Confederacy could agree to submit the slavery question to foreign nations, with the understanding that emancipation should be postponed at least twenty years. In that time he believed they could prove the "interest and justice" of the institution. If, however, the whole world was set against slavery, then they would have to make up their minds to fight the whole world.

The reporter writing the article on Alcorn's speech compared it to one he had given in the House of Representatives two years earlier in which he had predicted the invasion of the South. People had been astonished at its boldness, and, the reporter added:

We thought it at the time, and so characterized it in a notice in the Daily Mississippian, a wild effervescent of spleen, disappointment and prejudice. Since then, however, we have learned to think better of the man. . . . We listen to Gen. Alcorn now with the highest respect. He is a man whose sterling principles and loyalty are proof against both the indifference of his own Government and the tyranny and blandishments of the enemy. His predictions have been almost literally fulfilled, thus proving his superior sagacity to those who recklessly condemned him two years ago.[33]

The defiant quality of his speech indicates that publicly Alcorn was still "running with the maddened steed" and was gaining acceptance because of his actions. At the same time his letters for 1864 indicate an awareness of the changes which time and events were bringing with them. In March he paid an extended visit to General Buford at Helena during which he reviewed Negro troops, "truly a fine looking and well drilled body of men, their appearance marshall [sic], their step proud," and inspected two schools for

33 Newspaper clipping, no heading, no date (name, time, and place established by internal evidence), in possession of Mrs. V. A. Hain.

colored children: "intent upon their books, faces bright and joyous, the little fellows stole glances at me when I was presented to the mistress as a Confederate (the General jocularly calling me a 'rebel Gentlemen.') The little darkies seemed to say 'how do you like us Mr. Secesh.' "[34] On Sunday he attended an integrated church service, and described it in the same detached vein.

In spite of his friendship with General Buford, he continued to refuse to take the oath of allegiance to the United States. He recorded his first refusal in his diary on April 20, 1863, although many of his fellow Unionists, including Sharkey, did take it and appear to have escaped recriminations. Such an act would have made it easier for him to get necessities for his family and to sell his cotton. With General Buford's aid he and members of his family were allowed to travel to Helena without restrictions, but he wrote that the rules were rigid and he had to behave with honor. Mary, his oldest daughter, also refused to take the oath, a condition for visiting Memphis, whereupon Buford told her he admired her firmness and gave her permission anyway, provided she did not bring back any forbidden items. Alcorn was pleased to note that she acted with scrupulous honesty. He was unable to get clothing for his Negroes who complained that others took the oath and asked why he could not do likewise.[35] But he could not, since he continued to be fully committed to secession, even though he regarded it as a mistake.

The return of the Whigs to political power prompted Alcorn to think again in terms of military service, and he spoke of the possibility to his wife when he visited her in Alabama during the legislative session in the fall of 1863.[36] His name was still on the register of Commissions of the State Troops. Right after the close of the brief legislative session in the fall of 1864, he decided to enlist as a private, but Governor Clark asked him to accept the rank of colonel and organize militia units to prevent the escape of deserters and Negroes in Coahoma, Bolivar and Washington counties. "I would rather have served as a private," he wrote, "but as Gov. Clark told me I need not be so ambitious to become a private, that position is open to me at all times." His tour of duty lasted thirty

34  James Lusk Alcorn to Amelia Alcorn, March 22, 1864, in Alcorn Papers.
35  Alcorn to Amelia Alcorn, May 3, 1864, in Alcorn Papers.
36  Amelia Alcorn to Alcorn, August 30, 1863, in Alcorn File.

days, and he seemed anxious to have it end.[37] He later claimed that Clark had offered him command of the entire state militia, but that he had declined and gone "into the ranks" to show that although he had no confidence in the revolution, he would stand by his pledge.[38]

During the winter of 1864–65 the onus of Yankee rule pressed down harder on the Delta. Buford was freeing the Negroes and promising them justice in complaints against their former masters, and the whites were required to obtain permission before they could sell their cotton and buy supplies. Alcorn, nevertheless, continued to sell his cotton to smugglers,[39] and he refused to humble himself in order to buy supplies, although he did have to ask permission to remain on his plantation. Buford gave him the permission "provided I shall demean myself as a good boy—of which he is to be the judge—and the negroes of the neighborhood the witnesses." [40]

Under Federal rule the courts were beginning to function again, and Alcorn found his legal practice picking up. In January, 1865, he took over management of an estate for a widow in Sunflower County, and the following month he spent considerable time at probate court representing various clients.[41]

The Mississippi legislature also met early in February at Columbus and sat until March, but Alcorn made no attempt to attend, nor was he granted a leave of absence. Then, in early March he appeared in Columbus and made a speech in which he asserted that the whole civilized world was against slavery. He advocated an immediate declaration by the state legislature and the Confederate congress that the slaves would be freed at the end of twenty years, which he felt would obtain sympathy for them abroad, with its attendant advantages. Echoing proposals made earlier by General Robert E. Lee and Judah P. Benjamin, he also urged the recruitment of Negro soldiers, to be officered by white men and freed

37 Alcorn to Amelia Alcorn, September 6, 1864, in Alcorn File; and Alcorn to Amelia Alcorn, September 14, 1864, copy in Rainwater Collection, Box 3, Folder 32.
38 *Congressional Globe*, (46 vols.: Washington, 1834–73), 42nd Cong. 2nd Sess., Appendix, 392.
39 James Lusk Alcorn diary (Mrs. V. A. Hain), February 9 and 13, 1865.
40 James Lusk Alcorn to Amelia Alcorn, January 21, 1865, in Alcorn Papers.
41 Alcorn to Amelia Alcorn, January 22, 1865, and February 8, 1865, in Alcorn Papers.

at the end of the war.[42] A bill to this effect was then being debated in the Confederate congress and would be passed in an emasculated form less than a month before Appomattox.[43]

By that time the Confederacy was completely cut off from the outside world, and Alcorn could have had few illusions about its recognition by foreign nations. In line with the overall strategy planned by his handful of Whig Unionists at the beginning of the war, he was simply beginning to publicly urge acceptance of the changes he saw, so as to coax the "maddened steed" down the road he saw it would inevitably have to take.

The closing events of the war came rapidly. Lincoln's death elicited a special paragraph in the back of Alcorn's diary for 1865:

Thursday 20th April, 1865
On this day I heard of the assassination of President Lincoln & Secretary Seward. This atrocious and daring act in the drama of this bloody war has shocked me. I trust the assassins may be arrested and that it shall turn out that the conception was confined to the brain that performed the murderous deed. I cant think that any Southerner of character would be willing to turn assassin or become the accomplice of such. The deed illustrates the mutability of all things Terrene [sic] and shows how great a misfortune may be the elevation to high position. My heart is sad from this news. I see the future darkly, but Oh the scenes of blood! When and where will this strife end?[44]

The tragedy of the strife touched Alcorn in another way. His oldest son Milton enlisted at the beginning of the war and was elected captain of a company of Mississippi troops that joined the Confederate army. In the summer of 1863 he was taken prisoner at Port Hudson, Louisiana, then released a few months later from Johnson's Island prison on Lake Erie, and at the end of the war was mustered out as a major in command of the 1st Mississippi Regiment in Featherston's Brigade. He returned home with a hearing defect and a fondness for liquor which eventually led to his death by suicide.

Henry, Alcorn's younger son by his first marriage, ran away from home in January, 1865, to enlist in the Confederate army against his father's wishes. Almost immediately after joining up,

42  Montgomery, *Reminiscences of a Mississippian*, 228.
43  Clement Eaton, *A History of the Southern Confederacy* (New York: Macmillan, 1954), 275–76.
44  James Lusk Alcorn diary (Mrs. V. A. Hain), entry on Memoranda page of diary for 1865.

he contracted typhoid fever and was left behind by his unit near Murphreesboro, Tennessee, where he was captured. "If alive he is now I presume in prison," Alcorn wrote his wife. "Poor boy he will now have the reward for his disobedience." [45] Taken to Camp Chase near Columbus, Ohio, Henry made a partial recovery and managed to escape by answering to the name of a paroled prisoner who had just died. Somehow he found his way to Richmond where members of the Mississippi delegation to the Confederate congress which had just adjourned took him under their care and endeavored to bring him home. En route he suddenly died.[46] In later speeches Alcorn would refer to both sons as sacrifices he had made to the Rebel cause.

Once war ended, Alcorn acted quickly to transfer the struggle back to the political field. He decided to attend the special session of the legislature called at Jackson to consider the new state of affairs. On his way down to the capital he wrote his wife a letter indicative of the political strategy he was already working out. Several days before he had received a letter from "a committee of gentlemen" urging him to leave his retreat and give counsel:

Oh, my poor misguided country! here my views are sought with some avidity, they appear acceptable, I am opposed to Clark's idea and the popular idea of a convention. We seceded, said we had the right; Yankees denied this; said we were still in the Union and there we should remain, on this we fought; they whipped; we yield; you were right Yankee! You have established your power; we yield; we are and ever have been in the Union; secession was a nullity. We will now take the oath to support the Constitution and laws of the United States; elect our senators and representatives; claim that we have our slaves until slavery is abolished and upon the question of amending the Constitution for its prohibition Mississippi has a vote.[47]

The means they had taken to protect their way of life had been proved by force to be wrong; now they would take the struggle back into the political sphere. Alcorn was opposed to the idea of a convention to change the state constitution because he hoped to use the abolition of slavery as a bargaining point with which to win concessions from the North. A quick but not too thorough

---

45 James Lusk Alcorn to Amelia Alcorn, January 22, 1865, in Alcorn Papers.
46 H. C. Chambers to James Lusk Alcorn, March 24, 1865, in possession of Mrs. V. A. Hain.
47 James Lusk Alcorn to Amelia Alcorn, May 16, 1865, copy in Rainwater Collection, Box 2, Folder 33.

acquiescence would bring them back within the framework of the Constitution and the protection which they had abandoned with secession.

In Jackson, under the eyes of Federal troops, the state legislature after two days' attempt to convene finally made a quorum on Saturday, May 20. The legislators went to work "briskly and excitedly"; they passed a bill calling for a convention, and a resolution authorizing the governor to appoint commissioners to confer with United States authorities. This was their only meeting. President Johnson refused to recognize their actions as legal and ordered General E. R. S. Canby to disperse them. He did so on the following day, and by nine in the morning Alcorn found himself on a train headed toward Meridian, near the Alabama border. He crossed over into that state and traveled up to Eutaw, where he stayed with his wife and family until late in June.[48]

On July 4, 1865, he returned to Mound Place and began preparations to pick up the threads of his own life and that of his region to reweave them into the national cloth, with as few alterations as possible.

Persistently Whiggish in attitude, Alcorn was above all a conservative, looking back to what he believed were pre-Civil War Whig principles, and therefore he was alienated by the radical actions of both sides. He struggled realistically to preserve as much as he could of that network of beliefs and loyalties to which he had dedicated his life. He still believed strongly in his destiny to lead, but in order to do this he had not only to survive but he had to build up a position from which he could assume leadership. Alcorn succeeded in doing this without compromising his beliefs and loyalties. To call him an opportunist is to ignore the pragmatic consistency which underlay his actions during those war years.

48 James Lusk Alcorn diary (Mrs. V. A. Hain), May 18–22, 1865.

# 5

# Resumption of Peacetime Tasks

AS HOSTILITIES DREW to a close, Alcorn emerged relatively unscathed, with his lands and homes intact, and with a supply of gold to help him start anew. Even before the war ended officially, county courts had begun to function, and he resumed his law practice, attending probate court in Coahoma County, in February, 1865. Once peace came to the land, he kept busy preparing pardon petitions and election papers, and in August he received a retainer fee of $500 to represent a client in a murder case. As he observed dryly to his wife: "It is a bad wind that blows no good." [1]

The Union army released his home at Friar's Point that fall. When he brought his family back from Alabama he installed them there, and Friar's Point rather than Mound Place became the base of his postwar activities. He continued to operate his plantations, and he also began to accumulate land farther away from the river, east of Friar's Point and south of his holdings on the pass. These lands, acquired near the village of Jonestown in the years immediately after the war, became the nucleus of Eagle's Nest plantation, where he built a Victorian mansion in 1879.

In the 1860's Alcorn was still a vigorous man, with every reason to believe in himself and his destiny. His adroit responses to the challenges of the war years had enabled him to save a good part of his fortune. In 1867 he provided the cash to save from foreclosure the Glover plantation where he and Amelia had been

[1] James Lusk Alcorn to Amelia Alcorn, August 26, 1865, in Alcorn Papers.

married.[2] As the scope of his activities widened, he now applied to the new challenges which arose those qualities of self-confidence and practicality which had enabled him to cope successfully with the frontier.

In 1861 Alcorn had resigned as president of the board of levee commissioners as a gesture of defeat in the long fight for levees. Now, as he resumed the activities of his prewar life, he could hardly avoid the one involving an issue so close to home. He was one of a committee of three commissioners appointed by the Convention of 1865 to journey to Washington to enlist government aid in rebuilding the levees, or to try to raise money from private sources for this purpose. However, they were unsuccessful since the convention forbade them to pledge state aid in repaying such loans,[3] which discouraged private investors. Additionally, the hostility of the Thirty-Ninth Congress, then embarking on its own program of reconstruction, precluded any federal help.

Nevertheless, Alcorn looked more and more toward the Federal government for direct financial assistance and began to argue for levees in terms of national interest. An opportunity to present his feelings publicly presented itself the following summer when Congress began debate on a revenue bill. During the war Congress had passed a law placing a tax of three cents per pound on raw cotton and it now proposed to increase this tax to five cents.

The United States District Court for Northern Mississippi was in session at this time, and the lawyer-planters of the Delta who were attending it took advantage of the occasion to hold a protest meeting. The district judge adjourned court to accommodate them, and Alcorn dominated the proceedings. He opened the meeting by explaining its object; nominated and secured the election of his old friend and fellow-Whig C. D. Fontaine as chairman; and proposed a set of resolutions which were unanimously adopted. They urged planters, in view of the probable passage of the bill, to plow up unpromising stands of cotton and plant corn instead, since the country would probably not have the money to purchase food from the North and West. The meeting heard arguments on the value of cotton, as an important form of wealth, to the welfare

2 James Lusk Alcorn to Amelia Alcorn, September 18, 1867, in possession of Mrs. V. A. Hain.
3 *Journal of the Proceedings and Debates in the Constitutional Convention of the State of Mississippi, August, 1865* (Jackson: E. M. Yerger, 1865) 274, 276.

of the entire nation; as an instrument in foreign affairs; and as purchasing power for the South to buy Northern goods. The well-being of the South, as well as that of the newly freed Negroes, depended on cotton, according to this reasoning, because Southern commercial credit was based on it. A committee with Alcorn a member was appointed to prepare a memorial for Congress.[4]

Before this petition could be written, Congress voted to retain the cotton tax, but to decrease it by half a cent, thereby removing the main reason for the protest. Nevertheless, Alcorn proceeded to draw up a memorial which was presented to both houses of Congress on December 18, 1866, and carried his name alone as its author. In it he cited his own activities in levee improvement and wrote of the richness of the Yazoo-Mississippi Delta and its potential in tax revenues. He went on to warn of the danger to the cotton industry from cheap foreign competition, calling United States cotton production supremacy a necessity for its commercial greatness. Then he came to the purpose of his memorial, the cotton tax, which he felt the people of the South regarded "not only as a grievance, but as a wrong." If it had to be enforced, he asked that "it be disarmed, as far as possible from its irritating character and its alienating influences by its expenditure in the States contributing to it, whenever they present fields for its employment in works of such high general concern as those of the drainage of the great alluvians of the Mississippi." [5] In conclusion, he stated that the cotton tax collected in Mississippi, Arkansas, and Louisiana should be appropriated for the construction of levees in those states. Congressional action had made it necessary for Alcorn to change the tenor of his memorial, so he altered its contents from a tax protest into a plea for funds for internal improvements in the South. The national government seemed to be engaged in a policy of generous subsidies for internal improvements, particularly railroads, in the North and West. With his Whig background, Alcorn had no quarrel with such a policy, but he wanted to obtain a share in it for the South. Congress failed to respond.

Immediately after the war, without waiting to see if they could

4 Oxford (Miss.) *Falcon*, June 14, 1866; and Friar's Point (Miss.) *Coahomian*, June 15, 1866.
5 James Lusk Alcorn, *Memorial by J. L. Alcorn to both Houses of Congress* (Washington, 1866).

secure federal aid, a group of planters in Bolivar, Washington, and Issaquena counties, in the southern half of the old levee district, secured incorporation on November 27, 1865, of their own board of levee commissioners. Plans for reviving the prewar levee district had been discussed, but such an action would also revive the large, outstanding bonded debt against the old district. Further, many owners of large tracts along the river front still resented what they had considered Alcorn's dictatorial management and preferred if possible to keep the levee under local control. This new levee law provided for a tax on land, another on cotton. Tunica and Coahoma counties were invited to join but declined, in part perhaps because of Alcorn's vigorous opposition.[6] One reason for his dissent may have been bitterness remaining from the prewar controversies over levee construction. In addition, he disliked the localism inherent in this new board. He was on record as being against a tax on cotton. And his distrust of the use of bonds to raise revenue was an attitude formed in the days of the state's repudiation of the Planters' Bank bonds and the resulting damage to its reputation.

This financial conservatism was subsequently reinforced when he was afforded another close look at the problems created by contracting debts without adequately assessing the resources from which they would have to be paid. Early in 1867 the Mississippi legislature decided to dispose of unfinished levee business by creating the liquidating levee board to settle the claims still pending against the prewar board of levee commissioners. This new board was given the power to judge the validity of claims and to quiet them for from one-half to two-thirds of the amount requested by issuing bonds to the claimants to be financed by a land tax and the sale of forfeited lands.[7] Alcorn became president of this board and, until January, 1870, handled the complicated litigations and land sales over which it had authority.[8] Because of the inability of the planters to pay the required taxes during the preceding troubled years, almost every acre of land in the Delta was forfeit at one time or another. The board found itself in possession of thousands of acres of rich land and a maze of tangled tax titles,[9] testifying to the inability of the land itself, no matter how potentially valu-

6 Harrison, *Levee Districts,* 27–28, 33.
7 Wade, "Lands of the Liquidating Levee Board," 275–82.
8 Friar's Point (Miss.) *Weekly Delta,* February 10, 1869.
9 Harrison, *Levee Districts,* 41–43.

able, to meet requisitions on it. This experience, added to the Planters' Bank bonds fiasco and his antebellum financial struggles as president of the Board of Levee Commissioners, made Alcorn wary of any financing which seemed even remotely speculative or dependent on the resources of the Delta alone.

As in prewar times, the South began to hold commercial conventions to try to solve its economic problems. One of these which met at Memphis on May 18, 1869, provided Alcorn with an opportunity to continue his campaign for a unified, well-financed levee system. He was appointed chairman of a committee on Mississippi River improvements, with a membership representing states in the South, the Mississippi Valley, and as far east as New York. This committee presented resolutions calling on the national government to improve navigation on the Mississippi River, protesting the construction of low bridges over the river, and insisting that all future bridges and tunnels provide "double tracks for vehicles of every description." [10] Hoping to take advantage of his prominence, Alcorn worked hard on a speech to be given before the convention, but when the day came he had to submit it in writing because, as he disgustedly reported in his diary, "of the many windy speeches that members were disposed to make." [11]

Later that summer the *Weekly Delta* published his speech in full at a time when he was increasing his political activity. In it he developed the widened sphere of importance he would assign to the construction of levees. No longer would they merely benefit his region and state, but now they were "in the fullest sense of the term—national." Cotton he saw as the "Peace-maker of the World" because Britain's need for cotton kept her friendly. Before the war the United States had had a monopoly of the world cotton trade, but now he detected an international conspiracy, headed by the Manchester Cotton Supply Association, and including, besides the British Empire, France and Haiti (later he would include most of Europe and the Middle East), to keep the United States from regaining its dominant position.

The only way to meet the lower prices caused by this conspiracy was to increase the yield per acre, and this could best be done on the highly productive Delta lands—if the government would under-

10  Friar's Point (Miss.) *Weekly Delta*, May 26, 1869.
11  James Lusk Alcorn diary (Mrs. V. A. Hain), May 12, 18, 19, and 20, 1869.

take the construction of levees.[12] Correlation between the long
lists of statistics he presented on the lower prices and increased
production of foreign-grown cotton, and his optimism concerning
levees as the means to meet this rivalry may have been open to
question. But the speech showed a shrewd awareness of the strained
postwar Anglo-American relations in its hint of British-inspired
international conspiracies and its appeal to nationalism.

Through petitions to Congress, settlements of levee claims,
speeches at conventions, and political activity, Alcorn worked to
promote the interests of the Delta. The potential prosperity of
these rich bottom lands as a prime cotton-producing section was
the foundation upon which Alcorn wanted to reconstruct his world.
It was the frontier building a new civilization, but modeling it on
the old. His beliefs were the blueprint which would determine its
form. As he envisioned it, the prosperity of the Delta would produce
the new leaders of the South, a new class of intellect and wealth, to
follow in the footsteps of the antebellum aristocracy. And this class
would try to reproduce as closely as possible the previous social
structure.

This, of course, involved fitting the freedmen into the pattern.
Alcorn's prewar speeches and letters had given every indication
that he shared the general assumption that slavery was basic to
the Southern way of life. Yet, the more liberal influences to which
he may have been exposed in Kentucky, his own realistic frame
of mind, and the changes he observed during the war all helped
to produce in him a flexibility beyond that of most of his fellow
Mississippians. While this flexibility created an illusion of radical
action, Alcorn never fully understood the extent of the challenge
he faced, nor his own limitations in dealing with it. The removal
of slavery did not eliminate but only modified a problem which
has remained the basis of controversy to this day—a problem
which has been aptly described as the "lion of race-adjustment."
It had stood in the path of prewar gradual emancipation[13] and re-

12   Friar's Point (Miss.) *Weekly Delta*, July 21, 1869.
13   Allan Nevins, *Ordeal of the Union* (New York: Scribner's, 1947), I,
422, 504. Like many other historians, Nevins saw slavery as the principal
cause of the Civil War, but he also perceptively saw that it was "the
lion of race-adjustment" that prevented a solution of the problem. E.
Merton Coulter, *The Confederate States of America, 1861–1865* (Baton
Rouge: Louisiana State University Press, 1950), 9, also recognized the
basic racial issue by pointing out that the Negro himself, more than

mained a formidable obstacle. But Alcorn felt sure he would be able to deal with it.

Early in 1863 a suggestion of this more flexible attitude had appeared in a diary notation he made upon discovering that a particularly faithful slave had run away. He was mortified at being deceived, ". . . but can I in my heart blame him. Freedom is offered him, 'tis but natural he should accept. I feel that had I been in his place I should have gone, so good by Hadley, you have heretofore been faithful, that you should espouse your liberty but shows your sense. I wish you no harm." [14] The following year he described the activities of freed Negroes and their position vis a vis the whites at Helena with a complete lack of revulsion and an air of interested, if amused, objectivity.[15] After the war, members of the Ku Klux Klan burned down the buildings on a plantation of his because he had rented it out to freedmen.[16]

Slavery, as he had continued to insist, at least publicly, up to the end of the war, might be the best way to deal with the situation both socially and economically, but after Appomattox he was willing to consider alternatives. At the beginning of 1865 he had hoped to use the continued legality of slavery in Mississippi as a bargaining point in dealing with the North, but by the end of the same year he was urging his fellow Southerners to accept and ratify the Thirteenth Amendment which forbade slavery. Less than two years later he was willing to enfranchise the Negro, grant him full civil and legal rights, and even form political alliances with him. Eventually he would work to disfranchise him and would openly declare his belief in the racial inferiority of the Negro.

Basically he was not inconsistent. His way of life required a society of classes with gentlemen of wealth and intellect at the top and a permanently servile class on the bottom, be it slave or free. He differed from most of his contemporaries in being more adaptable in his means of attaining the desired goal, even to the point of attempting to use the instruments of change which defeat had

---

slavery, was a potent cause of the Civil War. Walter L. Fleming, *The Sequel of Appomattox* (New Haven: Yale University Press, 1919), 34, wrote that without the Negro there would have been no Civil War, and without his presence after the war, reconstruction would have been comparatively simple.

14 James Lusk Alcorn diary (Mrs. V. A. Hain), April 9, 1865.
15 James Lusk Alcorn to Amelia Alcorn, March 22, 1865, in Alcorn Papers.
16 Friar's Point (Miss.) *Weekly Delta*, April 7, 1869.

introduced into their midst in order to retain the configurations of the past.

Like all conservatives, Alcorn had a strong sense of continuity with the past. In the fall of 1862, within a few weeks after being captured by Federal soldiers, he had returned to their headquarters in Helena to file a protest against aid being given some of his runaway slaves. He had contended that this violated both the laws of the United States and his rights as a citizen of Mississippi, as if no war existed to change the relationships under which he claimed protection.[17] As soon as the war was over, his first idea was to resume the dialogue of controversy where the rebellion had interrupted it and on the same old terms. Mississippi would rejoin the Union (or had never been out of it), and under the protection of the Constitution would send her representatives to Congress where they would bargain with the North for concessions in return for the abolition of slavery.

Therefore he opposed the idea of calling a convention (to rescind the secession ordinance) which might acquiesce too readily in the face of emancipation, because if the Southern states had never really been out of the Union they still retained their rights as states. Like most politicians, he could make good use of a theoretical position when it appeared advantageous to do so, but he was realistic enough to abandon this approach as soon as it was apparent it would not work.

After the dispersal of the Mississippi legislature in May, 1865, Alcorn spent a month with his family in Alabama, and on July 4 returned to Mound Place. The trip marked his transformation from southern Rebel to southern American. While he had been in Alabama, President Johnson appointed Sharkey as provisional governor, and a civil government had begun to function. A few days after his return Alcorn noted in his diary that he had received Sharkey's proclamation ordering an election for delegates to a convention, but he refused to participate in the election.

Later that month he traveled to Jackson, meeting many acquaintances on the way. While there he stayed at the home of Judge William Yerger, a prewar Whig, met with the Judge's brother, J. S. Yerger, an old political ally, and visited with various friends, including Ethelbert Barksdale, then editor of the *Missis-*

17 "Protest of J. L. Alcorn . . . September 6, 1862."

*sippian* and later of the *Clarion*, both strongly Democratic news-papers. On July 26 he took the oath of allegiance to the Constitu-tion of the United States before Sharkey, noting the act in his diary without comment. A pattern of acquiescence settled on Coahoma County also, and a few days later his son Milton, his overseer Minga, and other neighbors living in the vicinity of Swan Lake gathered at the local church to take the oath.

Having concluded his peace with the Mississippi provisional government, Alcorn then made a pilgrimage to Washington to seek a pardon, since as an owner of extensive property he was exempt from the general amnesty.

In Washington he called on Attorney General James Speed to make his application for pardon, as well as Secretary of State W. H. Seward, Secretary of the Treasury Hugh McCulloch, and President Johnson, with whom he had several interviews, "some pleasant some not so much so." The role of petitioner was not an easy one for him to play. More congenial ones involved replen-ishing his wardrobe which must have lost much of its famous luster during the war years, and observing the ladies' latest hair and dress styles, information which he dutifully sent on to his wife. He noted with particular approval a drawstring arrangement whereby ladies could draw up their long skirts when walking on the dirty streets, which he quickly explained not only showed their feet, but also suggested cleanliness.[18] Washington was ob-viously not completely bereft of attractions.

While there he was also busy, as he tersely noted in his diary, with "visits to the departments, talks with acquaintances, form views, take an occasional drink, and so it goes, the weather is oppressive, the city filled with Southerners." He received his pardon on September 11 and on the thirteenth started for Mis-sissippi.[19]

Casual as his diary entries were for this trip, what Alcorn learned in Washington during the two weeks he was there caused him to make fundamental changes in the tactics he would use to try to preserve the past. From Washington he wrote his wife that the hatred of the extreme Republicans of the North toward the South was intense, and that while Johnson's course toward the South

18 James Lusk Alcorn diary (Mrs. V. A. Hain), August 19–26, 1865; James Lusk Alcorn to Amelia Alcorn, August 26, 1865, in Alcorn Papers.
19 James Lush Alcorn diary (Mrs. V. A. Hain), September 1–13, 1865.

might appear harsh, it was gentle compared to what the Radicals would do. He doubted that southern representatives would be admitted to the coming Congress, and believed that admission would be based on abolition of slavery, repudiation of Confederate debts, and some civil and franchise rights for the Negro. He felt it would be politic for Southerners to grant the Negro limited franchise based on property or educational qualifications, because if they did not make the Negro their friend, the path ahead would be "red with blood, and damp with tears."

The reasoning on which he based this proposition is the key to his actions for the next ten years:

> To let the negro approach the witness stand & the ballot box by no means implies his social equality; we dont recognize the social equality of the low and base of our own color who enjoy these prerogatives to an extent equal to the proudest. Political equality does not imply by any means social equality, the negro need not be made even politically equal, his testimony may be made to go to his credibility, & his suffrage may be based upon his property.[20]

Prewar Whigs had not hesitated to deal with what they considered the lowest free classes in order to gain needed political support, and Alcorn's willingness to act in similar vein can hardly be considered radical. He would in time increase his concessions to the Negro, but his flexibility in this regard was simply one of means. He ended his remarks on this subject with a prediction that the Southerners would not secure the friendship of the Negroes.

Meanwhile, in Jackson the convention called by Sharkey was meeting. It was composed mostly of Whigs, many of them men who had opposed secession before the war.[21] Some of the members reflected to varying degrees the conclusions to which Alcorn had come. Sharkey in July had told the people of Mississippi bluntly that regardless of their views on the constitutionality of the Emancipation Proclamation, the Negro was in fact free, and the wisest thing they could do would be to accept the fact. Judge Amos R. Johnston also urged acceptance of the conditions imposed by the Federal government, pointing out that resistance would only make the conditions more stringent.

20  James Lusk Alcorn to Amelia Alcorn, August 26, 1865, in Alcorn Papers.
21  Frank Johnston, "Suffrage and Reconstruction in Mississippi," *Mississippi Historical Society Publications*, VI (1902), 170; Garner, *Reconstruction in Mississippi*, 84.

Sharkey urged the convention to debate the extension of the franchise to colored men with certain education and property qualifications.[22] There is no indication that the convention even considered his suggestion. In this it behaved no differently than any other Southern constitutional convention which met in 1865. In each instance the conventions either completely avoided the issue or summarily rejected it by returning the proposal to committee. As in most of the other southern states, the convention in Mississippi abolished slavery and declared the secession ordinance null and void. In an unofficial way it also nominated Judge E. S. Fisher, an Old Line Whig, as a candidate for governor.

Before Alcorn left for Washington, he had refused to run as a delegate to this convention, although his law partner Walter L. Stricklin was a successful candidate and had conferred with him before the election.[23] He also refused to allow his name to be entered in the gubernatorial contest, but he did indicate that his supporters could nominate him as a candidate for the Mississippi house of representatives, and that he would be willing to serve as a United States Senator, a position to which the state legislature would have to elect him.[24]

His standing in Coahoma County was such that he was nominated, ran without opposition, and was elected, all while he was still in Washington. Coahoma County also cast 115 votes for Fisher and 95 for Benjamin G. Humphreys, a prewar secessionist Democrat,[25] but the state chose Humphreys, who would spearhead defiance of the Reconstruction measures. Mississippians also elected to the courts judges who were "secessionists" and ex-Confederates, and selected a legislature hostile to the extension of any rights to the freedmen. But in the same election, in a rare exhibition of political astuteness, the voters named four Whigs and one Union Democrat to be their representatives in Congress.

In the state house of representatives Alcorn was nominated to be speaker (without his consent, he claimed), and on the final ballot he received 26 votes to the 38 cast for the winner S. J. Gholson, a Democrat. He was appointed to several committees, but almost immediately the legislature went into joint session to elect

22  *Ibid.*, 78–84.
23  James Lusk Alcorn diary (Mrs. V. A. Hain), August 3, 1865.
24  James Lusk Alcorn to Amelia Alcorn, August 26, 1865, in Alcorn Papers.
25  Friar's Point (Miss.) *Coahomian*, October 6, 1865.

senators to represent the state in Congress. William Sharkey was elected on the first ballot for the short term, and Alcorn on the fourth ballot for the long term.[26] As in the case of his nomination for speaker, Alcorn claimed he had not solicited the position and therefore found the ease with which he had been selected over the nomination of the "most able men of the state" highly flattering.[27] The Democratic majority in the legislature, like the electorate, acted with singular astuteness. It sent two of its most acceptable members to Washington, and at the same time eliminated the two most powerful and articulate leaders of the minority from positions in which they might have influenced legislation.

One of the specific issues upon which the legislature had been elected had been the question of whether or not the Negro should be allowed to give evidence in a court of law. The composition of the legislature and its subsequent actions indicate that the electorate as constituted in 1865 was against extending even this fundamental right to the freedmen. Shortly after their election as Senators, Alcorn and Sharkey were invited to address the two houses. They both warned the members that it was a matter of policy as well as justice to allow the Negro to testify in court, and if they did not extend him this right the Federal government would.[28] They had hardly left Jackson when the legislature voted to permit the freedmen to testify only in cases in which a Negro was party to the suit, passed the Black Codes, and rejected the Thirteenth Amendment.

Since Alcorn already knew what the congressional temper was likely to be, and was aware of the disastrous course the Mississippi legislature was taking, it is difficult to see why he should have been so willing to leave an arena where he might have been able to modify legislative action for a scene where he would not even be officially recognized. Perhaps his earlier conversations with Johnson and the members of his cabinet led him to overestimate his ability to exert influence in Washington, the source of policy affecting Mississippi. In addition, Southerners customarily held the position of Senator in high esteem, and Alcorn may have simply

26 *Journal of the House of Representatives of the State of Mississippi, October–December, 1865*, (Jackson: J. J. Shannon and Co., 1866), 3–37.
27 James Lusk Alcorn to Amelia Alcorn, October 20, 1865, copy in Rainwater Collection, Box 2, Folder 33.
28 Garner, *Reconstruction in Mississippi*, 117.

been beguiled by the political and social distinction implied in the title.

As Alcorn and the other members of the Mississippi delegation had anticipated, they were not permitted to take the seats to which they had been elected. Congress had begun to take from Johnson the initiative in reconstruction, and finding themselves deprived of an official voice in the legislative-executive battle that was starting, the delegation decided upon a policy of "dignified silence." One member at least felt that if Southerners would only realize their actual condition and would behave with common sense, discretion, and prudence, it would be of great help to the delegates.[29]

Alcorn remained in Washington during December, visiting people and observing the situation as the intent and power of Congress under the leadership of the Radical Republicans became more and more evident. Acting in a more limited capacity, he obtained a post office for Friar's Point and presented claims to the government on behalf of clients.[30] L. Q. C. Lamar, discussing efforts to obtain the release of Jefferson Davis' private secretary, wrote to the chancellor of the University of Mississippi that he intended to write Sharkey in Washington, but that he had more hope "from Alcorn's energy than from Sharkey's influence." [31]

Early in 1866 Alcorn returned to Mississippi, apparently without having accomplished anything of note. The information he obtained, and the contracts he made during these two trips to Washington, together with his reemergence as a spokesman for the Delta, provided the basis for the political form his leadership would assume. It is doubtful that he returned from Washington the second time as a Republican,[32] but he had by then characteristically made a realistic assessment of the situation which was developing, and he had no illusions about the South's position in relation to the power struggle going on. The strength of the Republican party and its resemblance to the defunct Whig party must also have

29  Winbourne M. Drake, (ed.), "A Mississippian's Appraisal of Andrew Johnson; Letters of James T. Harrison, December 1865," *Journal of Mississippi History*, XVIII (1955), 45–46.
30  James Lusk Alcorn diary (Mrs. V. A. Hain), December 8, 14, and 18, 1865.
31  Edward Mayes, *Lucius Q. C. Lamar: His Life, Times and Speeches* (Nashville; Publishing House of the Methodist Episcopal Church, 1896), 121.
32  William B. Hesseltine, *Confederate Leaders in the New South* (Baton Rouge: Louisiana State University Press, 1950), 106.

impressed him. He returned home wiser and perhaps sadder, but also with some new ideas on methods for coping with the threats of change to his cherished way of life. Whether or not he yet considered himself a Whig and regardless of how radical his methods appeared to be, Alcorn responded to the changes around him in a manner that was distinctively and persistently Whiggish.

# 6

# Politics and a New Party

THE FRIAR'S POINT *Coahomian* noted Alcorn's return home early
in January of 1866 with the statement that: "His hopes of an early
restoration are not so strong we think as when he left for Washington." Some years later Charles Swift wrote that after his father-
in-law was refused the Senate seat, there was a "cessation in his
political aspirations and purposes." According to Swift, Alcorn
for a time then occupied himself principally in practicing law and
managing his plantations.[1] If there was such a cessation, it was
hardly more than a hiatus during the spring and summer of 1866.
It was during that summer that Congress passed the Fourteenth
Amendment—dealing with citizenship, due process, suffrage, representation, office holding—and sent it to the states for ratification.
Benjamin G. Humphreys sent it on to the Mississippi legislature
with a message urging its rejection, and the legislature quickly
complied. In late October Alcorn attended circuit court in Bolivar
County and was asked by some of the lawyers there, including
J. S. Yerger and James R. Chalmers, what the President's chances
were in the reconstruction struggle with Congress and what his
own prospects were for obtaining his seat in the Senate.

In reply Alcorn talked for an hour, telling them of Johnson's
loss of power and influence in his party. The legislature, he said,
had made a mistake in refusing to ratify the Fourteenth Amendment since it would be forced upon the state anyway and was a
logical result of the freeing of the Negro and the success of the

1 Swift, "James Lusk Alcorn," 19.

Federal government. He characterized resistance as "a childish display of spite, rather than a thoughtful earnest desire . . . to bring the states into full accord with the government. . . ," and said the result would be to bring harsher measures down upon them, to weaken the influence of friends and moderate men in the Republican party, and to give their enemies the excuse they wanted for a violent and extreme course.[2] The national congressional elections of the following month brought an increase in the Radical Republican majority in both houses of Congress, thus beginning the fulfillment of Alcorn's prophecy.

Early in 1867 Alcorn was invited to address the Mississippi legislature and in the speech he developed his views further. He advised against coalition with any faction of either party in the North, especially the Democrats who he felt could not help the South and, judging from their voting record on the sections of the Fourteenth Amendment, would not if they could. Referring to the opposition in the South to the section of the amendment which reduced representation when voting rights were restricted, he showed the hard, pragmatic line of reasoning characteristic of much of his political material during this period:

Of the second section . . . the Constitution as it now exists gives the South full representation for all her blacks, that the same Constitution gave us while these blacks were slaves, representation for but three-fifths. Could we expect to go back to Congress stronger than when we came away? Could we hope for an increase of political power as a result of the war? And could we contend for this increased representation when by every Southern State constitution, the freedmen were excluded from computation in the apportionment of representation. As the question now stood we denied that the negro should be represented in the political power of the State Government. How could we contend, with the hope of success, that the negro should be computed in estimating the representative power of the United States Government?

In speaking of the Fourteenth Amendment as a whole, he said he felt that it should be rejected if presented simply upon the question of its merit, but that if it were presented to the South as the final adjustment of all the obstacles in the way of complete restoration to the Union, "it then became a question of diplomacy, a question of expediency." In such a case he would be willing to accept all sections except the third (barring ex-rebels from

2 Montgomery, *Reminiscences of a Mississippian*, 265–68.

holding office), and he would be ready to debate the justice and propriety of it, presumably with the object of accepting it also if suitable concessions were made.[3] By accepting most of the amendment, but holding out on one section for bargaining purposes, he felt the whole reconstruction issue could be settled without dishonor to the South. Again he emphasized the South's straitened position in the matter of choice, and its need for restoration to the Union as a prerequisite for peace, order, and prosperity.[4] Apparently he did not know, or chose to ignore, the fact that a bill guaranteeing restoration of the South to the Union in return for ratification of the Fourteenth Amendment had been tabled and allowed to die in Congress that previous summer.[5]

Alcorn's views on Negro suffrage were becoming clearer and apparently more radical, and because of this he began to lose his long-time political associates. Earlier, in November, 1866, a correspondent to the Vicksburg *Herald* noted that Senator Sharkey had indicated his opposition to colored voters, and wrote: "It would be equally gratifying to the people of Mississippi to know that their other Senator, Gen. Alcorn, had also placed himself in opposition to this nefarious measure . . . last year he addressed a letter to a distinguished citizen of our State in which he boldly advocated that doctrine!" [6] While Sharkey and most of the prewar Whigs hesitantly played the role of conventional conservatives, Alcorn moved down the path of what appeared to be outright radicalism.

Events could not have helped but confirm him in his belief that something positive and unusual had to be done. Johnson had attempted to complete reconstruction in Mississippi by relieving Sharkey of his duties and recognizing Humphreys as regularly elected governor on December 14, 1865. However, Federal troops remained in Mississippi, and while civil government functioned almost unimpeded, the influence of their presence was used to prevent enforcement of discriminatory laws and to prohibit the institution of any suits or prosecutions arising out of the war.

3 Jackson *Daily Clarion*, January 29, 1867.
4 Johnston, "Suffrage and Reconstruction in Mississippi," 187.
5 Howard K. Beale, *The Critical Year* (New York: Harcourt, Brace, 1930), 206–207.
6 J. S. McNeily, "From Organization to Overthrow of Mississippi's Provisional Government, 1865-1868," *Publications of the Mississippi Historical Society, Centenary Series*, I (1916), 235–36.

Then in 1866 the southern states had rejected the Fourteenth Amendment, while the country at large confirmed and increased the Radical Republican majority in Congress. This led to the passage of the Reconstruction acts under which Mississippi became part of the Fourth Military District. Military rule became the dominant authority, with civil rule continued on a provisional basis. Military authorities were also given the responsibility to register a new and broader electorate, and to guide it in establishing a more representative government. This was expected to be accomplished by the election of delegates to a convention to draw up a new constitution for the state. Negro suffrage and the power of the Negro vote became a political reality which had to be faced.

By the summer of 1867 Alcorn's political plans began to take shape. In July he spoke in Memphis to a small audience composed mostly of old Whigs and others without political affiliation. According to the newspaperman who reported his speech, he seemed to be calling for a reorganization of political parties in the South to avert formation of a white party and an opposing Negro one controlled by Northerners. He would not object to a Democratic party composed of the traditional Southern radicals, and suggested another one containing staunch Whigs and Douglas Democrats, the two to share the Negro vote. The only way to rescue Mississippi would be through the creation of a new party. Even the reporter, who seemed to be wary of him because of his reputation, conceded that he should be heard.[7]

A full presentation of Alcorn's plan for dealing with the situation was provided in a pamphlet he issued on August 8, 1867, titled *Views of the Hon. J. L. Alcorn on the Political Situation of Mississippi.* He appealed to his fellow citizens to be realistic and to try to deal with their problems as rational men rather than as partisan zealots. Even though he had been called radical, "does it follow that when we are looking around for counsel against the dangers impending over us all, my words, unpalatable tho' they are, may not, after all, be the words of wisdom and sound policy?"

To emphasize the danger, he cited figures to show the Negro majority which had elected Governor William G. Brownlow in Tennessee, and similar majorities shown by voter registration in

7 Jackson *Daily Clarion,* July 11, 1867.

Alabama and Louisiana. Voter registration in Mississippi under the new military bill would show similar results, making the governorship, the legislature, and even the courts subject to the Negro vote. "The brute force which lies ready to sustain that state of affairs we have no means of wrestling with save that embodied in our *brains.*" The so-called influence of the former masters on the freedmen he called nonsense. The Negro majority would fall "by political gravitation" under the influence of the radicals, and a constitutional convention was inevitable. The only way to avert material and political ruin was to negotiate. "I stand ready to ask terms from the radicals."

Congress, he further pointed out in the pamphlet, was more than ordinarily partisan. The Republicans were aware that a sectional party was short-lived, and while they feared Negro suffrage because of its possible effects on their popularity in the North, they needed it in the South. They would like to escape the implications of representatives in Congress who were Negro or represented purely Negro constituencies, and therefore would welcome white support. No more than the Republicans could Mississippians afford two parties based on racial distinctions, and he proposed to negotiate on the basis of this common problem.

There follows immediately the most quoted paragraph in Alcorn's political writing. In the light of his reasoning, it assumes a much less radical color than when quoted without reference to the balance of his pamphlet:

The colored man comes, as well as the white man, within the scope of my proposed negotiation. Free, erect, enfranchised, with all the rights of American citizenship attaching to him, the terms which I seek to obtain shall not be one iota more to your advantage or to mine than to his. All that Congress has given him I accept as his with all my heart and conscience. I propose to vote with him; to discuss political affairs with him; to sit, if need be, in political counsel with him; and from a platform acceptable alike to him, to me, and to you, to pluck our common liberty and our common prosperity out of the jaws of inevitable ruin.

Even though his "platform" included this controversial core, that is, his proposal to include Negroes as allies, it nowhere hinted at anything remotely suggesting equality or admitting them to leadership. By guaranteeing them their rights as citizens, he hoped the "influential and respectable mass of white people" would be able to "maintain their position as advisers of the old and devoted servants of the South—the colored people." Politically they were to assume a similar position to that expected of them in the economic and social realms, that is, to be the "mud sill" on which the structure would be built. While their consent would have to be obtained, the actual governing would be done by their betters.

Alcorn wrote further of his concept of the terms on which he and his fellow members of this proposed party might negotiate to give the Republicans their needed white support. He suggested abolition of the cotton tax, rebuilding of the levees, and a general amnesty. These would be demanded in return for support for a constitutional amendment which would settle the question of reconstruction, guarantee the bonded debt, "and of all rights vested, whether North or South." In the matter of a presidential candidate, while he preferred General Grant, the "new organization" ought to acquiesce in the selection of the congressional party, provided only he endorse the terms of the proposed negotiations. In this struggle between the President and Congress, the Constitution was entitled to no more attention that it would receive from an antiquarian. "My reflections as to the means of saving the State take no notice of those fossils of the pre-secession period." He therefore advised discarding such older methods, and "as bold man does in the case of a runaway horse whose bridle he essays to grasp, *we first run on with it for a distance sufficient to check its speed.*" [8]

In order to be acceptable to the Radicals, this new mixed party which he suggested would have to be free from any association with ex-secessionists. Only those who had been Old Line Whigs or Douglas Democrats could be admitted, although he was anxious to see full political rights restored to all Mississippians. "A mixed party of unionists," he wrote, "can obtain for us that great remedy of all our troubles—representation." [9]

8  This analogy closely resembles the one Alcorn used, according to Frank A. Montgomery, in explaining why he joined the secessionists. It might also be related to a family story that Alcorn, Lamar, and a third party held a conference soon after the war on how to help Mississippi. They agreed that a Southerner would have to join the radicals to find out what they were doing and to try to influence them. Both Lamar and the other person declined the honor, so Alcorn agreed to do it.

9  James Lusk Alcorn, *Views of the Hon. J. L. Alcorn on The Political Situation of Mississippi* (Friar's Point: n.p., August 8, 1867).

This new political organization Alcorn saw as the means for dealing with the changes imposed upon the South and for preserving the desired form of society. It would be autonomous and would be his personal party, since to Alcorn political loyalties were largely personal loyalties and destiny intended him to be the leader, in the gentlemanly Whig tradition, to whom these loyalties would be owed. His party would then give the Radical Republicans needed support in return for concessions. In a sense, his was a practical proposal which followed long-standing political practices, and it was ingeniously designed to reap the advantages of being allied with the party in power while at the same time trying to modify changes that party wanted to introduce into the state.

How far Alcorn had come, from the viewpoint of another prominent ex-Whig, can be seen from a letter William Sharkey wrote to the editor of the Columbus, Mississippi, *Index* at about the same time. In it Sharkey urged the people of Mississippi not to ratify the Reconstruction laws passed by Congress. Since secession was impossible, he said, the states had never been out of the Union, and therefore were not in the position of defeated nations forced to accept the terms of their conqueror. The United States government was a limited constitutional government, and their oath to the Constitution demanded that they resist. They might even have to back away from universal suffrage, that "splendid theory." It has not been possible to find a single prominent pre-war Whig or Union Democrat who actively supported Alcorn in his proposed new party at this time.

Neither did the national Republican party appear to pay any attention to him. Within Mississippi a regular state organization was set up, and it held its first state convention on September 10, 1867. Among its founders were men who would continue to be prominent in its activities: George C. McKee, Jonathan Tarbell, J. L. Wofford, H. R. Pease, and the Reverend James Lynch, a Negro minister.[10] Alcorn continued to present his views throughout the fall but without noticeable effect, often to hostile audiences.[11] A large proportion of the white voters took no part in the November elections, with the result, as Alcorn had foreseen, that the majority of those who did register under military super-

10 Garner, *Reconstruction in Mississippi*, 181.
11 James Lusk Alcorn to Amelia Alcorn, September 18, 1867, in possession of Mrs. V. A. Hain; Grenada (Miss.) *Sentinel*, April 14, 1869.

vision voted in favor of a constitutional convention and selected the delegates to it.

Out of this convention came a new constitution for Mississippi which, discounting the garish atmosphere in which it was supposed to have been written, was a good one. It eliminated, of course, all distinctions due to color as well as all property and educational qualifications for any functions of citizenship. Remembering the Planters' Bank scandal, its authors entered a clause absolutely forbidding the legislature from pledging the state's credit. The powers of the governor were expanded, salaries were increased, and in a spirit of change, a lieutenant governor, a superintendent of education, a commissioner of immigration and agriculture, a board of equalization, state and district printers, and special treasury agents were added to the roster of state officials. The number of judges was tripled. It was a more democratic constitution, but contrary to Jacksonian Democratic precepts it also governed more.[12] This constitution was then to be submitted to the voters for approval.

Alcorn took no direct part in this convention, but his cousin Robert J. Alcorn, representing Yalobusha County, attended as a Republican member and was quite active. He had also been born and reared in Kentucky, and had come to Mississippi in 1852. Apparently he had been able to avoid military service during the Civil War, but in 1863 he acted as an agent to procure livestock for the Confederate army in Mississippi.[13]

After the convention the state Republican party held a nominating convention and selected Robert Alcorn to be its candidate for secretary of state on an all-white ticket composed mostly of Northerners. In the broadside which announced his candidacy he also urged adoption of the new constitution as a means of bringing prosperity to the state, while admitting that some of its harshest features could be modified. Presumably he had in mind its wholesale proscription of the rights of anyone who had taken part in the rebellion (and who had not redeemed himself by taking the oath of allegiance to the Constitution of the United States), and he reminded his readers of Mississippi's unenviable position as a

12  Garner, *Reconstruction in Mississippi*, 281; Jesse Thomas Wallace, *A History of the Negroes of Mississippi from 1865 to 1890* (Clinton, Mississippi: n.p., 1927), 60–61.

13  Receipts dated November 8 and December 1, 1863, in Robert J. Alcorn Folder, National Archives.

defeated state. On the whole, his presentation was a milder version of the views of his cousin James.

James Alcorn seems to have kept clear of the actual Republican organization during this campaign, but he did speak on behalf of the Republican ticket.[14] This widened the gap between him and most of his long-standing associates and enemies. Some of them, such as A. G. Brown, Ethelbert Barksdale, and William Yerger, had, as late as the fall of 1867, also been urging acquiescence in the Reconstruction acts and participation in the election for delegates to a constitutional convention. These men were now among a group who advocated active opposition to ratification of the new constitution, and who openly called for a party to "vindicate alike the superiority of their race over the negro, and their political power to maintain constitutional liberty." [15] As Alcorn drew closer to the Republican party, most of his old associates moved into the reshaped Democratic party.

The support Alcorn had hoped to recruit apparently did not materialize during the winter of 1867–68, and as the centrifugal force of politics impelled both parties away from the center, he began to turn toward the already organized Republican group as the only practical alternative since his proposal for an autonomous party had not elicited any response. The presence of Robert Alcorn and possibly other pro-Alcorn delegates at the constitutional convention of 1868 suggests this. The delegate from Coahoma County, A. S. Dowd, would be the one officially to propose his name the following summer for nomination for governor. Yalobusha County, which Robert Alcorn represented, may have functioned as a sort of temporary "pocket borough" for the Alcorn group, because the following year it was one of the three counties carried by Alcorn's opponent in the gubernatorial race.

Early in 1868 Robert was again in Coahoma County founding the first of two short-lived newspapers that vigorously supported Alcorn. These activities together with Alcorn's conduct during the campaign strongly suggest that the efforts of the two cousins were related; that as Alcorn's first idea to form a new party proved unsuccessful, he began to infiltrate the rival Republican group.

In the fall election of 1868 Robert Alcorn, the Republican

14  Jackson *Daily Clarion*, June 24, 1868.
15  Natchez *Democrat*, January 28, 1868.

ticket, and the proposed constitution were defeated through the efforts of the revitalized Democratic party. Robert's defeat did not reflect on James personally, and the failure of the Mississippi Republican organization placed the latter in a position where he could effectively bargain for a position of leadership within it, a position from which he could carry out his original plan. There no doubt is considerable superficial truth in John R. Lynch's succinct explanation that when Alcorn's public advice to the people of Mississippi to accept Congressional reconstruction was rejected by the Democrats, there was nothing left for him to do but join the Republican party.[16] However, in spite of statements by Lynch and Alcorn himself later, there is every indication that this step was carefully planned, and that Alcorn had never seriously considered building his organization within the framework of the Democratic party.

Almost immediately after the Republican defeat Alcorn's name appeared among those of the party leaders. A party convention which met in Jackson on November 25 prepared a petition to Congress which charged fraud and violence at the recent election and asked that the constitution be declared ratified and the Republican ticket elected. A committee was appointed to take the petition to Washington and lay it before Congress with a request for the readmission of the state. Alcorn was named as one of the sixteen members on this committee, which also included at least two Negroes.[17] Congress responded by keeping Mississippi under military rule until such time as it would adopt an acceptable government and constitution.

Early in 1869 things began to happen in Friar's Point. On February 3 a new newspaper, the *Weekly Delta*, appeared, edited by Robert J. Alcorn and published by F. S. Belcher. In March, James Alcorn resigned from the law firm of Alcorn, Stricklin and Harman, and the issue of the *Weekly Delta* which carried the announcement of this resignation also informed the public that Belcher had sold his interest in the paper to George R. Alcorn, another cousin. Although this paper vehemently insisted that it was an independent organ, not controlled in any way by James Alcorn, it fully endorsed and consistently defended him and the national Republican party.

16  John R. Lynch, *The Facts of Reconstruction* (New York: Neale Publishing Company, 1913), 84.
17  Garner, *Reconstruction in Mississippi*, 219–20.

George Alcorn at this time was also clerk of the Chancery Court of Coahoma County and Robert Alcorn was a judge. Both men therefore were acceptable to the military authorities under the terms of the Reconstruction acts.

In April a Democratic paper, beginning to be alarmed at Alcorn's growing accord with the Republican party, attacked him as the most dangerous man in the state because of his charm, bravery, and integrity which would be employed on behalf of the radical party. The *Weekly Delta* rebutted with a glowing reply, stressing Alcorn's independence of spirit and his identity with the South.

On June 2 the same newspaper expressed the hope that Alcorn would be selected as the Republican gubernatorial candidate. A week later its hopes began to take tangible form. The local Republican organization held a meeting which Robert Alcorn called to order and for which George Alcorn served as secretary. The group adopted a series of resolutions which pledged fidelity to the Union, belief in equality, free schools, and the Republican party as the party of progress. It gave its support to President Grant and the Congressional party, and approved the appointment of Adelbert Ames as military governor of Mississippi. Then Dowd, who had been Coahoma County's delegate to the constitutional convention of 1868, presented a resolution that Alcorn be nominated as a candidate for governor. Alcorn responded with an hour-long speech and urged that a Republican club be organized. Robert Alcorn was selected to be the delegate to attend the state Republican convention at Jackson.[18]

By the beginning of August, 1869, without waiting for endorsement by the state organization, or possibly with its tacit backing, Alcorn was openly campaigning for the national Republican party, although not expressly for the governorship. He was also active in creating a faction that would have the support of the national party and would be loyal to him. He warned against "Conservative Republicans" who were ready to betray the party to the Democrats and negate the results of reconstruction, and spoke of rejecting the advances of a group which included J. L. Wofford, one of the founders of the party in Mississippi. This group, he hinted, had been responsible for the defeat of the previous year.[19]

On September 29 he was nominated by acclaim at the Republican

18 Friar's Point (Miss.) *Weekly Delta*, June 9, 1869.
19 Hernando (Miss.) *Press*, August 19, 1869.

state convention to be its gubernatorial candidate, a nomination which took place in the presence of General Ames, the commander of the military district including Mississippi.[20] In his acceptance speech Alcorn acknowledged that his convictions had placed him for twenty-five years in opposition to the majority of the people of his state, but he stressed that above all else he wanted to work to promote the common good. He felt his nomination commissioned him to make a generous offer of alliance from the Negroes to the whites. He denounced the hypocrisy of the opposition Democratic party which claimed it wanted the cooperation of the colored people but at the same time declared null and void the Reconstruction acts which gave them their rights. The Democrats, he charged, were responsible for the separation of the political parties on the basis of race, and he tried to show the fairness of the demands of the Negroes. At his insistence the demand for universal suffrage was linked with that for general amnesty.

In the last part of his acceptance speech he again turned hungry eyes toward the federal treasury. "Under the policy of internal improvements by the general government, we hold moral claims for large subsidies from the treasury of the United States." Republican accession to political power in Mississippi would, he believed, result in "generous cooperation" from Congress. He listed aid for the cotton industry, subsidies for railroads within Mississippi, construction of a harbor at Ship Island in the Gulf of Mexico, and, of course, the building of levees in the Delta region.[21]

This latter part was an appeal to old Whigs, based on the fact, as Alcorn had repeatedly pointed out, that to share in the national internal improvement projects Congress was so generously endowing, one had to belong to the party in power. In a long letter published earlier that month he had explained at great length why Whigs should join him in the Republican party, using the impotence of the Democratic party as well as its traditional hostility to such improvements to argue his point.

Internal improvements, by the general government, is as much as ever a subject of Democratic hostility. Whigs of the South can find no reason for siding with the Democracy on that question now. . . . Public

20  U. S. Senate, 44th Cong. 1st Sess., *Senate Report No. 527* (Washington: Government Printing Office, 1876), I, 451.
21  Friar's Point (Miss.) *Weekly Delta*, October 13, 1869.

improvements by the general government has ceased, recollect you, to be simply a question of theory. It has become a question of fact. The issue in that case is no longer one of logic, but of money—of enormous sums of money!

The South, he insisted, was entitled to its share of this outlay. Whigs should stand by their principles at least until their region had collected a few hundred thousand dollars for improvements of its own.

His distaste for the Democratic party was as strong as ever. It had been responsible for shattering the peace and prosperity of the 1850's with its insistence on secession; it was still the party of destruction, and would only pull down the state's chance for restoration of civil government and sweep it back into political chaos. It was the party of the Jacksonian mob, given to irresponsible and unrealistic acts. "I am still led, as I ever have been, to do battle with the Democracy because of that common complexion of mind by which you and I had been placed, years ago, side by side in the splendid line which has so often withstood them to the death." [22] In another address he reminded them how the English nobles had "bent to the storm that burst on them in the Reform Bill of 1832," and had taken their places as the "natural leaders of the people" to moderate the democratic power which would have improverished them[23]—nice analogy for the role he saw for Whig leaders in the Republican party.

A local historian from Coahoma County, Mrs. Mary Fisher Robinson, wrote that Alcorn followed his "party line" into moderate Republicanism.[24] There is nothing in his speeches or writings to indicate that he had abandoned any of his Whig principles. He probably was correct when he charged that he was far truer to Whig principles than his associates who were frightened into the Democratic party by the prospect of Negro suffrage. For him the freedmen were simply another class, somewhat inferior to the others, which he was to lead. He would be their spokesman and the defender of their rights. Their inarticulate power could be used to keep friend and foe in line, and he was confident it was a

---

22  *Ibid.*
23  James Lusk Alcorn, *Address of J. L. Alcorn (Republican Candidate for Governor) to the People of Mississippi* (Friar's Point, Mississippi: n.p., November 10, 1869).
24  Robinson, "A Sketch of James Lusk Alcorn," 28.

power he could control. Alcorn, in his own mind, felt he had found the way to deal with the "lion of race-adjustment."

The prospect of stepping from membership in a defunct party to possible leadership in a very promising one no doubt helped to make the move an attractive one. To this leadership he would bring the Whig ideal of service and his own sense of personal destiny. Several years later in a speech in the Senate when his loyalty to the Republican party came into question, he declared, not quite accurately, that although he had been offered the candidacy by the "victorious Democrats," he had preferred to support the "defeated Republicans" since in this way he felt he could aid the Negro and his state, and do his duty to his country.[25] Practicality, idealism, personal ambition, and Whiggery all had a part in his decision to seek and accept the nomination by the Republican party.

Alcorn's decision to run made a favorable impression in the state. One contemporary's reaction was that his nomination "was a surprise to everyone and a very gratifying one to many. He [Alcorn] had lived in Mississippi since early manhood, had accumulated a large estate, was a man of great ability, and one of the best speakers on the hustings in the State." He added that Alcorn was "an imperious, fearless man, who could not be cajoled nor bought nor intimidated."[26] An "Old Whig" wrote the *Weekly Delta* that he did not like either party, but admired Alcorn because he was a gentleman of strong character, great eloquence, and lofty courage, concerned with the interests and institutions of the South. He ended by saying that, "Since I must choose between two *men* and there is only *one* in the race, I am for Alcorn."[27]

Alcorn gave his opening speech at Hernando and began an energetic campaign, reminiscent of his prewar career. The executive committee of the Republican party published a schedule which called for him to deliver a speech in a different town throughout Northern and Central Mississippi every day from October 11 to November 16. The latter part of this schedule included joint debates with Lewis Dent, his opponent. Dent was President Grant's

25 *Congressional Globe*, 42nd Cong. 2nd Sess. (Washington: Government Printing Office, 1872), Appendix, 405.

26 W. H. Hardy, "Recollections of Reconstruction in East and Southeast Mississippi," *Mississippi Historical Society Publications*, VIII (1904), 145.

27 Friar's Point (Miss.) *Weekly Delta*, September 29, 1869.

son-in-law, and primarily for this reason had been nominated by the "Conservative Republican Party," a coalition of Democrats, ex-Whigs, and conservative Republicans, including the rebuffed Wofford. The strongest weapon in Dent's speechmaking arsenal was sarcasm, delicate and cutting. While it made a good impression on the oratorically discerning audience of that day, it could not outfire the heavy artillery of Alcorn's booming voice, theatrical gestures, and bandbox appearance. One opposition newspaper nicknamed him "Dandy Jim."

Color was added to the campaign by an element of personal danger, for the Ku Klux Klan was active in the state, contributing to an undercurrent of widespread lawlessness. J. F. H. Claiborne, among others including Alcorn's wife, tried to persuade him not to run, believing that he "would fall a martyr under a cloud that would cover [him] in [his] grave." [28] Adelbert Ames attempted, against his wishes, to use soldiers to protect him.[29]

Even his audiences sometimes felt the danger. While addressing a group in Ripley, he had an altercation with a local political leader whom he called a liar. Expecting violence, the audience scrambled out through the door and windows while Alcorn called after them not to leave, that his opponent was "a drunken cowardly vagabond." [30] He won over an audience in Aberdeen by coolly drawing a six-shooter out of his satchel when he heard the click of pistols near the rostrum, and challenging any would-be assailant to stand up and face him.[31] At Winona "several of the more desperate whites" wanted to kill Alcorn with a rifle while he was speaking from the railroad depot platform to a large crowd composed mostly of demonstrative Negroes, but "conservative Democrats" prevented them from carrying out their plan.[32]

Almost immediately at the end of the joint debates Dent left the state without waiting for the results of the election. The *Weekly Delta* happily speculated on his hasty departure, calling him "Mysterious Jerry." [33] Dent had no chance at success. He

28  Montgomery, *Reminiscences of a Mississippian*, 283.
29  *Congressional Globe*, 42nd Cong. 2nd Sess., Appendix, 405.
30  James Lusk Alcorn to Amelia Alcorn, October 17, 1869, in Alcorn File.
31  Robinson, "Sketch of James Lusk Alcorn," 43.
32  Fred M. Witty, "Reconstruction in Carroll and Montgomery Counties," *Publications of the Mississippi Historical Society*, X (1909), 124.
33  Friar's Point (Miss.) *Weekly Delta*, November 17, 24 and December 1 1869.

was a non-Southerner who faced an experienced orator acutely in tune with regional nuances and the psychology of his audiences. His non-identity with the state was further emphasized by a widely circulated letter which repudiated his claim of Mississippi residence through the leasing of abandoned lands in Coahoma County. This letter was signed by George R. Alcorn as clerk of the probate court and stated that he was not on the tax rolls of that county.[34] In addition, President Grant refused to support Dent in spite of their relationship. On August 6 the President had granted Jonathan A. Tarbell, secretary of the state Republican committee, an interview which he permitted him to have published and in which he unreservedly endorsed the regular Republican ticket.[35] Alcorn was also given personal assurances that the administration would continue to back Ames, which it did.[36]

Since both parties had similar platforms, which promised protection of Negro rights, universal suffrage, and complete amnesty, the contest had to revolve around the candidates. To offset Dent's weaknesses, his backers did their best to discredit Alcorn by publicizing apparent ambiguities in his past, which have bothered historians ever since. "Gen. Alcorn was a Whig up to '59, a Union man in '60, a secessionist in '61, a fire-eater in '62, a peace-man in '63, a growler in '64, a rebel in '65, a reconstructionist in '66, a scalawag in '67, a radical in '68, and a bitter-ender in '69." [37]

Nevertheless, Alcorn won by an overwhelming majority, and carried with him a large majority in both houses of the state legislature. Grant had the constitution of 1868 resubmitted to the voters, with the proscriptive clauses against ex-rebels and rebel sympathizers listed separately. The electorate ratified the constitution and rejected the clauses. Alcorn began his term of office with a Republican legislature and a new constitution.

A major factor in his victory was the active support of Adelbert Ames, who was identified, through his marriage to the daughter of Benjamin F. Butler, with the radical wing of the national Republican party. Ames had come to Mississippi in the summer of

---

34  A. T. Morgan, *Yazoo, or, On the Picket Line of Freedom in the South* (Washington: author, 1884), 281.
35  Allan Nevins, *Hamilton Fish; The Inner History of the Grant Administration* (New York: Dodd, Mead, 1936), 291–92.
36  James Lusk Alcorn to Amelia Alcorn, October 17, 1869, in Alcorn File.
37  Amos R. Johnston, *Speech of Hon. Amos R. Johnston, at Sardis, Mississippi, October 13, 1869, on Alcorn's Record* (n.p., n.d.).

1868 when he was appointed military governor by General Irwin McDowell, and in March 1869 he became commander of the Fourth Military District. He was the son of a Maine ship captain and retained a good deal of New England in his attitudes and mentality. He had graduated from West Point in 1861, fifth in his class, and was wounded at the First Battle of Bull Run, earning through his bravery the Congressional Medal of Honor and eventual promotion to brevet brigadier general. In Mississippi he considered himself the protector of the freedmen and found it hard to understand Southern disregard for the sabbath and love of hard drinking. There could be little basis for real understanding between Alcorn and the young New Englander.

Immediately after the election Ames tried to take the initiative by appointing Alcorn provisional governor prior to his inauguration. He had as a precedent Grant's action the previous summer in appointing Henry C. Warmoth governor of Louisiana following his election but prior to his inauguration as civil governor. But Alcorn had other ideas. "I have not accepted, nor will I," he wrote his wife, and added significantly, "I have thus far dictated my terms and will continue to do so." [38] Publicly he announced that he refused to accept the appointment since it came from military authority and was subject to military power for its support. He stated that he held in immediate prospect the position of civil governor, a position much more acceptable to him since he had received it as a result of popular choice.[39]

Undoubtedly he felt his election had given him, not Ames, political control of the state, especially since the legislature almost immediately after the election selected Ames to be one of Mississippi's Senators to Congress. Presumably this was to be his reward for helping to elect Alcorn, as well as an effective way of removing him from the scene. Alcorn's temperament indicates that he would not have been likely to accept a position second to Ames. His actions and comments show that he felt he had direct support from Washington and that he would be the head of the Republican party in Mississippi. Therefore he could now proceed to form it into a neo-Whig party which would work under him to rebuild the kind of Mississippi in which he believed.

38  James Lusk Alcorn to Amelia Alcorn, December 27, 1869, copy in Rainwater Collection, Box 3, Folder 38.
39  Garner, *Reconstruction in Mississippi*, 248.

# 7

# Governor of Mississippi

AS ALCORN STOOD up in the state capitol at Jackson to deliver his inaugural address on March 10, 1870, he had every reason to believe he would be successful in the role of governor. He had shown himself to be indispensible to the Republican party and was now the political hope of a whole new class of constituents. For the first time in his career he was the leader of a majority party, and under the new constitution he was assuming more power than any of his predecessors had ever had. Further, because Mississippi was just being readmitted to the exercise of civil government and elections for local offices were not scheduled until the fall of 1871, Alcorn inherited from the military government the right of appointment, with the consent of the senate, to all those normally elective offices.

These factors provided the state's chief executive with an exceptional opportunity to build a strongly centralized political organization with himself in firm control. Alcorn had always had a Federalistic appreciation of the benefits of strong government, and a good part of his contempt for Jefferson Davis had stemmed from his belief that Davis was a weak, if tyrannical, leader. During his gubernatorial campaign he had attacked the civil-military government in Mississippi because of its divided authority, and he had blamed it for the rise in crime. He felt that if the people could not reconstruct the state, the civil government should be abolished and the military authorities given full power to curb the lawlessness that threatened life and property.[1] He had written his wife

1 Friar's Point (Miss.) *Weekly Delta*, September 1, 1869.

that if the opposition succeeded in capturing the legislature so as to counteract his election, he would advise Congress to continue the military government.[2] As he had demonstrated in his interpretation of the position of president of the Board of Levee Commissioners and later in the strong disciplinary measures he took during his brief military career, and as he would attempt to show in his conduct as governor, he believed in a strong executive equipped with the power to act as he saw fit. He belonged to that class of planters who were accustomed to commanding others and who did not tolerate opposition easily. Sure of himself and his cause, Alcorn would accept leadership only if it brought with it power, and this the governorship seemed to do.

Inaugurated along with him were R. C. Powers as lieutenant governor, James Lynch as secretary of state, Henry Musgrove as auditor, W. H. Vasser as treasurer, Joshua A. Morris as attorney general, and Henry R. Pease as superintendent of education. Powers, Musgrove, and Pease were former officers in the Union army who had settled in the state since the war. Vasser and Morris were pre-war Mississippians, and Lynch was a Negro minister from the North.[3]

Flanked by his official family and bolstered by a sense of political power, Alcorn early in his inaugural speech voiced a viewpoint few Southerners shared and many detested to the point of violence.[4] In voting for secession, he declared, he had sacrificed conviction. "Secession, I have ever denounced as a fatal fallacy. In casting my lot with my own people in the late war, I sought not justification behind logical subleties." He repeated his belief that he had been liable for punishment as a rebel, and after expressing his pleasure at "bowing out" military rule, he spoke, with reference to the national government, of "a magnificent mercy never shown before by a government since established authority first dealt with rebellion after the fierce fashion of 'a short shrive and a long rope.' "[5]

He seemed aware that rebellion cannot be justified unless it is

2  James Lusk Alcorn to Amelia Alcorn, October 17, 1869, in Alcorn File.
3  Rowland, *Mississippi*, I, 64–65.
4  Garner, *Reconstruction in Mississippi*, 278; J. S. McNeily, "The Enforcement Act of 1871 and the Ku Klux Klan in Mississippi," *Mississippi Historical Society Publications*, IX (1906), 135.
5  James Lusk Alcorn, *Inaugural Address of Gov. J. L. Alcorn, Delivered at Jackson, on Thursday, March 10, 1870, to the Legislature of Mississippi* (Jackson: Fisher and Kimball, 1870), 4.

accompanied by reasonable hope of success or caused by extreme provocation. Since his position before the war had been that such provocation did not exist, and he had realized that the rebellion would fail, his position, and parenthetically that of the South, had been unjustifiable. He was one of the few Southerners on whom the reality of the preceding events had made an impression, and he may have hoped to shock recalcitrant Mississippians into an appreciation of the situation.

And this situation involved deep changes with which the new civilian government would have to cope. Alcorn tried to make the people aware of these changes by pointing out how the duties of the state had increased. It must now consider the welfare of individuals rather than just the heads of a few favored "families." He warned that, because of this concern for a wider group, taxation would be much greater. However, the application of these taxes would tend to enrich the state, particularly through the promotion of industrial colleges and public schools because of the principle "that the highest production of wealth follows the combination of muscle and intelligence." In the interest of economy he was not in favor of large expenditures on public works, and he planned to inactivate the militia. As an inducement to keep the peace, he warned that he would call out the militia if an outbreak of lawlessness made it necessary, and this in turn could result in heavier taxation.

He advocated equality at the ballot-box, in the jury box, and in the distribution of public offices to colored persons and to poor whites. Then he softened this equalitarian stand by adding: "Wealth, intelligence, social position have always [been], as I trust they ever shall be, great power in the state."

In order to promote the "material interests" of the state he felt taxation should not bear too heavily on industry, there should be no increase in the public debt, and the productive powers of the state should be developed. He contrasted the more practical accomplishments of the North, such as construction of canals, harbors, and railroads, with the intellectual abstractions of the South and told his listeners that Southerners "must abandon their political theorizing for the wiser statesmanship which devotes itself, in the first place, to the fosterage of material interests."

Considerable Whig flavoring comes through in this inaugural speech, a seasoning which would appeal primarily to the palates of the Delta planters and prospective industrialists, but could not have tasted quite so savory to small farmers and poor whites. He urged public education for the children of the poor whites as well as the colored people, and spoke approvingly of the newly inaugurated system of free labor. Both of these developments would aid the industrialization of the state; but the overtones of equality at the lower levels of society which they carried must have sounded disquieting to poor white ears. Such reforms had greater appeal to the upper classes who would be indirectly benefited by them, and to the Negroes who were looking to him for leadership. For the former, he also promised not to increase the public debt, and he hoped for public improvements with Federal aid. In the old Whig idiom he spoke of his love of the Union, "of [his] heart swelling to the dimensions of the patriotism of Henry Clay." [6]

He delivered his speech with the brisk air of one who is about to get to work in a businesslike manner on the accumulated problems of his state. This practical approach, plus his mildly hierarchical view of society—an Anglo-Saxon class of intellect and property at the top, the Negro at the bottom, others in between—was probably a fairly accurate reflection of the American mind at that time. The overall impression he made was that of being the man for the moment, the person best suited to direct affairs at this transitional point in Mississippi history.

The situation in Alcorn's state in 1869-70 indicates that whether or not he was ideally the man best suited for the moment, he was the only one available who could breach the gap between the "alien" radicals and the native conservatives, at least long enough to get Mississippi started again as a fully functioning state. Even under the restrictions imposed upon them, the conservatives had demonstrated enough voting strength to defeat the constitution in 1868. Had the radicals been forced to run a carpetbagger or a native Republican of less stature for the governorship, the conservatives might have made a better showing and, as Alcorn feared they might do, captured one or both houses of the legislature. In such an event their action, with the support of conservative Republicans, could have caused Mississippi to be placed again under military rule, as occurred in Georgia when a conservative coalition in the legislature in 1870 took the initiative from a radical governor.

The problems with which Alcorn had to deal were similar to

6   *Ibid.*, 3–12.

those faced by the governors of the other reconstructed southern states, and dominant among the issues was that of finance. As he had warned in his inaugural speech, the government for the many was a more expensive enterprise than it had been before the war. The auditor's books showed that he started his administration with a public debt of $1,177,339.46. [7] He had to meet the increased expense of an expanded court system and executive department, of the inauguration of a public education system, and of repairs to the lunatic asylum, the state capitol, and the executive mansion.

To cover these expenses and to stimulate business, he issued $500,000 in state warrants, popularly known as "Alcorn money." They bore interest at 8 percent and were designed to resemble greenbacks, with an engraving of the state capitol on one side and vignettes of Governor and Mrs. Alcorn on the other. In order to encourage wide circulation, they were issued in small denominations and state officers were required to receive them at face value in payment of taxes and other state commitments. The railroads also cooperated by accepting and using them at par value. Their acceptance within the state and by Memphis banks at face value, helped to restore confidence in the state government, whose financial reputation had suffered ever since the repudiation of the Planters' and Union bank bonds. These warrants were gradually called in and cancelled, but as an emergency currency they served their purpose well by helping to put the state on a better financial footing. [8]

In a further effort to improve the financial condition of the state, Alcorn turned his attention to the companies busy harvesting the postwar increase of interest in life insurance policies. Since close to a million dollars was leaving the state annually in insurance premiums, he recommended that insurance companies be required

7  Mississippi began her period of Republican rule in better financial condition than some of her sister states. In South Carolina the first Republican governor began his administration with a public debt of $5,407,306.27; in Arkansas, with a debt of $3,363,503.19; and in Alabama, he was burdened with one of $6,848,400.00. Perhaps a partial answer to some of their financial problems might be found elsewhere than in wholesale charges of corruption.

8  James Lusk Alcorn, *Annual Message of Gov. Jas. L. Alcorn to the Mississippi Legislature, Session of 1871* (Jackson: Kimball, Raymond, 1871), 40–47; Rowland, *Mississippi*, I, 69; Garner, *Reconstruction in Mississippi*, 130–31; Amelia Alcorn to Rosebud Rector, January 26, 1907, in possession of Mrs. William Swanson, Hot Springs, Arkansas; Swift, "James Lusk Alcorn," 36–37.

to make adequate deposits within the state to cover the money taken from the state. These deposits would be made in state warrants which could be bought on the market at a discount and, since they bore interest, represented an investment. The passage of this measure, without an additional taxing provision he had wanted, resulted in deposits being made to an amount of over $200,000, and helped to increase the market value of the state warrants.[9]

During the first year of Alcorn's administration operating expenses jumped about $500,000 over those of 1869, and the state debt by the end of the year had risen about $600,000. But Alcorn argued that these figures compared favorably with the administration of 1861: "When the exceptional demands incident to the wreck of war are considered, when the fact is considered that the duties of the State Government of 1870 are not only fuller, but that they apply in that fuller degree to double the number of people, I insist that the cost of the State Government, whatever may be the fact as to its absolute economy, was relatively very decidedly less in 1870 than it was in 1861." [10]

Attorney General Morris turned his defense of the administration's financial operations into an attack on its principal critics, the Democrats. He believed the state's financial condition compared favorably with that of the prewar administration of the men who now criticized it: "The Government of the United States committed to the hands of these same men and their associates large donations of money and lands for educational purposes, for internal improvements, &c. nearly all of which they squandered and stole—a very small percentage of which was ever appropriated to the objects designed by the Government in the donation." [11]

A congressional investigating committee found the increase in rate of taxation in Mississippi to pay for these increased expenses far less than in some northern states where no serious complaints were made.[12] During the entire Reconstruction period Mississippi

9 Rowland, *Mississippi*, I, 67–68; Jackson *Weekly Mississippi Pilot*, April 30, 1870; *Journal of the Senate of the State of Mississippi* (Jackson: Kimball, Raymond, 1870), 7–12.
10 Alcorn, *Annual Message . . . 1871*, pp. 43–44.
11 U. S. House of Representatives, 42nd Cong. 2nd Sess., *House Report No. 22* (hereinafter referred to as "KKK Report"), (Washington: Government Printing Office, 1872), XI, 307.
12 U. S. Senate, 44th Cong. 1st Sess., *Senate Report No. 527* (Washington: Government Printing Office, 1876), I, x.

financed its state governmental activities almost entirely through taxation, starting with a nearly empty treasury and with what, under the circumstances, was a considerable debt.[13]

In contrast, every other southern state tried to meet the increased expenses of reconstruction and expanded government by issuing bonds. This led to market saturation and corruption in the handling of the sales, so that by the end of the Reconstruction period many of them, notably South Carolina and North Carolina, had been forced to repudiate at least some of their tax bond issues or refund them at a loss to the bondholders.

According to the reports of the Mississippi state auditor, expenditures reached their peak during Alcorn's second year with a total of $1,729,046.34, dropped to $1,430,192.83 in 1875 (the last year of a Republican administration), and in 1878, during the first Democratic administration, stood at $707,022.46. Receipts followed a roughly parallel line, dropping below expenditures only once, during 1871. [14]

With regard to railroad legislation, Alcorn's administration was also able to show a comparatively good record. Like most Southerners attempting to get their states to emulate the North's industrial growth, Alcorn believed in the power of railroads as a sort of magical growth-and-prosperity stimulant for the areas through which they would go. But while many of his southern fellow governors outdid each other in extending the hospitality of their states to railroad promoters, he was wary of granting them too much power. In a message to the state senate in 1870 he recommended that the job of inspecting railroads be added to the duties of the board of public works. He also wanted the board to be able to regulate connections between railroads, and to have the right to inspect and, if necessary, condemn railroad structures.[15]

13  Vernon Lane Wharton, *The Negro in Mississippi* (Chapel Hill: University of North Carolina Press, 1947), 179; Garner, *Reconstruction in Mississippi*, 322–23. The author, a Dunning student and Southern historian, writes that the Republican regime maintained a remarkable record of honesty, with no evidence of a major embezzlement such as marred the immediate postwar records of so many states, North as well as South.
14  *Annual Report of the Auditor of Public Accounts to the Legislature of Mississippi for the Year 1871* (Jackson: Kimball, Raymond, 1872), 16; *Annual Report of the Auditor . . . for the Year 1875* (Jackson: Pilot Publishing Company, 1876), 2; *Biennial Report of the Auditor . . . for the Years 1878–79* (Jackson: J. L. Power, 1880), 7.
15  *Journal of the Senate . . . of Mississippi*, 1870, pp. 42–43.

In June, 1870, he vetoed a railroad bill partly on the grounds that it gave too much power to corporations, made misdemeanors against railroad property penal offenses, and failed to protect the property through which the projected railroad might go.[16] His veto was sustained after a bitter fight in which railroad privileges were obscured by the civil rights issue. He was supported in his position by Jason Niles, the chairman of the state Republican committee who was at that time in the house of representatives.[17] The only railroad legislation passed during Alcorn's administration which obligated the state financially was an act to encourage the building of railroads by authorizing the payment of $4,000 per mile to any railroad which would construct at least twenty-five miles of road within the state and have it equipped and in running order by September 1, 1872. The constitution prohibited pledging the state's credit, so Mississippi never had to repudiate worthless railroad bonds as North Carolina, Alabama, and Arkansas were forced to do.

Nevertheless, in keeping with the national picture and activities in other states, Mississippi had its touch of railroad scandal. Colonel Henry S. McComb, an enterprising citizen of Delaware, persuaded the legislature to turn over to him the state's stock in the New Orleans, Jackson and Great Northern Railroad upon his agreement to build a certain amount of road. The stock involved was equally described as worthless because the company was about to go into bankruptcy, and as being very valuable since the railroad was the only one running the full length of the state, from Memphis through Jackson to New Orleans. The bill was passed by a bi-partisan majority and Alcorn signed it without protest.[18] The charge was later made that a loan of $30,000 by McComb to the state played a part in its passage, to which the official Republican newspaper, the *Pilot*, replied by asserting that the loan had been repaid.[19]

That same summer the energetic Colonel McComb, who later was implicated in the Credit Mobilier railroad stock scandal, went

16 *Ibid.*, Appendix, 1–2.
17 Friar's Point (Miss.) *Weekly Delta*, June 29, 1870.
18 *KKK Report*, XI, 32–33, 207.
19 J. S. McNeily, "War and Reconstruction in Mississippi, 1863–1890," *Publications of the Mississippi Historical Society, Centenary Series*, II (1918), 412.

to Louisiana and persuaded the state and the city of New Orleans to sell him their stock in the same railroad at one-eighth of its book value. He eventually sold his holdings to the Illinois Central Railroad at a substantial profit.[20]

In addition to encouraging railroad construction, Alcorn had other suggestions to attract prosperity back to his state. He asked for a reduction in the property exemption laws of the state, on the grounds that they removed too much property from the use of credit and creditors.[21] In his annual message of 1871 he tried to get the legislature to economize on its expenditures. And to make local conditions more attractive to investors, he suggested a limitation on the taxing powers of the county boards of supervisors. He also wanted land assessments to be based on the classification of lands according to production, in order to remove the whole process from local pressures. With considerable foresight, he sought the abolition of the lien law of 1866 which gave a merchant advancing credit to a planter a lien on his crop. Yet, that summer he refused to approve a bill which would have granted an exclusive right of ferrying for fifty years as a monopoly, and another which would have exempted a railroad from taxes for eight years.[22] Local power might be restricted in order to encourage business, but not that of the state.

The constitution of 1868 provided for a commissioner of immigration and agriculture as a further means of promoting economic health. Alcorn preferred to emphasize agriculture and minimize immigration. The Democratic press was campaigning for white immigration to offset the Negro franchise, but Alcorn opposed sending an agent to Europe and regretted the "political passions" which were trying to "forc[e] . . . a stream of settlement into the State from Europe." Perhaps some Whig–Know-Nothing distrust of foreign "hordes" still clung to him. He wanted the legislature to designate the main duties of the commissioner as being agricultural, i.e., improvement of seeds, methods of planting and stock

20 Donald Bridgeman Sanger and Thomas Robson Hay, *James Longstreet* (Baton Rouge: Louisiana State University Press, 1952), 349.
21 James Lusk Alcorn, Message to the Senate and House of Representatives of the State of Mississippi, July 15, 1870, in Governors' Correspondence, 1870–75, Series E, Folder No. 89, Mississippi State Archives.
22 *Journal of the Senate of the State of Mississippi* (Jackson: Kimball, Raymond, 1871), 678–79.

James Lusk Alcorn, about 1843, when he was in the
Kentucky legislature.

Rosemount, the family home of Amelia Walton Glover in Alabama.

Amelia Glover Alcorn and James Lusk Alcorn, from a daguerreotype taken in 1851, about a year after their marriage.

The Mississippi Secession Convention of 1861.

The newly-constructed mansion at Eagle's Nest, just after Alcorn moved his family into it in 1879. Figures from left to right are: Aunt Cynthie, a Negro maid; Justina and Gertrude Alcorn; two cousins; and Amelia Alcorn.

Mississippi state warrants which circulated as money while Alcorn
was governor.

James Lusk Alcorn, in the United States Senate.

Statue of Alcorn atop the Indian mound which serves as the family cemetery, near Jonestown, Mississippi.

breeding. In addition, the commissioner might aid in settling immigrants, should they come.[23]

The legislature took no action during Alcorn's term in office, and when a commissioner was finally appointed during Ames's administration, he had little success in attracting white immigration. Almost every southern state shared Mississippi's efforts and lack of success. Georgia even experienced a slight decline in the number of foreign born in her population, and the bulk of Arkansas' white immigration was composed of Easterners who came each winter to escape their own more rigorous climate.

Both houses of the state legislature passed a resolution calling on the Federal government to appropriate $2,000,000 and a grant of five million acres from public domain to aid in the restoration of levees in the Yazoo–Mississippi Delta. Along with the resolution Alcorn sent the Mississippi delegation in Congress a long letter which he had written out himself, reiterating his views on the importance of cotton to the national welfare. It was an echo of the prewar Southern belief in "King Cotton." He painted a utopian picture of the upper Mississippi and Ohio valleys which would, because of the increased cotton production, flourish as the providers of foodstuffs for the lower South and as the manufacturers of cotton textiles. All this activity would be of great social benefit, since it would cheapen "those great civilizers, the cotton shirt and the calico dress." On the international scene American cotton supremacy would thwart that European "conspiracy," would strengthen United States diplomacy, give volume to its commerce, and bring in gold to its treasury.[24] It was a good try that brought no results. The following year Alcorn approved a joint resolution, which no doubt he also had inspired, asking Congress to refund to the people of the cotton-growing states the amount of tax collected on cotton during the years of its existence.[25] This move likewise was futile, although Southerners continued to hope for years that their money would be returned.

On the state level, Alcorn continued to disapprove of the activities of the board of levee commissioners for Bolivar, Washington,

23 *Journal of the Senate . . . of Mississippi,* 1870, pp. 37–40.
24 James Lusk Alcorn, message in his own handwriting to Adelbert Ames and Hiram R. Revels, n.d., in Alcorn Official Papers, Series E, Folder No. 90-A, Mississippi Department of Archives and History.
25 *Congressional Globe,* 42nd Cong. 2nd Sess. (Washington: Government Printing Office, 1872), appendix, 411.

and Issaquena counties. Under pressure because of an imminent flood and unfinished levees, this board had exceeded its authorized limit of $1,000,000 in bond issues, and now wanted the legislature to legalize an over-issue. The legislature passed a bill amending the earlier incorporation act by raising the ceiling on the issuance of bonds to $2,000,000. Alcorn vetoed this bill and in his message attacked the original act. He felt that it gave the board unconstitutional taxing powers, and also that it conflicted with his views of sound policy since it authorized a cotton tax which was "a tax on production, a tax in fact on labor, and as such violates what I hold to be the best interests of the State and people." [26]

He also indirectly attacked the whole idea of financing levees by issuing bonds. A few days before his veto he spoke to the Committee on Public Works advocating passage of a bill by which the state would undertake directly to build the levee, taxing landowners in proportion to the benefit they would receive, and using the tax resources of the state to underwrite the project. This bill "made every landholder a share-holder according to the quantity of his estate. It was a system of agricultural insurance in which the taxpayers mutually became underwriters one for another." He described it as "just an honest plan by simple land-owners to build a levee." Their own agents would direct the work, and they knew from experience how much time and money would be required, and how high the embankment should be.

He warned against becoming involved in the issuance of bonds. This, he told them, was an age of speculation, of bonds, of credit, and of corruption. Mississippi should retain its "simple purity. . . . The reconstructed States have been charged with being corrupt. We had no share in this accusation and our government had no sins to answer for on this score." He pointed to Louisiana where, over Governor Henry C. Warmoth's objections, the legislature had chartered a private company to build and maintain the levees, but whose stock was being sold to speculators at a nominal price.[27] Although Louisiana had only just embarked on its venture, Alcorn's example was well chosen. As time passed, the company, which had received a million dollars initially and the annual proceeds from a

26 James Lusk Alcorn, Message to the Senate and House of Representatives of the State of Mississippi, June 8, 1870, in Governors' Correspondence, 1870–1875, Series E, Folder No. 89, Mississippi State Archives.
27 Friar's Point (Miss.) *Weekly Delta*, June 8, 1870.

tax on all property within Louisiana, failed to live up to its obligation to build and maintain levees, and to be responsible for damages to the planters. The work it did accomplish was two to three times as expensive as that done previously, and somehow it never had any money to meet suits for damages.[28]

Arkansas attempted to finance a levee construction program by selling bonds, but found itself in 1874 with a three-million dollar debt and little completed work to show for its efforts. Mississippi's constitution of 1868 forbade pledging the public credit, but this did not prevent the authorization of agencies which could issue bonds on their own behalf. Alcorn's attitude undoubtedly protected the state from a source of scandal and debt, but he was unable to obtain legislation for levee construction which would have committed the whole state in the direct manner he advocated. Political infighting, local rivalries in the Delta, and the opposition of the hill counties combined to defeat him.

One of the most vulnerable parts of Alcorn's administration was its attitude on civil rights. After his inauguration the remaining sections of the Black Codes of 1865-66 were quickly repealed. The codes were statutes passed in southern states dealing with the social and economic conditions of the freed slaves. The various laws were attempts to adapt the restraints of slavery to the Negroes' new status. In June, 1870, an act rescinding the last section closed with a declaration that it was its intention to remove from the record all laws which in any way discriminated between citizens of the state on the basis of race. Also in 1870 a commission appointed by Alcorn codified the state laws incorporating the same prohibition against discrimination.

To all this Alcorn no doubt gave his approval, but Negro leaders wanted to go further and eliminate discrimination in transportation facilities, although at this time only three or four states in the Union had passed laws specifically prohibiting such segregation. In a general railroad bill passed by the legislature in late June, these leaders succeeded in having a clause inserted which would make it a penal offense to compel any person to occupy any particular car or section of a car. Although Alcorn based his

28 Francis Byers Harris, "Henry Clay Warmoth, Reconstruction Governor of Louisiana," *Louisiana Historical Quarterly*, XXX (1947), 574–76; Charles Nordhoff, *The Cotton States in the Spring and Summer of 1875* (New York: Appleton, 1876), 58.

veto on other undesirable features in the bill, he also objected to this section on the grounds that the apparent meaning of the clause was inconsistent with a later section which declared the bill was not to mean that any railroad company might not provide "separate cars for ladies and gentlemen and separate cars for smoking." According to his reasoning, this left the decision for placing passengers to the discretion of the brakeman or conductor.[29]

In a message to the senate, a few weeks later he asked that this bill be amended to have the railroad companies furnish "equal accommodations for the two races, the white race to be assigned to the one and the colored to the other." This amendment was voted down, 4 to 15.[30] Then two Negro senators, Robert Gleed and William Gray, succeeded in getting enough reluctant white Republican votes to pass a law against discrimination on any type of public transportation. In an attempt to avert such legislation, Alcorn had the presidents of the railroads in Mississippi meet the Negro members of the legislature at the executive mansion and offer to provide them with equal but separate facilities. Alcorn is supposed to have lectured them on their refusal and to have warned them that their demands could not be enforced without bloodshed.[31] What actually happened was that although the law passed, it was ignored in practice, and Negroes continued to accept segregated travel facilities.[32] Jason Niles also supported this portion of Alcorn's objection to the general railroad bill, and later tried to get the antisegregation bill tabled.[33]

Alcorn concerned himself with still another violation of human rights. The convict leasing system, begun in the Reconstruction period, continued to be an ugly aspect of Mississippi society for the balance of the century. The practice was introduced into the eastern part of the United States early in the nineteenth century, and became accepted procedure in the South during the Civil War. It was not adopted in Mississippi until 1866 and 1867, when acts passed by the Democratic legislature had empowered Governor Humphreys to lease the convicts in the state prison for work outside the walls under certain conditions. He does not appear to have taken advantage of this, but later General Alvan

29 *Journal of the Senate* . . . *of Mississippi, 1870*, p. 203.
30 *Ibid.*, 545–47.
31 Garner, *Reconstruction in Mississippi*, 286.
32 Wharton, *The Negro in Mississippi*, 231.
33 Jason Niles diary, XLI, Southern Historical Collection.

Gillem, while commander of the Fourth Military District, made a contract with Edmund Richardson, a planter and speculator, whereby, along with payment for upkeep, he received almost absolute control of the state's convicts until November, 1871.

In a message to the senate early in his administration Alcorn attacked the system, claiming that it was "repugnant to public virtue" to have men working under guard outside the prison walls and away from the discipline and keeping of those having authority over them. He urged the appointment of a commission to investigate cases of unduly harsh or unjust sentences and to select those convicts deserving of executive clemency.[34]

Later he himself named a commission to examine into the conditions of the prison and its inmates. On June 23, 1870, this commission submitted a long report on its findings. Only eighty prisoners, mostly white, were in the prison, and the balance, mostly Negro, were working on the plantations owned by Richardson. The commissioners found the leased convicts well cared for, supplied with ample food and clothing. Since lack of room within the prison would result in overcrowding, they recommended that the prisoners be permitted to remain on the plantations for the remainder of the year. In justice to Richardson, they felt it necessary to point out that the high prisoner mortality rate fell six months after he took over, and that prior to this the convicts had been at work "under other parties" on the levees where they had been exposed to inclement weather and had been poorly clothed and fed. The commissioners closed their report with a long list of convicts whom they recommended for pardon, together with their reasons.[35] Alcorn, however, according to one report used his pardoning powers sparingly.[36]

Later that year the legislature passed and Alcorn signed, a bill granting Richardson a new lease for fifteen years. Charges of bribery were made, and also that more financially attractive offers for the convicts had been rejected.[37] But Alcorn may have changed his position because of the report of his commission, and the un-

---

34 *Journal of the Senate . . . of Mississippi,* 1870, pp. 57–59.
35 Report signed by P. B. Starke, chairman, Thomas W. Stringer, and T. J. Mitchell, to James Lusk Alcorn, June 23, 1870, in Alcorn Official Papers, Series E, Folder No. 90-A.
36 *KKK Report,* XI, 452.
37 *Ibid.,* 208.

deniable fact that the state prison was too small for the number of inmates assigned to it. If, as the report indicated, Richardson was a comparatively humane lessee, both Alcorn and the legislature may have merely chosen the lesser of two evils. In his annual message the following spring Alcorn urged that means be found to use the convicts on public works so as not to overburden the limited capacity available for their confinement.[38]

Alcorn's successor, Lieutenant Governor R. C. Powers, upon taking over the administration of the state, also attacked the leasing system, and under his leadership the legislature provided for the establishment of a system of prison farms and limited the employment of the convicts outside the walls to public works. These reforms were abandoned during the last year of Republican rule when the Ames administration was trying to economize, and the legislature again authorized leasing the convicts to private persons. The Democrats continued the leasing system, turning the convicts over to a contractor who subleased them without regard to their welfare. The resulting abuses continued until after 1890, when a clause prohibiting the system was written into the new constitution.[39]

Under the new constitution, because of changes and increases in the judiciary, Alcorn had a wide field for new appointments in a most important area of state government. As justices on the newly-created state Supreme Court he appointed Jonathan Tarbell, E. G. Peyton, and as chief justice, H. F. Simrall. The former was a Northerner, the latter two long-time residents of the state and prewar Whigs. No charges of corruption or incompetence were ever made against any of these men. He recruited his appointees to the enlarged circuit court system from among the leading citizens of the state, natives as well as newcomers, and few of his appointments brought forth objections from his opponents. Witnesses testifying before a congressional investigating committee in 1872 could make no charges against his appointees, and some

---

38 Alcorn, *Annual Message . . . 1871,* p. 33.
39 Wharton, *The Negro in Mississippi,* 238–39. Eventually, with the advent of the automobile and the need of good roads, convicts began to be used on public improvements, particularly in the South, as both Alcorn and Powers had recommended. What they did not foresee was that this would lead to the cruelties of the chain gang.

felt that they were at least as good as Mississippi had had before the war.[40]

Alcorn's annual message of 1871 devoted considerable space to optimistic comments on the social conditions of the state. As an exslaveholder, he confessed that he had had lingering doubts about the adequacy of the "restraints of *reason*" on a people who had been held under "the life-long restraints of force." But the evidence clearly showed that the Negroes in Mississippi were capable of "well ordered freedom." He urged that the marriage license fee be kept at the 1857 rate in order to encourage morality. He found the increase in the number of churches gratifying, but he regretted the increase in "dramshops." He also hoped that the statistics showing fewer horses in the state meant fewer "indolent equestrians."

He felt that the freedom of the Negro had expanded the freedom of the white. The wage system would stimulate "quick sales and light profits" incident to cash sales, resulting in an increase of business. Although agricultural production had declined, the agricultural resources of the state were as great as ever and the supply of labor was as available as ever. The "elevation and protection of labor is the true means for increasing that productive result which is the measure of the value of material wealth." All in all, he was convinced that "reconstruction goes forward to the sure consummation of moral and material triumph." [41]

On the whole, the optimistic tone of Alcorn's message could be justified, since to all appearances his administration had gotten off to a good start during its first year. He had taken effective steps to improve the state's financial condition and could show considerable success in preventing speculation in state bonds. He was actively trying to encourage agriculture and industry. No major scandals marred his administration, and if there were flaws in the optimistic picture he drew, they appeared susceptible of mending. As chief executive of his state, Alcorn attacked the numerous problems by bringing into play those same characteristics which had enabled him to rise to a position of esteem and wealth in the frontier country of Coahoma County—a high code of personal

---

40 *KKK Report*, XI, 312–13; Garner, *Reconstruction in Mississippi*, 283, considered the judiciary "of fair ability."
41 Alcorn, *Annual Message . . . 1871*, p. 6 ff.

ethics, shrewdness in his dealings, a puritanical dedication to hard work, and extraordinary energy. Apparently responding to the drive of that energy, Mississippi seemed to be moving back into its place as a regularly functioning state within the framework of the Union. Alcorn's practical approach, influenced by his persistent Federalist-Whig viewpoint, appeared to show that the past could be successfully invoked to meet the changes of the present.

# 8

# Growing Trouble

ALCORN COULD WELL claim credit for the modest successes of his first year as governor of Mississippi since the improving economic conditions and comparatively clean bill of political health the state enjoyed were due largely to his personal efforts. But these accomplishments were obscured even as they were being achieved by three interrelated problems which did not respond so readily to his efforts at solution. They were the controversy over public education, his inability to build the kind of political structure he had envisioned, and the wave of violence which occurred during the spring and summer of 1871. Coming in the aftermath of the Civil War and permeated by the all-pervasive question of race adjustment (which Alcorn was so sure he could handle), these problems were highly charged with emotion and lay like a train of dynamite underneath everything he was trying to accomplish.

The first of them involved the inauguration of a system of public education, an innovation, provided for in the constitution of 1868. Interwoven as it was in the political, economic, and social life of the state, it proved to be close to the heart of the challenge Alcorn had to meet if he wanted to succeed as governor. Before the Civil War Mississippi had had no public education system, and the only funds set aside strictly for education, other than those for the University of Mississippi, came from the Chickasaw School Fund. Money for this fund was provided by lands set aside after one of the Indian treaties and was available to counties in the northeastern part of the state where the lands involved were located. Federal funds which accrued to the state for educational purposes had been given to the University of Mississippi, were used for the maintenance of a few private academies, and lost through mismanagement, or squandered.[1]

The Freedmen's Bureau had paved the way to some extent for setting up a public school system for both races. It had awakened in the Negroes an awareness of the need for education and had provided at least rudimentary instruction for a considerable number, enabling them in turn to become instructors in the schools the state would furnish for colored children. In addition, the bureau had begun a state-wide educational system by drawing up school districts and furnishing them with school buildings when funds permitted, so that the state acquired a geographic plan as well as some buildings and furniture. Henry R. Pease, who had been in charge of education in Mississippi for the bureau, was elected superintendent of education in the new administration, and brought with him the knowledge and experiences he had acquired in initiating the bureau's system.[2]

During the period of Alcorn's administration, Pease was the only elected official in the education system. The state board of education, which consisted of the secretary of state, the superintendent of education, and the attorney general, supervised the funds to be spent, and appointed the county superintendents of education. At the local level, the school directors were appointed by the county boards of supervisors, and they directly managed the schools. However, at this time the members of the boards of supervisors were appointed, either by Ames or Alcorn, and these boards also levied the local taxes which provided the bulk of the funds used for setting up the schools. Some income came on a state-wide basis from fines, the granting of liquor licenses, and the poll tax, but most of the money came from local taxes levied on local property by appointed boards of supervisors, and was now to be used for an innovation with which many were not in sympathy. The ingredients of discontent were inherent in the circumstances.

1  *KKK Report*, XI, 307; Garner, *Reconstruction in Mississippi*, 365; James Lusk Alcorn, *Special Message of Gov. James L. Alcorn on the Subject of the Establishment of a University for the Colored People, Etc.* (Jackson, Miss.: Kimball, Raymond, 1871), 5.
2  Stuart G. Noble, *Forty Years of the Public Schools in Mississippi with Special Reference to the Education of Negroes* (New York: Columbia University, 1918), 26–27.

Public education brought to the foreground the delicate and unresolved problem of race relations. Alcorn made his position perfectly clear in his first message on education. In it he discussed the question of whether the local boards of education should be racially mixed or whether each district should maintain two separate ones. But he did not doubt that the legislature would bring to the problem "that correct spirit of justice to both races which demands that the schools themselves shall be kept absolutely separate." [3] The constitution of 1868 was silent on the question, and Alcorn found his legislature tended to have a different interpretation of the spirit of justice. The result was that the laws passed to implement the public education program simply stipulated that a school would be established in a given area upon application for one by the parents or guardians of twenty-five children of school age. In practice these schools were always segregated,[4] as they were elsewhere in the South, although most southern constitutions written in 1868 and the laws implementing public education avoided specifying segregated schools.

When it came to higher education the problem became thornier. Alcorn's election caused uneasiness in the state's stronghold of higher education, the University of Mississippi. "Chancellor [J. N.] Waddel [sic], Lamar, and others at the University at Oxford have sent overtures to me," he wrote his wife in late December, 1869. "Lamar thinks I will not turn him out as we have been personal friends. Waddel relies on my magnanimity. 'We shall see what we shall see.'" [5] Waddell remained in office, but Lamar, then a member of the faculty, submitted his resignation in protest over Alcorn's appointments to the board of trustees, and it was accepted.[6] Since Lamar was the son-in-law of Augustus B. Longstreet, esteemed literary figure and former president of the university, the action did not improve Alcorn's standing on campus.

During the summer of 1870 a rumor began to circulate that this Alcorn-appointed board of trustees of the University would permit the registration of a Negro student. The professors issued a statement that they would resign rather than accept such a student.

3 *Senate Journal,* 1870, appendix, 13–14.
4 Noble, *Forty Years of Public Schools,* 30; *KKK Report,* XI, 88.
5 James Lusk Alcorn to Amelia Alcorn, December 27, 1869, copy in Rainwater Collection, Box 3, Folder 38.
6 Edward Mayes, *History of Education in Mississippi* (Washington: U. S. Department of Education, 1899), 164.

Alcorn published a reply to their statement in which he linked their reaction with the policy of the Democratic party and indicated that while he wanted to maintain the university at Oxford as "a subject of honorable tradition to my own race," this might not be possible if they insisted on indulging in racially inflammatory language. He closed by pointedly advising them to keep out of politics. Dr. Waddell followed up Alcorn's letter with a conciliatory statement in which he pointed out that the Republican party was committed to the maintenance of the university and to Alcorn's own policy as contained in his messages. If there was any doubt as to the intention of the administration to retain it as an institution for whites, the doubters should await the legislative action in the matter of establishing a university for colored people.[7]

A harbinger of this came in Alcorn's first message on education. In it he asked the legislature to establish a normal school for teacher training, and since the white teachers obtainable were more advanced than the Negro ones, he suggested that the first normal school "be devoted to the education of teachers of color," and that three-fifths of the federal grant be allocated for it, with the other two-fifths going to the University of Mississippi for the establishment of a chair of agricultural chemistry and the working of a model farm.

Also on his recommendation, Oakland College, a former missionary school in Claiborne County, was purchased and renamed Alcorn College. Hiram R. Revels, who had served briefly as Senator from Mississippi, became its first president, and the school eventually developed along the lines of Tuskegee Institute.

Before the end of the first year of Alcorn's administration criticism of the school system began to mount, and was underscored by increasing violence against Negro schools in the northeastern hill counties. This violence, organized by the Ku Klux Klan and acquiesced in by the more influential white portion of the communities affected, was directed mainly but not exclusively against free schools. The protest it embodied was an explosive mixture of social, economic, and political factors. White members of the communities felt they were being disproportionately taxed, since they were the principal property owners, to maintain schools and teachers which mainly benefited Negro children. Poor whites saw a social threat in such education. Charges of extravagance were

7 McNeily, "War and Reconstruction in Mississippi," 402–403.

made against local school directors, and boards of supervisors were accused of abusing their taxing power. Often county officials, such as the sheriffs who collected the taxes, were brought in from other counties and therefore lacked the local identification which would have made their actions more acceptable. Frequently they found themselves powerless or too timid to take effective action against perpetrators of Klan violence. Since almost all of these officials had been appointed by Alcorn, the onus of their actions or inactions passed on to him, and he suffered more politically from the accusations than he probably realized at the time.

He tried hard to provide answers to some of these criticisms. In 1870, early in his administration, he suggested that in view of the heavy expense involved in setting up schools, they should be established first in populated districts and the results studied.[8] The following year he again called for an economical common school system without "frills" such as walnut desks or high salaries for teachers.[9] In another message to the legislature he aroused the ire of Lafayette County by using it as an example of the extravagance boards of school directors could indulge in because of the unlimited power allowed them by existing laws.[10]

In his annual message of 1871 Alcorn warned against a "spirit of centralization" in the school system. He indicated that the office of county superintendent of education should be elective, and spoke out in favor of local control which would help reconcile the people to the innovation of public education. He also felt that school lands should not be leased for more than twenty years at a time to prevent exploitation "as practiced by half a century of political corruption," and stated specifically that they should not be sold but rather kept as an inalienable heritage for the children of the state.

Remembering the agitation of the previous year, he looked forward to the founding of a university for Negro boys, and suggested Shaw University, located in the Delta, which had the single drawback "of its situation in the same section of the State as the University at Oxford." He wanted the same system of

8 *Senate Journal*, 1870, appendix, 13–14.
9 Alcorn, *Special Message . . . on the Subject of the Establishment of a University*, 5
10 Anonymous, *To the People of Lafayette County, Mississippi. A Plain Talk and a Few Truths* (n.p., n.d., apparently published by the Board of School Directors), Alcorn Official Papers, Series E, Folder No. 93-A.

scholarships established for Negro youth as for white, so that the University of Mississippi could be "placed superior to all clashes of party or of race, a perpetual glory of the Mississippians of my own blood." [11]

In a pamphlet published that same spring, he elaborated his "separate but equal" position with further recommendations for educational facilities for Negro students. After another attack on the Democratic party for its mishandling of prewar Federal land grants, he pointed to the Negro people as joint heirs of those bequests and said he felt that they should be compensated by the immediate establishment of a high school which could be developed into a college as they advanced in learning.

He reported that on a recent trip to Washington he had arranged for the issuance of the agricultural college land scrip due Mississippi, and now he wanted it invested in United States or state bonds. The income should be divided, with two-fifths going to the University of Mississippi and three-fifths to a Negro university, to be used to maintain schools of agricultural and mechanical sciences in each university. He also wanted to establish a system of scholarships, one each for a white and Negro boy in each county.

Then he repeated the recommendation made in his annual message that Shaw University be converted to a colored counterpart to the University of Mississippi, and closed by stating that he could see no reason why such a university should not be set aside "formally" for colored students. This would allow "distinctions of race to run their course in their character of social sentiments," and would set up an "honorable rivalry" between the two institutions.[12]

Alcorn's attempt to placate both sides in this question of segregated education had already become evident in all its ambiguity in the spring of 1870. An article appeared in abolitionist-journalist Frederick Douglass' newspaper, the *New National Era*, attacking him for advocating separate schools, and accusing him of prejudice and promoting racial strife. In a letter to the Jackson *Pilot* Alcorn denied the charge of prejudice outright, and then attempted to

11 Alcorn, *Annual Message . . . 1871*, pp. 17–24.
12 Alcorn, *Special Message . . . on the Subject of the Establishment of a University*, 5 ff. The state also contributed to the support of normal schools for Negro students at Tougaloo University and Shaw University.

explain the position of the Southern whites in the face of what he termed a social revolution. Those charged with making the principles of such a revolution acceptable to the people "shrink from every unnecessary violence to popular will, in recognition of the fact that their success has no other power worth considering at its back, save that of the pressure of necessity under the gentle urgings of moral force." He felt that very great progress had been made in acceptance of the new order of things, and he protested against stirring up old prejudices which were beginning to settle. Public schools were an experiment in Mississippi and "we must learn to walk before we attempt to run."

He accused the *New National Era* of being over-sensitive on the subject of social equality. Any protest against the school system, he believed, ought to come from white taxpayers who would have to bear the burden of it, and he hinted that the expense of separate schools might cause them to consider a dual system too much of a luxury. He felt that mixed schools which contained a majority of colored children would exclude white children, and *vice versa*, while he wanted all to be educated. He closed with this advice: "A little foresight will certainly show that any tampering with an accomplishment of a result so important, to gratify an impatient sentiment of race-pride, while endangering a great substantial benefaction, is but an unwise attempt to force the sure fruitation of events." [13]

Placed alongside his sharp admonition to the trustees of the University of Mississippi which was delivered that summer, this earlier statement makes it possible to see at this point the degree of ambiguity Alcorn was obliged to employ to keep both extremes in line. "Separate but equal" was the obvious compromise, and there is no reason to doubt that Alcorn intended, so far as he was able, to make educational facilities equal. If nothing else, the very complexity of the dilemma in which he was placed would have necessitated it. He was deeply committed to the belief that education was vital for the progress of his state, and this education had to include the lowest segment of the population if it were to become a productive part of the whole. Also, he had been elected largely by Negro voters and an integral part of his plan was to be their leader and represent their interests, as he saw those interests. On the other hand, the kind of genuine equality Negro

13 Jackson *Weekly Mississippi Pilot*, May 21, 1870.

leaders were beginning to demand was abhorrent to him, and he was quite conscious of the undercurrent of violent reaction which threatened.

Since his compromise reinforced the racial separation his colored supporters wanted to eliminate, his tactics were to try to mollify the left with apparent concessions and silence the right while actually fighting the essential part of their battle for them. The result was a cloud of ambiguity in the confusing depths of which both sides worked to undermine his position.

Still, this precarious position contributed materially to the steady progress that was made in educating the children of Mississippi during the period of Republican control. By the end of 1871, 230 schools had been constructed for Negroes and 252 for the whites. The Republican administrations under Powers and Ames continued his policies, and even when the Democrats returned to power they made no changes in his system, although eventually their economizing penalized Negro schools, particularly those engaged in higher education.[14]

Through his speeches and actions, particularly with regard to education, Alcorn won the support of J. F. H. Claiborne, already a prominent Mississippi historian, who became convinced that Alcorn's approach to the problem of how to reconstruct the state was the only feasible one.[15] Support from a man of Claiborne's standing was encouraging, but the type of political backing he needed to form the moderate Whig-Republican organization he had in mind was less apparent.

Alcorn had hoped to recruit prewar Union Democrats, such as those who had supported him in his fight against secession, but

14  Wharton, *The Negro in Mississippi*, 246–47; James Byrne Ranck, *Albert Gallatin Brown, Radical Southern Nationalist* (New York: D. Appleton-Century, 1937), 263. Ranck who had little good to say of Reconstruction, considered the public school system "the most constructive achievement of the radical Republican regime in Mississippi." Although Alcorn's school system started out with a much more centralized organization than those in other Southern states, it seems to have prospered and not to have been hampered to the same extent by the intrusion of politics, taxpayer resistance, and extravagance. Several states, notably Arkansas, Alabama, and South Carolina, began closing down schools before the end of reconstruction due to lack of funds.

15  In the preface to the chapters on Reconstruction for the second volume of his *History of Mississippi*, Claiborne wrote that he intended to vindicate Alcorn's position and to show that among Mississippi's leaders, he alone was "equal to the crisis."

they rejoined the Democratic party. For them the old issue of Union versus secession faded into memory in the presence of such questions as the revived rivalry between the hill counties and the Delta, and Alcorn's apparent racial policy.

The Whigs to whom he had appealed so strenuously in his political campaign seemed to sit on the fence. The Republican newspaper, the *Pilot*, accused them of hating the Democrats but of having a dread of being identified as Republicans.[16] A reply to this accusation suggests some of the facets of Republicanism which Whigs found uncongenial. They disliked, so the writer righteously claimed, the Democratic doctrine of "To the Victor belong the Spoils." In addition, he wrote, Whigs believed in the depravity of human nature and the need of laws to restrain it, while Democrats believed that the majority could do no wrong and minorities had no rights that needed to be respected. Therefore, it was quite obvious from their actions that radical Republicans were really ultra-Democrats.[17]

Buried in this querulous reply is a suggestion of the conservative Whig's distaste for the political and social changes the Republicans were introducing. Yet, in order to turn the tide of reconstruction so that it would rebuild Mississippi the way he wanted, Alcorn had to identify his organization firmly with the Republican party. He shattered the hopes of one Whig who had looked forward to a revival of the prewar Whig-Democrat rivalry by telling him bluntly that Whigs would have to join the Republican party "in good faith" if they wished to share in the rewards of being in power.[18] In Mississippi, as elsewhere in the South, conservative Whigs were beginning to overcome their distaste for the Democratic party. They were attracted by its opposition to Republican inovations and they found its position on the race question more direct and congenial. Its simply reactionary stand was a great deal easier to understand than Alcorn's more sophisticated attempts to use the instruments of change for what was actually the same ultimate goal—a preservation of as much of the past as possible.

A further handicap Alcorn faced in trying to build his organization was that the Whig party in the disintegrating period of the fifties had failed to attract young leaders of Alcorn's generation

16 Jackson *Pilot*, May 21, 1870.
17 *Ibid.*, May 28, 1870.
18 McNeily, "War and Reconstruction in Mississippi," 389.

to follow in the footsteps of Seargent S. Prentiss, George Poindexter, A. K. McClung, and William L. Sharkey, and to oppose his
contemporaries within the Democratic party, like Robert Lowry,
Ethelbert Barksdale, and L. Q. C. Lamar. Walker Brooke and
Sharkey were too old, and younger men like Amos R. Johnston
and the Yergers had opposed Alcorn in the gubernatorial campaign.[19] Whigs whom Alcorn found to appoint to office were for
the most part men not identified with prewar leadership and
unable to bring followers into his organization.

His failure to acquire within the Republican party a substantial
following in support of his brand of Republicanism proved to be
a weakness which appeared almost immediately after he had taken
the oath of office, and which increased steadily during the period
of his governorship. After working to put him into office, a large
portion of the party found itself opposing many of his views.

These differences show up most clearly in his relations with
the state legislature. Early in 1870 differences over railroad and
school desegregation policies appeared, as well as in matters of
economy, aid for levees, and concessions to businesses. Alcorn used
his veto power freely and a rumor began to circulate that he was
disillusioned with the "carpet-baggers." [20] On July 1 he vetoed
a printing bill that would have "starved out" local Democratic
newspapers by restricting local printing patronage to "loyal" papers.[21] An unsuccessful attempt to pass the bill over his veto
widened the estrangement between chief executive and legislators.

He conceded in his annual message of 1871 that he and the
legislature had not always agreed,[22] and the legislature confirmed
his admission by becoming more intransigent that spring. It ignored
his requests for economies, and refused him legislation he wanted
to cope with the rising tide of violence. Then the opposition found
its spokesman when some of the legislators appealed over his head
to Mississippi's Senator Ames in Washington because they were
critical of the governor's efforts to suppress this violence. This
appeal placed Ames openly in the position of champion of the
Negroes and of challenging Alcorn's leadership of the Republican
party in Mississippi.

19  During Alcorn's administration Johnston served on his commission to
    codify the state laws.
20  Friar's Point (Miss.) *Weekly Delta*, August 3, 1870; *KKK Report*, XI,
    450–51.
21  McNeily, "War and Reconstruction in Mississippi," 369.
22  Alcorn, *Annual Message . . . 1871*, pp. 3–4.

A break between these two men, one who had come to Mississippi after the war as a military officer and the other who had lived there since 1844, was almost inevitable. Each looked at Mississippi through the focus of his background, beliefs, and sense of duty, and each formulated a plan in which he would use the state Republican party to reconstruct the state. The goals of the young New Englander with his sense of mission to the Negroes, and those of the older, more experienced Southerner with his memories of the past and his class and sectional identity, were bound to clash. Alcorn had no intention of modifying his aims by sharing leadership of the party with Ames, as indicated by his earlier refusal to accept an appointment as governor from him. Also that winter began what Ames, the newly elected senator from Mississippi, described as Alcorn's "social hostility" toward him when they were both in Washington.[23] The phrase suggests that Alcorn was unwilling to accept Ames as an equal at the social gatherings they both no doubt attended.

One of Mississippi's leading Negro Republicans, John R. Lynch, claimed that the trouble between them was purely personal and had no connection with party or politics.[24] But the Republican party was hardly in power in Mississippi when the contention took on a distinctively political coloring. Because of the conditions surrounding Mississippi's readmission to the Union, no municipal or county elections were scheduled until the fall of 1871, and all such offices, normally elective, were to be filled by the governor with the consent of the senate. The situation gave Alcorn a rare opportunity to build up his organization, and over the twenty-one months of his administration he appears to have replaced virtually all of the local officials Ames, as military governor, had appointed. Ames saw clearly what Alcorn was attempting to do, and of course interpreted his actions as replacing "good" Republicans with men whose loyalty was questionable, and as slighting Negroes.[25]

Alcorn's appointments provide some basis for Ames's contentions, as well as furnish an idea of the kind of party he was trying to form. Out of 536 appointments, 247 went to Republicans and 217 to Democrats. Few Negroes received appointments, and those who

23 Blanche Butler Ames, *Chronicles from the Nineteenth Century: Family Letters of Blanche Butler and Adelbert Ames* (Clinton, Mass.: Colonial Press, 1957), I, 332–33.
24 Lynch, *The Facts of Reconstruction*, 81.
25 Ames, *Chronicles from Nineteenth Century*, I, 174, 289, 349.

did were mostly named to be county supervisors, although they were seldom in the majority on any given board. One only was appointed to be a mayor, and none received higher judicial positions than justice of the peace.[26]

While it is true that Negroes with the educational background to make them efficient officeholders were exceedingly few, Mississippi did have a small but outstanding group of Negro leaders against whom no charges of corruption were ever made. One of them, James Hill, a native Mississippian, was born a slave on a plantation near Holly Springs. He became the most influential politician of his race in his state, remaining a person of power in the Republican state organization long after the end of Reconstruction. Another, Blanche K. Bruce, was a former slave from Virginia who came to Mississippi in 1868, settled in the Delta, and was aided by Alcorn during the early part of his political career. He was the only Negro to serve a full term in the United States Senate where he was highly regarded by his colleagues. The best known of these leaders was John R. Lynch, who was born a slave in Louisiana and sold to a resident of Natchez. After obtaining his freedom during the Civil War he entered politics, served several terms in the United States House of Representatives, was highly esteemed by Republican party leaders, and went on to distinquished careers in the army and as a lawyer after 1876. The Negro leader who appears to have supported Alcorn actively the longest was Hiram R. Revels. He had been born to free parents in North Carolina and came to Mississippi as an African Methodist Episcopal minister. He was drawn somewhat reluctantly into politics, served a brief term as United States Senator, and was named by Alcorn to head the first Negro college in the state. Others whose names appear briefly and without recriminations were W. T. Stringer, a native of Ohio who played an influential role in the writing of the constitution of 1868, and J. Aaron Moore, Robert Gleed, and William Gray, who were members of the legislature while Alcorn was governor.[27]

Yet with the execption of Revels, whom historian Vernon Wharton describes as more of a scholar than a politician, and James Lynch, secretary of state during his administration, Alcorn failed to use his appointive power to win continuing active support

26  Wharton, *The Negro in Mississippi*, 167.
27  *Ibid.*, 159–64.

from these men who, in the political realties of that time, represented a majority of the citizens of Mississippi.[28]

The appointments he did make proved a weak frame for a political organization. Dyed-in-the-wool Republicans did not like the manner in which Alcorn replaced Ames appointees with his own, and Negro leaders resented his neglect of their race. In many localities his appointees became known as "Alcorn Republicans," with the implication that they were something less than true Republicans. On the other hand, Democrats derisively called them "scalawags" and grouped them with the Radical Republicans for purposes of social ostracism. Too often an "Alcorn Republican" was regarded as a politically ineffectual person, one who was neither fish nor fowl, and his misdeeds or ineptness were laid directly at Alcorn's door.

While few charges of corruption were made against these appointees, they were often described as incompetent, and it appears that Alcorn had trouble finding able men within the group from which he wanted to draw his appointments.[29] He appointed Democrats in some counties, to the disgust of radicals, and carpet-baggers in others, to the dismay of the local residents. In addition, lack of acceptable local talent often caused him to send "strangers" into small isolated communities where they met less than friendly receptions.[30] Increasing resentment at the local level, particularly in the hilly northeastern section of the state, united with the dislike of the expense and, often even the idea, of public schools to bring into the open increasing numbers of violent acts, and the ugly operations of the Klan.[31]

28  The Federal census of 1870 lists the population of Mississippi as consisting of 382,896 whites and 444,201 nonwhites.
29  Later Alcorn claimed that he had become estranged from the white people when he became governor, and since he had to set his government "in motion," he was compelled to appoint some officials whom he realized were unfit. Jackson *Clarion*, September 4, 1873.
30  Alcorn appears to have practiced a certain amount of nepotism during his administration. In Coahoma County George R. Alcorn was chancery clerk and D. F. Alcorn was sheriff. William A. Alcorn was sheriff of Tallahatchie County and Robert J. Alcorn, besides editing a newspaper, was a judge and a trustee of the Deaf and Dumb Asylum. A. Moore, a brother-in-law, was sheriff of Noxubee County where he had considerable trouble with Klan violence.
31  *KKK Report*, XI and XII, ff.; McNeily, "The Enforcement Act of 1871," p. 144. He claimed that Alcorn sowed the "dragon's teeth of uprisings" by his appointments.

Violence was already lying close to the surface in Mississippi when Alcorn assumed the office of governor. He had seen evidences of it during his campaign, and appears to have realized the great threat it posed to his plans and to the welfare of the state. Less than a month after he began his term of office the *Pilot* complained of Klan outrages. It described Tishomingo County, in the northeastern corner of the state, as the most lawless county and predicted that it would be there that Governor Alcorn would first be required to use the militia in order to enforce the law.[32]

Alcorn, however, used a different approach to his problem. Upon his recommendation the legislature passed a Ku Klux Klan act, although it did not name the organization, making it unlawful to wear masks and disguises. The act provided heavy penalties for entering houses and committing assaults in disguise. Alcorn also induced the legislature to vote him a "special contingent fund" of $50,000, which, even before the act passed, became known as the Secret Service Fund and produced vociferous opposition.[33] With this money Alcorn established a Secret Service Department, appointed a chief, L. M. Hall, and engaged agents to investigate cases of violence. One of these men went to elaborate lengths to get evidence in a Klan murder near Oxford and sent in a report naming over a dozen men whom he believed were implicated. Another sent in a detailed report on the murder of the mayor of Winona.[34]

The department remained in operation well into 1871. During the fall of 1870 it employed approximately seven agents including the chief, but seems to have had a high turnover in personnel. The November payroll listed two Negroes. Besides employing investigators, Alcorn used money from his fund for rewards for information, and to employ special prosecutors when the perpetrators of crimes were actually caught.[35]

In spite of this activity, how much he accomplished with this fund is difficult to ascertain. No convictions were ever obtained

---

32 Jackson *Pilot*, March 19, 1870.
33 *Ibid.*, March 26, 1870.
34 L. M. Hall, Chief, Secret Service Division, Jackson, Mississippi, report to James Lusk Alcorn, November 5, 1870, in Alcorn Official Papers, Series E, Folder No. 90-A.
35 Mayor H. Mask to Governor Alcorn, April 19, 1871; A. Worley Patterson to Governor Alcorn May 5, 1871; various receipts and expense sheets, all in Alcorn Official Papers, Series E, Folder 93-A.

under the state Klan act,[36] and in his annual message of January, 1871, Alcorn had to ask for additional help. He wanted the amounts of rewards for information raised from $500–$5,000 to a maximum of $25,000, and recommended that bowie knives and pistols be taxed and the carrying of them concealed made a misdemeanor punishable by fine and imprisonment. He announced that he was taking measures to activate the militia in the counties afflicted, and suggested that it might be advisable to make the counties involved pay the rewards, presumably to induce the citizens to be more cooperative in law enforcement.

At the same time he denied that the crimes which were inspiring these measures "represented any organized opposition to the officers of the law." [37] An English reporter who interviewed him soon after he delivered this message found him busy removing sheriffs who had failed to maintain order in their counties and considering measures to call out the militia. He wrote that "Mr. Alcorn was ill enough pleased at the prevalence of murder and homicide in Mississippi, but maintained that the powers of Government within the State were amply sufficient to enforce an impartial execution of the law." Alcorn also complained to him of the difficulty along the state borders "where violent and lawless persons had an opportunity of organizing and perpetrating crimes, and escaping from justice with provoking facility." [38] In all his public utterances Alcorn denied the presence of organized Klan activity, in contradiction to his own Secret Service reports, and he insisted that the state government could handle the situation.

No doubt he was anxious to forestall outside interference, not only from the Federal government but also from Adelbert Ames, who did not consider his removal to Washington as dismissing him from the Mississippi scene. Young and inexperienced, Ames remained pretty well in the background in the United States Senate until early in 1871 when that body began consideration of the Third Enforcement Act which would give the President the power to suspend the writ of habeas corpus and to use Federal troops to suppress Klan outrages. For his maiden speech Ames decided

---

36  North Carolina, Alabama, Louisiana, and Arkansas also passed state anti-Klan laws which were as unsuccessful.
37  Alcorn, *Annual Message . . . 1871*, pp. 31–32.
38  Robert Somers, *The Southern States Since the War, 1870–1871* (New York: Macmillan, 1871), 248–49.

to argue on behalf of this bill as spokesman for the Negroes of Mississippi. Shortly before he was scheduled to speak he received unexpected and dramatic support for his position when a riot occurred in Meridian, Mississippi.

In this small railroad community near the Alabama border tension between whites and Negroes had been building toward a climax for some time. During his administration as military governor, Ames had removed the mayor of Meridian William Cathey, who was native to the area and popular with the white residents. In his place he appointed William Sturges, who became a favorite with the Negro citizens. To add to the ensuing resentment, groups of armed white men from across the nearby Alabama line came frequently into Meridian in search of Negroes who had fled from work contracts. These men apparently also engaged in agitation. A committee of Negro residents went to Alcorn to complain about the situation, but according to one report, received no satisfaction from him. Upon their return they held a meeting to report the results, a fire broke out as the meeting was adjourning, and several Negroes were arrested. During their trial two days later, March 6, 1871, a riot occurred. The Negroes being tried and the presiding judge were killed, and a group of "good citizens" escorted the mayor to the county line and persuaded him that it would be best for him and the community if he did not return. The following night three prominent Negro citizens who had been taken into "protective custody" were removed from the jail and murdered.[39] Two days after the riot Alcorn sent a detachment of troops to Meridian and four days later recalled them to Jackson.[40] Meridian became quiet after that, but the problem which its actions publicized remained.

Alcorn was probably correct when he said that as a riot it was no worse than others which had occurred in the past, and not as bad as some during Ames's military administration, but the repercussions went far beyond what its size would indicate. The Meridian riot became a vehicle for calling attention to the acts of violence, approximating a reign of terror, which were occurring

---

39 *KKK Report*, XI, 6 ff.
40 Second Lieutenant Charles Jordan, 16th Infantry, Jackson, Mississippi, to Governor Alcorn, March 8, 1871; certification, that transportation be paid for thirty-one soldiers from Meridian to Jackson, March 12, 1871, no signature; both in Alcorn Official Papers, Series E, Folder No. 92-A.

mainly in the northeastern tier of counties, along the Alabama line. The counties in which this terrorism became publicly known were Lowndes, Monroe, Noxubee, Oktibbeha, Choctaw, Winston, Kemper, Itawamba, Tishomingo, Alcorn, Prentiss, Pontotoc, Lee, Leake, Tippah, Union, Chickasaw, and Lauderdale. The violence was directed mainly against the newly established free school system, particularly those schools set up for Negro children. Murders occurred in Monroe, Noxubee, and Lowndes counties, in addition to those in Meridian, Lauderdale County. Buildings used as schools for Negro children were burned, many of them churches or privately owned property, and in some counties, notably Oktibbeha, not a single school for Negro children remained standing by the summer of 1871. Teachers in these schools were threatened by letter and by night visitors. For some the warnings were underlined with whippings. A young Scotsman, Cornelius McBride, teacher in a Negro school near Sparta, in Chickasaw County, was given 150 lashes and threatened with death if he did not leave. An ex-officer in the Union army. Colonel A. P. Huggins, who had settled in Monroe County and became an assistant assessor of internal revenue and county superintendent of schools, was severely beaten and driven out of the county, resulting in the disorganization of the entire school system.[41]

In an attempt to cope with this situation, on March 20, 1871, Alcorn persuaded the senate to pass an act giving him the power to change the venue for a person charged with a felony whenever he felt an impartial trial could not be had in the county where the crime was committed. He also wanted the power to raise a cavalry regiment and personally to pay the militia. A coalition of the more radical white and Negro Republicans, aided by the Democratic minority, successfully blocked passage of these measures in the lower house of the legislature, and also refused to renew his Secret Service fund.[42] Alcorn later claimed he could have enforced the law if the legislature had given him power, particularly the change of venue law. He charged that Ames's adherents and the Democrats conspired against him, the radicals joining

---

41 *KKK Report*, I, 73–80, 1187–89. The minority report did not deny the presence of violence, but described only the feelings of the whites and the circumstances including lack of elections and charges of local corruption. *Ibid.*, 369–79.

42 McNeily, "The Enforcement Act of 1871," pp. 132–33.

because they needed federal intervention to restore their waning power.[43]

By the beginning of April the Secret Service Department was unable to meet its obligations, and bills were beginning to accumulate. With the use of his regular contingent fund, Alcorn managed to keep some agents on the payroll and to continue to employ special prosecutors in an effort to obtain convictions under the state Klan act, but without success.[44]

In the meantime, the sounds of the Meridian riot reached Washington—and Ames. A group of Republican legislators appealed over Alcorn's head to Washington for troops "which the governor would not ask for." [45] Ames supported them by incorporating the Meridian riot into his maiden speech on behalf of the proposed Third Enforcement Act. He started by defending the policies of the Republican party in Mississippi, and he attacked Alcorn for attempting to create the impression that he had things under control. The numerous proclamations offering rewards proved the extent of the outrages, according to the senator, and although Alcorn claimed he had the power to enforce the law, no one had yet been convicted of Klan violations. Ames read a telegram from H. W. Warren, president of the Mississippi Republican caucus, calling the Meridian riot a "combined effort of the whites to overthrow the city and county government." Colored refugees from Meridian who went to the governor asking what they should do, according to Ames, were invited to go to Coahoma County where he would guarantee them good wages and protection. The main themes of his speech were Alcorn's impotence and the intransigence of the rebels.[46] For both of these ills federal intervention as embodied in the Third Enforcement Act was the only remedy.

Horace Greeley's New York *Tribune* now joined the attack and charged Alcorn with failure to suppress the violence. In reply Alcorn published a pamphlet, *The Case of Mississippi Stated*, in which he tried to prove statistically that violence was diminishing, and that conditions had been much worse during the period of military rule under Ames. Continuing, Alcorn declared: "I pledge

43 *Congressional Globe*, 42nd Cong. 2nd Sess., appendix, 409.
44 Chief L. M. Hall to Governor Alcorn, April 7, 1871, in Alcorn Official Papers, Series E, Folder No. 90-A.
45 McNeily, "The Enforcement Act of 1871," pp. 126–27.
46 *Congressional Globe*, 42nd Cong. 1st Sess. (Washington: Government Printing Office, 1871), 194–98.

my honor as a man before the whole country that, save on the border of Alabama, I can at this moment recall but a single instance of Ku Klux outrage in this State for the last six months; whereas the Commanding General, Ames, gives character to the military administration of the year preceding my inauguration, when he believed that Ku Klux were then attempting to create a reign of terror!" [47]

He included in his pamphlet a copy of a letter Ames had sent to a Negro member of the Mississippi house of representatives in which he said that Alcorn was permitting his friends to be killed by "tens and hundreds," in order to gain favor with the Democrats. Ames, Alcorn charged, was inflaming the passions "of a poor people struggling up amongst us to the moral and intellectual level of free Government."

The pamphlet closed with a statement indicative of the independent political role in which he had cast himself:

I suppose I understand the course you have seen proper to pursue in reference to me personally. "Lashing into traces" is, however, an unpromising performance in the case of a man given so inverterately [sic] as I am, to work in no harness save his own. A Republican I am for reasons satisfactory to my judgment and conscience; and not—pardon me for saying—because of any consent of yours. While I shall be very happy to receive that consent at your leisure, I shall nevertheless continue—if you will excuse my bluntness—to be a Republican without it.[48]

On April 2, Alcorn sent a telegram to the Mississippi delegation in Congress using statistics, based on coroners' inquests, to show that violence was decreasing. However, the following day Ames received a telegram from four members of the legislature refuting those figures with others obtained from the auditor's books and including some murders not officially reported. According to Ames, there had been at least sixty-three murders during the past six months, rather than the nineteen Alcorn claimed to support his theory of diminishing violence. These figures were given added weight by a telegram to Ames from Henry Pease, the superintendent

---

47 His defense was somewhat disingenuous, since most of the violence reported to the congressional investigating committee did occur along the Alabama border, which takes in considerable territory.

48 James Lusk Alcorn, *The Case of Mississippi Stated (Governor Alcorn to the Editor of the New York Tribune),* (Jackson,: n.p., April 5, 1871), 1–4.

of education, that thirty churches and schools had been burned during Alcorn's administration.[49]

Shortly thereafter, Ames made another speech in the Senate in support of the Klan bill. In it he returned to Alcorn's statistics, remarking sarcastically that the state was rarely burdened with inquest claims on Klan victims, and he pointed out the inconsistency in Alcorn accusing the military government of producing anarchy, yet asking the state legislature for authority to organize a militia regiment. Alcorn was anxious that Congress not legislate against the Klan, but as Ames pointed out, he had found it necessary to send Federal troops to Meridian.[50]

On April 20, 1871, Congress passed the Enforcement Act providing Federal troops to suppress violence and extending federal jurisdiction to the prosecution of Klan outrages. Under this act a large number of persons were indicted in the Federal district court at Oxford, Mississippi, starting on June 28, but convictions were few. Later Ames accused Alcorn of refusing to aid the Federal district attorney, G. Wiley Wells, and Alcorn retorted that Wells had been too inexperienced for the job.[51] Also in June a congressional investigating committee began hearing witnesses testimony on violence in Mississippi, and in early July Alcorn found it necessary to ask that Federal soldiers be sent to Pontotoc because of a Klan disturbance.[52]

The turmoil obscured Alcorn's position and actions. On the congressional investigating committee, majority members were intent on proving the Klan origin of violence and minority members on refuting them. When the questioning touched on the politics of the local officials involved, often the blame came to rest on "Alcorn Republicans," with no attempt by either side to bring out information favorable to him.

The policy of the *Clarion*, Mississippi's leading Democratic newspaper, provides another example of the governor's anomalous position. One week it reprinted a letter to the New York *Tribune* by Allen P. Huggins, the Federal tax assessor and school superintendent for Monroe County who had been whipped and driven out by the Klan. Huggins charged he had been "sold out" by Alcorn and

49 Ames, *Chronicles from the Nineteenth Century*, I, 256–57.
50 *Congressional Globe*, 42nd Cong. 1st Sess., 569–70.
51 *Ibid.*, 2nd Sess., appendix, 407.
52 *KKK Report*, XI, 460–61.

that Alcorn "went too far" when he denied that there had been any opposition to the collection of taxes. The *Clarion* followed the letter with a statement that he was lying and that his account of the whipping was "greatly exaggerated." But the following week it published a virulent editorial attack on Alcorn, writing of him as the "Eminent Man" and his "gang of mongrels." [53] He had the support of neither side in an increasingly bitter struggle in which the two sides were drawing further and further apart and the middle ground was becoming more and more untenable.

During the summer of 1871 violence in Mississippi reached its climax, and then that fall, reacting to a combination of factors, it suddenly abated. The first local elections were scheduled to take place in November, thereby removing one of the causes of discontent. Another factor was the wider support that the system of public education began to gain from the white population. As schools continued to be established, equipped, and staffed, attacks on the system became increasingly unpopular.[54] The threat of military force also helped. Grant had made effective use of troops in South Carolina under the Klan act, indictments had been handed down in the federal courts in Mississippi, and a subcommittee of the congressional investigating committee was preparing to visit the state in November.[55]

While a semblence of peace descended upon the state, the struggle between Ames and Alcorn within the Republican party continued, with Alcorn apparently successfully resisting Ames's initial challenge. In June, 1871, he induced the legislature to remove Kimball, Raymond and Company, Ames supporters and publishers of the *Pilot*, as official printers. Charges of corruption appear to have facilitated the action against them, and Alcorn had the support of many regular Republicans, including Jonathan Tarbell,[56] who later retreated to a position of neutrality in the Ames-Alcorn struggle.[57] To receive the state's printing patronage Alcorn named Alcorn and Fisher, the former being his ubiquitous cousin Robert,

---

53 Jackson *Weekly Clarion,* May 2 and 9, 1871.
54 Wharton, *The Negro in Mississippi,* 244–46.
55 Ames, *Chronicles from the Nineteenth Century,* 344–45; *KKK Report,* XII, 721.
56 *KKK Report,* XI, 451. Tarbell tried to take a neutral position in the controversy.
57 Ames, *Chronicles from the Nineteenth Century,* I, 291.

and the latter a Northerner who had helped publish the *Pilot* in its early days.[58]

On the strength of the appointment, Alcorn and Fisher, on July 5, 1871, started a new newspaper, the *State Leader*, in support of Alcorn. The few extant copies indicate it was moderate in tone, and singularly lacking in race consciousness in contrast to the *Clarion*.

Besides being governor, Alcorn was also Senator-elect. A provisional civil government, with the newly elected legislature in session, had begun functioning in January, 1870, and one of the legislature's first acts had been to name Senators to represent Mississippi in Congress. As a result of a preelection understanding, it elected Alcorn unanimously, to serve for the period of office beginning in March, 1871. Ames was chosen, also without opposition, to finish out the senatorial term which would have begun in 1869, and Hiram Revels was selected to fill the short term which would expire in 1871.

Ames Republicans began to apply pressure to try to force Alcorn to resign from the governorship and take the seat in the United States Senate to which he had been elected. But in order to strengthen his organization, Alcorn saw that he would have to remain in the state until after the fall election. His official explanation was that it had been understood when he became a candidate for governor that he would be elected to the Senate and would serve there rather than in Jackson. But then he found that to be elected he had to promise to remain in Mississippi until the people had had an opportunity to select their own officials in a regular election without the presence of troops. By refusing to resign he was simply complying with that promise.[59]

On the surface, the campaign in the fall of 1871 had the appearance of an interparty struggle, with Alcorn in his favorite element fighting the Democrats. On the hustings he encountered old friends who were also old opponents—L. Q. C. Lamar, Ethelbert Barksdale, and Robert Lowry. Democratic leaders hastily called Lamar out of political retirement when Lowry was unable to keep an engagement with Alcorn. The clash between the two was remi-

---

58  *Ibid.* Ames complained of this removal of his supporters to his wife and indicated that one of those appointed was "a stranger to the principles of our Party."
59  *Congressional Globe*, 42nd Cong. 2nd Sess., 3702.

niscent of the 1857 campaign. Lamar wrote that his sudden appearance so disconcerted Alcorn "that he was unable to get along in his reply, though usually a most irrepressible 'slang-whanger.' " [60] But Alcorn, in a letter that sparkled with self-confidence, reported to his wife that when Lowry could not appear he challenged the Democrats to put up anyone they chose. Lamar was the one person above all that he would have had them choose. "I think—and it was the judgment of every fair minded person, that I whaled both Lowry and Lamar badly—very badly indeed." Lowry, he added, would not be with him that day, and he understood his physician to say that he was not able to speak. "I thought I would make him sick. I will make anyone sick that undertakes to follow me up. . . . You will see a report of the speeches in the Memphis Appeal and while they say Lowry skinned me you can see from even their own report that he did no such thing." [61] Alcorn was obviously enjoying himself.

At the urging of the radicals, Adelbert Ames also returned to Mississippi that fall to take part in the campaign, the first experience of its kind for him. His letters to his wife bristle with hostility toward Alcorn, who appeared to him as a dishonest schemer trying to betray the Negro and the Republican party. He was heartened to discover a solid phalanx of friends headed by O. C. French, one of the most prominent white Radical Republicans. "Everything looks well for a united party. Alcorn is intensely disliked by all true Republicans." [62] Ames found his relationship to Benjamin F. Butler helpful. After one speech the audience first cheered him and then his father-in-law. Later his constituents drank his health and also that of his new born son Butler Ames, "whose name seemed to carry with it the very quintessence of all that is loyal and true—so far at least as relates to Republicanism and friendship for the oppressed colored man." [63]

Ames felt he was launching himself with considerable success upon "the boisterous sea of *talk*," and he showed adeptness at the art of mending political fences, as when he regained the personal friendship of Henry Pease who had begun to oppose him.[64] The

60 Mayes, *Lucius Q. C. Lamar*, 136.
61 James Lusk Alcorn to Amelia Alcorn, October 11, 1871, in possession of Mrs. V. A. Hain.
62 Ames, *Chronicles from the Nineteenth Century*, I, 315.
63 *Ibid.*, 334–35.
64 *Ibid.*, 342.

Radical Republicans conceded to him the position of leadership, and began making plans to run him for governor in 1873 and then reelect him to the Senate.[65]

Both Alcorn and Ames spent the major part of their efforts in parallel attacks on the Democrats, rather than in internecine contests. However, in late October Ames predicted that while the Republicans would probably retain control of the legislature, the Democrats would make large gains due to "the Andrew Johnson policy of our governor." He "has made a war on carpet-baggers —in fact on all who would not bow the suppliant knee to him." He also accused Alcorn of giving offices to ex-Confederates, from which vantage points they were now fighting the Republicans.[66]

The outcome of the election, described by the Memphis *Avalanche* as the most orderly one ever held in the state, was pretty much as Ames had predicted. The Republicans retained control of the legislature, but they lost members in both houses and held onto control of the house of representatives by a slim majority only.

On November 30, Thanksgiving Day, Alcorn resigned his office and turned it over to Lieutenant Governor R. C. Powers. He had Thanksgiving dinner with his cousin Robert, and after receiving praise and farewells from his admirers, he left for Washington, reluctant to depart from friends and an office in which he felt he had performed a service for his state.[67]

No doubt Alcorn did serve his state well, but not well enough. When he took the oath of office as governor, he was presented with an opportunity few political leaders have. His powers were exceptionally great since, besides the enlarged executive power given by the constitution, he had unusual appointive powers which reached into every town and county in the state. He had demonstrated that he was indispensible to the Republican party, and added to this was his personal prestige and wealth which identified him with the propertied upper class in a society in which classes were taken seriously.

In spite of all this he failed during his term as governor to build the middle-of-the-road Republican Whig organization which he had envisioned. With the Negro population, and probably the

65 *Ibid.*, 320.
66 *Ibid.*, 344–45.
67 James Lusk Alcorn to Amelia Alcorn, December 2, 1871, in possession of Mrs. V. A. Hain.

Negro vote, representing a majority, no political organization could be built without at least some support from it, but Alcorn discovered that his colored supporters, whom he was sure he understood, turned out to be far less pliant than he had expected. His appointments at the local level which should have been the backbone of his party were disappointing. No doubt he received considerable support from surviving Whigs, but they showed a reluctance to assume the name of Republican, much less to assume leadership in the Republican party under him. Probably even if they had backed him wholeheartedly they would not have been an effective foundation for his organization since they were primarily identified with one region and one class.

His own class consciousness prevented his assessing properly the explosive social situation which the recent changes had brought into being. He appears to have failed to understand the attitude of the small farmers and poor whites of the hill counties toward the freed Negro. Having lived for years in the Delta where the Negro was accepted as a necessary and often welcome part of the economic scene, and having achieved a secure position in the aristocratic planter class, Alcorn did not appreciate the antagonism of the lower class whites for whom slavery had offered the consoling reminder that they were not at the bottom of the social ladder. Soon after the war he argued that giving the Negro political equality did not make him a social equal, any more than it did the "low and base of our own color." [68] He failed to realize that it was precisely this lack of distinction which would cause the trouble. Contemporaries described him as a proud and imperious man, and Ames referred to his dictatorial ways and "social hostility." A man conditioned to the prewar aristocratic concept of a ruling class would not easily understand the fears of a lower, less socially secure class, or recognize the effect his attitude might have on those with whom he had political contacts but whom he considered beneath him socially. In the long run Lamar, with his unkempt appearance and homespun trousers, was more politically astute than Alcorn with his careful grooming and imported broadcloth. The former had learned the lessons of Jacksonian democracy and endeavored to identify himself with the people; the latter never lost his belief in the Hamiltonian-Jeffersonian concept of the democratically chosen ruling elite. While Alcorn's adherence to

68 James Lusk Alcorn to Amelia Alcorn, August 26, 1865, in Alcorn Papers.

Whig-flavored ideas provided him with a method of dealing with changes, it also prevented him from truly understanding the changes. Persistent Whiggery, in effect, betrayed him.

Alcorn's legislative program was most successful in the fields of finance and education. He failed to attract industry to Mississippi, to aid the state's potentially rich Delta, or to deal with the violent elements of the population within the state without Federal interference.

As he had realized from the start, the single biggest threat to his administration was the possibility of violence. Critics have claimed that Alcorn could have handled the situation, that he need not have made it appear so serious.[69] Evidence tends to refute this charge, since it is clear from the testimony given the congressional investigating committee, that a program of terror against Negroes and radicals did exist. With the pattern of local justice as it was, and still is, Alcorn was no doubt correct when he complained that his hands were tied by the refusal of the legislature to give him a change of venue law and additional funds. He was well aware that his inability to handle the situation played into the hands of his enemies. The strongest single prop for his personal organization would have been his ability to maintain law and order in Mississippi without either the help of the Radical-controlled national government or the Klan-inspiring Democrats.

By the time this violence subsided it had contributed substantially to thwarting Alcorn's dream of a Southern Republican organization in his state. The actions of the congressional investigating committee indicate that Alcorn had lost vital national party support. The investigating members concerned themselves almost exclusively with the question of the Klan's part in the violence—the Radical Republican members trying to prove it was Klan-directed, and the Democrats trying to refute them—and neither side concerned itself with what Alcorn was attempting to do. The committee heard witnesses almost exclusively from about eight counties in the northeastern section of Mississippi, and most of the testimony was either an unrelieved picture of terror or a complete denial of any outrages. Witnesses referred to "Alcorn Republicans" in disparaging terms, but no one on the committee attempted to defend him or bring out information favorable to his administration.

---

69 Dunbar Rowland, *History of Mississippi. The Heart of the South* (Chicago-Jackson: J. S. Clarke, 1925), II, 174; McNeily, "The Enforcement Act of 1871," 125.

However, Alcorn did try to remove incompetent officials and the few extant reports of his agents indicate they were active in the central and northern regions of the state, where they may have had limited success in checking violence. The committee made no inquiries about these areas, the Delta, the Natchez region, or the southern counties. In any of these a pattern of violence may have been inhibited by Alcorn's actions. As a result anything constructive he may have been able to accomplish never became known.

Instead, this violence became the instrument by which Ames rose to prominence and gained the support to challenge effectively Alcorn's leadership of the state Republican party. Alcorn's controversy with the young New Englander, in which the latter became more and more identified with civil rights and the cause of the Negro, alienated the Grant administration, while his complicated maneuvering with respect to racial segregation and education caused him to be mistrusted by his Negro supporters and misunderstood by Whigs and Democrats.

It would have taken a much more ruthless and knowledgeable man to succeed where Alcorn failed, and in one sense he did not fail. Friends and critics have since conceded that he gave his state a good administration, and was both sincere and successful in keeping corruption to a minimum.[70] He failed in that his administration, the first in the new era and equipped with unusual powers, had a unique opportunity to turn Mississippi's face toward the future. Shrewdly as he analyzed political and economic changes arising out of the war, he did not appreciate the social changes in the main current of American life that had washed away the cornerstone of what he was trying to preserve—a ruling planter-aristocracy. What little he was able to accomplish to bring his state abreast of the times was lost again in the white revolution of 1875 to which he unwittingly contributed. The pendulum swung far to the right, pushing Mississippi into a backwater in which were drowned economic advancement, a true two-party system, and the aspirations of the freedmen.

70 Montgomery, *Reminiscences of a Mississippian*, 275–76; Lynch, *The Facts of Reconstruction*, 85; Johnston, "Suffrage and Reconstruction in Mississippi," *Mississippi Historical Society Publications*, VI (1902), p. 189; Peter J. Hamilton, *Reconstruction*, Vol. XVI of *The History of North America*, ed. Guy Carleton Lee (Philadelphia: George Barrie, 1905), 395; Garner, *Reconstruction in Mississippi*, 322–23; Donald, "The Scalawag in Mississippi Reconstruction," 451.

# 9

# Politics in Washington and Jackson

HISTORIANS HAVE TENDED to see in Alcorn's resignation and assumption of his senatorial duties a negative act in the sense that he resigned in defeat and took the position of senator as a sort of consolation prize.[1] While it is now evident that he had already failed in his attempt to construct a neo-Whig, semi-autonomous party in Mississippi under his leadership, when he left Jackson he did not see the sequence of events in that light. In the governor's mansion he left a man sharing his views, he still wanted the Negro vote, and he continued to be identified with the regular Republican party organization. His actions during the first years of his term of office indicate that he regarded his move to the United States Senate as simply another phase of his strategy to use the Republican party to reconstruct the state in accord with ideals in which he believed.

En route to Washington he wrote his wife a letter in which he revealed something of his views on the situation. He hated to leave his friends and to give up the position of governor: "It was my place; I had won it, and while weary of it and glad to get away, I nevertheless felt a jealousy that another had come to take my place . . . ." He spoke of all those who came to pay their

1 Clayton Rand, *Men of Spine in Mississippi* (Gulfport, Miss.: Dixie Press, 1940), 196–97; Rowland, *History of Mississippi,* I, 167; and in Johnston, "Suffrage and Reconstruction in Mississippi," 189, see Alcorn's resignation and removal to the Senate as a retreat or a case of "abandoning" (Rowland's term) the state to the opposition. Johnston calls it "retiring." Montgomery, *Reminiscences of a Mississippian,* 275; and Hamilton, *Reconstruction,* 394, seem to feel he was "tempted" into becoming a senator.

respects and say goodby: "I discovered an earnestness in their extravagant praise that stripped the ceremony of the appearance of formality. Among the democrats, the most prominent who called was Wiley P. Harris who expressed his approbation of my administration in decided terms. Said my career as Governor had been a brilliant success: that in the history of Mississippi I would stand prominent as one of her great men." But all this made him sad because it seemed as if he were taking his "departure to that land from whose shore there is no return."

The melancholy he felt during his trip to Washington was that of a gregarious political man leaving behind him a familiar arena and a network of relations with friends and enemies. Like an orchid drawing life-sustaining moisture from the air, Alcorn drew animation from the challenges and responsibilities of executive power and from the excitement and demands of the hustings. Even in his assurances to his wife that he would much prefer to be with her in the peace and quiet of their plantations (she spent most of her time supervising their management), some of this crept in.

This reluctant departure from a congenial political scene did not have in it any sense of defeat, nor did he see the acquisition of the position of Senator as simply a personal prize. "My struggle for position has not been prompted by selfseeking—I have ever felt I was but discharging a public duty—I feel it a duty to go forward." [2]

Alcorn arrived in Washington for the opening meeting of the second session of the Forty-Second Congress where, unlike his previous experience, he was well received. Senator Henry Wilson of Massachusetts (who would be Grant's running mate that fall) presented his credentials, and he was sworn in without delay, although there had been some rumors that his right to the seat might be challenged.[3] Afterward members of both the Senate and House gathered around his desk to greet him, including Senator Oliver P. Morton who "hobbled across the chamber saying he desired to take me by the hand."

Evidently Alcorn believed that the fall elections had strengthened his wing of the Republican party and that his political position in Washington was a strong one. In that same letter he remarked to

---

2 James Lusk Alcorn to Amelia Alcorn, December 2, 1871, in possession of Mrs. V. A. Hain.
3 *Ibid.*; McNeily, "The Enforcement Act of 1871," p. 127.

his wife that Ames also had greeted him cordially: "He sees how the land lies and surrenders like a man." [4]

Ames's appraisal of how the land lay was similar to Alcorn's. "The prospect here is not the brightest," he wrote from Jackson a few weeks later. "We have the large majority of my way of thinking, but our party majority over the Democracy is so small that a few bolters from us will hold the balance of power. These few are men who (the majority) bow to Alcorn and who are ready to do his bidding." Powers, who succeeded Alcorn as governor, had denounced him during the campaign, but had now changed sides again. "His influence is being thrown as no one heretofore suspected it would be." And Ames indicated that the radical branch of the party had served notice that it would fight the new governor if he opposed it.[5]

The first indication of friction came quickly. Alcorn's followers attempted to make use of their balance of power when the time came to organize the state house of representatives. They united with the Democrats in opposition to the Republican nominee for speaker, John R. Lynch, the prominent Negro leader, and succeeded in producing only a deadlock. In a show of solidarity with Ames, Alcorn returned from Washington and succeeded in talking the "bolters" back into line by pointing out the practical need they had of the Negro vote. Lynch's opponent for the position had been an "Alcorn Republican" who had received the backing of the Democrats, and Alcorn broke the deadlock by inducing him to withdraw his name from nomination.[6]

As the Democrats had already discovered, they were the ones who could make effective use of the balance of power. Early in January they united with the Radical Republicans to oust Alcorn and Fisher as state printers, and restore Kimball, Raymond and Company.[7] On January 25, 1872, the *State Leader*, after characterizing the action as "a fusion of extremes," [8] ceased publication. The Alcorn-Ames controversy now moved, along with its two protagonists, to Washington.

4  James Lusk Alcorn to Amelia Alcorn, December 4, 1871, in possession of Mrs. V. A. Hain.
5  Ames, *Chronicles from the Nineteenth Century*, I, 350–51.
6  Lynch, *The Facts of Reconstruction*, 61–65.
7  *Congressional Globe*, 42nd Cong. 2nd Sess., appendix, 408.
8  William D. McCain, *The Story of Jackson. A History of the Capital of Mississippi, 1821–1951* (Jackson: J. F. Hyer, 1953), I, 228.

In the nation's capital Alcorn, with the skill of a knowledgeable politician, moved quickly and easily into the active life of the Senate. He was named to membership on the Naval Affairs Committee and the Committee on Mines and Mining; later he remarked in a speech that he was undoubtedly put on the latter committee because Mississippi was the one state in the Union utterly devoid of mineral wealth. In recognition of an important part of his public life, he was appointed chairman of the Select Committee on Levees of the Mississippi River,[9] from which position he conducted a six-year assault on the public treasury on behalf of his region, but with slight success.

Unlike Ames, Alcorn quickly made the members of the Senate aware of his presence by taking an active part in pleading for quick passage of the amnesty bill proposed early in 1872. He was particularly articulate in opposing a civil rights amendment proposed by Senator Charles Sumner which he felt would delay its passage. Ames voted for the amendment and Alcorn against it, but they both voted in favor of a section denying pardon to those who had been members of the Ku Klux Klan. He was not present when, as separate bills, both measures were passed in May, but he later declared that he would have voted for them.[10]

With both men in the Senate, the rivalry between Alcorn and Ames, which had been apparently smoothed over by their common support of Lynch, soon rose to the surface again. A bill to extend the fourth section of the Klan act was presented to the Senate, and the antagonists assumed the positions they had taken following the Meridian riot. Ames charged that Klan activity was still interfering with civil rights in Mississippi and that federal intervention was needed; Alcorn continued the hands-off-Mississippi stand he had taken as governor.

On the evening of May 20, 1872, the Senate chamber was treated to the spectacle of a verbal battle between the two senators from Mississippi. Each made a speech giving his views on the proposed bill while the other heckled from his seat, and even the matter-of-fact reporting of the *Congressional Globe* cannot conceal the cold fury generated between them.

9 *Journal of the Senate of the United States of America*, 42nd Cong. 2nd Sess. (Washington: Government Printing Office, 1872), 5, 28.
10 *Congressional Globe*, 42nd Cong. 2nd Sess. (Washington: Government Printing Office, 1872), 246, 247, 3258, 3268–69, 3421, 3762.

Alcorn led off by lashing out against Ames for his criticism of the handling of the Meridian riot, going from that into sarcastic remarks about Ames's quick change from the uniform of a brevet brigadier general to the senatorial toga. Speaking of Ames's lack of residence in Mississippi, he drew laughter from the senators by remarking that although Ames listed Natchez as his home, he had never been in that city long enough to wash out a shirt.[11] As Alcorn developed his argument that there had been no organized Klan activity during his administration, he had to stop often to engage in rapid-fire skirmishes with Ames, and at one point when a remark of his brought Ames to his feet with an accusation of "another false statement," Alcorn paused and commented almost sadly on his colleague's lack of courtesy. He closed his long speech by asking that Mississippi be left in its "state of repose" and not be discriminated against in the family of states. He felt that if left alone, it could work out "a freedom of social harmony and public peace." [12]

Ames's reply was more openly bitter in its sarcasm. He struck at what was apparently as much Alcorn's attitude as his actual phraseology by referring to his use of "I," "my state," "my people," "my plantation," as if he and other prewar Southerners were the only ones entitled to be there. He also emphasized the ambiguity of Alcorn's attitude during the Civil War, saying that he "was never Union in his heart," that when he failed to fulfill the ambition for which he supported the rebellion (presumably a position of leadership in the Confederacy), he retired to his plantation. Therefore he had little idea of the changes which took place in politics during the intervening years and, as a result, was unable to consent to Northerners settling in the state unless they conformed to the wishes of "my people." [13]

Alcorn had the last word the next afternoon in another long speech in which he defended his administration, denied again that the Meridian riot had been Klan inspired or that the Klan still existed in Mississippi. Ames, he contended, knew nothing about the state and had no interest in it except to hold office. He painted

11 Ames, *Chronicles from the Nineteenth Century,* I, 107. In 1870 Adelbert Ames felt he "must" buy property in order to become more intimately connected with the state. On November 10, 1872, he wrote that he had just bought a house in Natchez, *ibid,* 446.
12 *Congressional Globe,* 42nd Cong. 2nd Sess., appendix, 402–11.
13 *Ibid.,* appendix, 393–96.

a rosy picture of life there with whites and blacks as copartners in agriculture, a greater demand for laborers than the supply, and justice for all. There was, he felt, no need to extend the Klan act, and if Congress would leave his state alone, problems would be solved satisfactorily.[14] Congress thought differently and passed the bill extending the Klan act.[15]

In this clash between the two Mississippi senators, Alcorn's experience as a stump speaker gave him the advantage where quick thinking was required. Twice he forced Ames to modify his statements, and in general his responses were longer and more balanced, and showed a greater awareness of his audience. During the two years they were in Congress together Alcorn was far more articulate than Ames. He participated in discussions on a much wider range of subjects, and he showed himself to be more adept at off-the-cuff responses and humorous quips.

Of course, this was not necessarily indicative of their relative strength within the party, but Alcorn does appear to have had more tact and to have made effective use of his personal charm in obtaining political patronage. Ames, on the other hand, still had quite a bit to learn. In the course of considering a nominee of his for a consular position, the State Department wrote him asking how long his candidate had resided in Mississippi. The question touched a sore spot, and Ames replied in a long tirade on the irrelevancy of a person's length of residence in a state when being considered for a position. He accused the State Department of drawing "distinctions between members of the same party because of birth," and, dropping openly into politics, reminded the Department that it had been the Republican party which had gotten the votes without asking how long the voters had lived in the state. Democrats and Rebels set great store by long residency in one place. Mississippi, "the best reconstructed state in the South" had only received "one petty consulate" and could not expect more, so in the future "we . . . will make our communications to the President, who, whether he can grant our request or not, will not insult us and our party by questions he would not put to applicants from other states." His letter provoked angry reaction in the office of the Secretary of State, where someone drafted and redrafted a reply which was a mixture of denial of Ames's charges

14  *Ibid.*, 3701–3704.
15  *Ibid.*, 3736.

and conciliation, with overtones of sarcasm, but there is no indication it was ever sent.[16]

Earlier in the same month that Ames was ruffling State Department feathers, Alcorn received a letter over Hamilton Fish's signature offering one of his constituents the consulate at Valencia, Spain. It included a request that he not make the offer public, since it was not yet generally known the post was available, indicating that he was being given preference in naming someone to the position.[17] He also had the Friar's Point postmaster removed and his candidate installed, and appears to have been shown consideration in other appointments.[18]

When the Forty-Second Congress met in December, 1872, for its third session, Alcorn was also appointed to the important Committee on Privileges and Elections. Ames, however, resigned his position on the Military Affairs Committee because a senator who had less seniority and military experience had been given second place on it.[19]

If the Republican party appears to have supported Alcorn, it can be said with greater certainty that Alcorn supported the Republican party. He may have cast a doubt upon the sincerity of this support by his declaration that it had been his duty to become a Republican in order to aid the Negro and to serve his state and country, and that as he had dared to be a Republican in 1869, he would now dare to be a Democrat if he felt it his duty.[20] But his record shows steady support for Grant's administration and no inclination whatsoever to move in the direction of the Democrats. During his hurried trip back to Mississippi to settle the speakership dispute between regular Republicans and his followers in the legislature, he also found time to accept an invitation to address the state house of representatives. In his speech he ridi-

16 "J.," Department of State, Washington, to Adelbert Ames, March 19, 1873; Adelbert Ames, U. S. Senate Chamber, to the Secretary of State, Washington, March 1873; and draft of letter, n.d., addressed to Adelbert Ames, Letter File, Hamilton Fish Papers, Library of Congress.

17 Hamilton Fish, Department of State, to James Lusk Alcorn, March 1, 1873, in Letter Book No. 7, No. 327, Hamilton Fish Papers, Library of Congress.

18 Hamilton Fish, Department of State, to James Lusk Alcorn, May 15, 1872, in Letter Book No. 4, No. 735, in Hamilton Fish Papers, Library of Congress; James Lusk Alcorn to Amelia Alcorn, April 8 and 13, 1872, in Alcorn File, and in possession of Mrs. V. A. Hain.

19 Bonneville (Miss.) *Prentice Recorder*, January 2, 1873.

20 *Congressional Globe*, 42nd Cong. 2nd Sess., appendix, 405.

culed and denounced the incipient reform movement in the Republican party as a "Dent movement" on a larger scale and announced that he would support Grant's nomination for a second term as President.[21]

When it became evident that the Republican party would renominate Grant, the leaders of the reform movement bolted the party and called their own convention at Cincinnati for May 1, 1872. One of the contenders for the presidential nomination, Supreme Court Justice David Davis, a political independent, attempted to lure Alcorn into supporting him. "The Cincinnati convention folks have made a set for me," he wrote Amelia. "Judge Davis has offered if I will come in, to give me the best place within his gift should he be elected. I play mum, but I intend that Grant shall let me control affairs in Mississippi as I will make him feel my weight." Then he added characteristically, "There is no telling which side I shall be on. My nature rebels at the idea of *following*. I wish to fall out with any party that says I must follow. I was not made for this. I had rather be *first* in *Coahoma* than stand second to any one." [22] Alcorn was not a man for whom party loyalty came before all else. Unlike many of his contemporaries, he tended to see parties and leadership in personal terms, related to his belief in his destiny and the network of social ties into which his life was woven. He saw himself more as affiliated with, rather than a follower of, the Republican party.

With considerable shrewdness he remained loyal to the Grant forces, but his attitude and his determination to "control affairs in Mississippi" were not lost on Ames. During their debate over the extension of the Klan act Ames charged that Alcorn was "not a true Republican," that the carpetbaggers had lost confidence in him, and that he did not represent the party in Mississippi.[23] Alcorn reminded the party leaders of whose side he was on in the coming election by referring to Greeley's attempt after the Meridian riot to "read [him] out of the Republican Party," and added that he would not disturb Greeley's devotions to what came out "from the conventicle of Cincinnati." [24]

---

21  Jackson *Daily State Leader*, January 6, 1872.
22  James Lusk Alcorn to Amelia Alcorn, April 13, 1872, in Alcorn File. This letter contradicts Rowland, *History of Mississippi*, II, 175, 179, who claims he joined Greeley and the Liberal Republicans.
23  *Congressional Globe*, 42nd Cong. 2nd Sess., 396.
24  *Ibid.*, appendix, 407–408.

Nor did the scandals which developed in the administration dismay him. In a speech in Jackson early in 1873 he lightly referred to the mounting revelations of scandal as one of those periodic recurrences in "governmental excitement." While some were really guilty of complicity in the Credit Mobilier affair, most were only guilty of concealing their knowledge of it. He reminded his audience that in the past it had not been considered venal for Daniel Webster to take money from the manufacturers of Massachusetts whose interests he had looked after, nor for Henry Clay to have his debts paid by those whose affairs he had or could promote. The members of Congress involved had been legitimately interested in legislation on a Pacific railroad, and it would be difficult to broach any matter in which some congressman did not have a stake.

He again complained that the prospect for Mississippi was "not as bright as I would be glad to see it. . . . We need to wake up here. We are too sleepy. Too slow." And he contrasted his state with the more energetic North. In closing his speech he endorsed Grant for a third term and called on the young men of Mississippi to desert "the party of the dead past—the Democracy" and join the Republican party, "the party of progress, activity, life and reform." [25]

The previous fall in the presidential election of 1872 Grant had carried Mississippi since, with both Alcorn and Ames supporting him, their feud did not weaken the state party in a national election. Alcorn does not appear to have campaigned actively for Grant,[26] but Ames did so with vigorous attacks on Greeley and the Democrats who also backed him.[27]

In addition, Ames did some substantial groundwork in promoting his wing of the state organization. All that fall, as he campaigned for Grant and discovered that "less effort is needed each time I speak," he also discussed and analyzed the possibility of strengthening his position by becoming his party's candidate for governor in 1873. He believed that the colored voters "as a class" were for him, but that some carpetbaggers, his "personal enemies," together with "the weak-kneed Southern Republicans are bitter and active

25 Jackson *Weekly Mississippi Pilot*, April 12, 1873.
26 J. S. McNeily, "Climax and Collapse of Reconstruction in Mississippi, 1874–1876," *Publications of the Mississippi Historical Society, Centenary Series*, II (1918), 437.
27 Ames, *Chronicles from the Nineteenth Century*, I, 380–81, 399–400, 402, 407–408.

against me." He felt that his opponents were suggesting a gubernatorial ticket renominating Powers as governor and George C. McKee to replace him as senator. His own supporters were insisting on a Negro for lieutenant governor, which would create difficulties. Many white Republicans would refuse to vote for his return to the Senate since this would leave a Negro as governor of the state. Revels, he discovered, was going about the state promoting Alcorn's interests, an activity which later cost him the presidency of Alcorn College.[28]

After a winter's activity in Washington, Ames returned to Mississippi in April, 1873, and discovered that the *Pilot* had already come out in favor of his candidacy. He reported with evident satisfaction Governor Powers' failure to force the *Pilot* back into line by threatening to veto a printing bill, although the editor was obliged to retreat to a position of neutrality for the time being. Powers was also unable to prevent passage of a railroad bill being promoted by the persistent Colonel Henry McComb. The governor was "losing ground" and had approached him for a compromise which he rebuffed, and he added: "The atmosphere is all I could ask." [29]

Alcorn was also in Mississippi that spring, and in April he gave a speech in Jackson for which he was introduced by Governor Powers. In spite of the fact that interest in the fall gubernatorial election was already high, and Powers was on the platform with him, he failed to endorse anyone.[30] He seems to have taken no notice of the hard political spadework in which his opponents were engaged.

Shortly before the end of June, Ames again appeared in Mississippi where he found political activity being stepped up, both by his friends and his opponents led by Powers, but he felt "as sanguine as ever." His faction was successful in having the state convention moved up from September to the middle of August, and as the counties began to hold conventions to elect delegates to the state conclave, he noted that the first two delegates chosen pledged themselves to him. By the middle of July he was campaigning actively and claimed he had the allegiance of the majority of the delegates, representing the Negro vote, Northerners, and "the most

28 *Ibid.*, I, 377–78, 379, 383–84, 386, 419.
29 *Ibid.*, I, 442–43, 444–46, 448.
30 Jackson *Weekly Mississippi Pilot*, April 12, 1873.

substantial of the scalawags." On July 26, Powers declared himself a candidate for the governorship but, according to Ames, the following day in Aberdeen he so aroused the hostility of his audience that Ames's friends had to intercede for him. A few days later McKee, trying to make a speech on behalf of Powers, was shouted down in Jackson. The *Pilot* now came out openly for Ames.[31]

On August 27 the Republican state convention nominated Ames, 187 to 40, and also chose A. K. Davis to be its candidate for lieutenant governor, W. T. Cardozo for superintendent of education, and James Hill for secretary of state. The latter three were Negroes. Powers' thorough defeat brought Alcorn into the foreground, and two days later in a speech to the same convention he announced that he would also run for governor. He charged that Ames needed a condition of "quasi-war" in the state in order to maintain his position, and therefore was opposed to his, Alcorn's, efforts to bring peace to the state and white voters into the Republican party. He accused the men nominated to run with Ames of being dishonest, and declared himself a candidate to save the state from Ames.[32]

Alcorn does not appear to have wanted to leave his post in Washington, and he reluctantly entered the race only because the opposition to Ames, led by Powers, failed to carry the convention. On September 18 he called a convention of his own (Ames called it a caucus), which nominated him on an "Independent" ticket and named Henry Musgrove as its candidate for lieutenant governor. In spite of this Independent label, the schism was strictly an intraparty struggle, and Alcorn remained in the national Republican party.[33] The Democrats held a convention at Meridian on September 17 during which they decided to put no ticket in the field, although they did urge unofficial support for Alcorn.[34]

Lamar probably expressed the view of the pro-Alcorn Democrats when in a letter to a friend he wrote: "I am for Alcorn, and perhaps it will surprise you to learn that I am as warmly in his favor

31 Ames, *Chronicles from the Nineteenth Century*, I, 463, 466, 468, 471, 488, 496, 510.
32 Jackson *Clarion*, September 4, 1873.
33 Lynch, *The Facts of Reconstruction*, 76, 81; it is difficult to find evidence that Alcorn ever considered himself as leaving the party, nor did the national organization, contrary to the statement in Garner, *Reconstruction in Mississippi*, 292.
34 Ames, *Chronicles from the Nineteenth Century*, I, 564, 571.

at this time as I have been in times past opposed to him." He had objected to Alcorn's use of Negroes and carpetbaggers to restore harmonious relations with the Federal government, but Alcorn was evidently now satisfied that the continuance of the "radical party" headed by Ames would be "a terrible evil to the State. I was opposed to the *introduction* of these people into the government of the State. I am ready to cooperate with him in their *expulsion*." Because of his character, actions, and position, Alcorn had assumed the leadership of the conservatives, and was entitled to their "cordial and unstinted support." [35]

As always when Alcorn participated, the campaign was a vigorous one.[36] But Ames, seasoned by two previous campaigns, at least by his own account, rose to the occasion. He encountered enthusiastic audiences, including whites and Democrats, successfully met Alcorn in joint debate, and routed Musgrove during one of those oratorical contests. In one letter he gleefully reported to his wife how he had used one of Alcorn's tactics against him, that of maneuvering himself into being first speaker and then using up most of the allotted time. Alcorn, he felt, was trying to get the Negro vote but would be unsuccessful.[37]

In his campaign Alcorn centered his attacks on Ames's lack of residence in the state, and his relationship with Benjamin F. Butler, which he interpreted as meaning that if Ames won, Mississippi would become "simply a province of Massachusetts." He also continued to accuse Ames's supporters of dishonesty, particularly G. H. Gibbs and O. C. French, secretary of the Republican state committee, and he recounted the excessive sums of money the *Pilot* had received for public printing.[38] The *Pilot* retaliated by comparing his campaign to that of Dent in 1869. [39]

In the meantime Ames was evidently making the sort of impression he had optimistically predicted he would. Early in October Governor Powers, with the support of Attorney General Joshua Morris, called the legislature into special session in an effort to have the election postponed. Such a bill was introduced and started

35 Mayes, *Lucius Q. C. Lamar*, 177–78.
36 Hardy, "Recollections of Reconstruction in East and Southeast Mississippi," 148; U. S. Senate, 44th Cong. 1st Sess., *Senate Report No. 527* (Washington: Government Printing Office, 1876), I, 981.
37 Ames, *Chronicles from the Nineteenth Century*, I, 583, 597, 600, 602–604.
38 Jackson *Clarion*, September 25, 1873.
39 Jackson *Pilot*, September 25, 1873.

through the legislative mill, to be killed only five days before the election was held. Ames was sure Alcorn, Powers, and Musgrove had planned this maneuver months before, to be used only if he were nominated, and he felt that the confusion it engendered among the electorate would cut down his margin of victory.[40]

The balloting was light, but Ames won by a majority of about 20,000 votes, and Republicans secured a clear majority in both houses of the legislature. While Ames's victory was not overwhelming, there seems to have been a grassroots abandonment of Alcorn. Claiborne in July had actively supported Ames's gubernatorial ambitions;[41] Coahoma County sent a delegation to the Republican state convention pledged to Ames;[42] and in the election its citizens cast 1281 votes for Ames and 426 for Alcorn.[43]

Alcorn's defeat ended any hopes for a conservative, homegrown Republican organization in Mississippi. Several factors appear to have contributed to this decisive defeat. In spite of his appeals to Negro voters and the support of Negro leaders Hiram Revels and T. W. Stringer, he failed to win a substantial portion of the Negro vote.[44] Some of this disaffection, on the part of both colored and white voters, could have come from the manner in which he waged his campaign, and from certain basic character traits. Lynch, who never was one to criticize a fellow Republican too severely, wrote that Alcorn erred in making opposition to Ames a test of loyalty to himself, that he was not supported by many of his warmest personal and political friends, and that he never forgave those who opposed him.[45] He was still the genial but proud and imperious man described by his contemporaries, and had a Southerner's strong sense of personal loyalty, which in this instance he felt should have taken precedence over what men of Lynch's way of thinking considered their primary loyalty to the regular party machinery.[46]

40 Ames, *Chronicles from the Nineteenth Century*, I, 504–505, 577, 616, 623–24.
41 Adelbert Ames to "Mr. Casey," July 19, 1873, in Box 1, Folder 2, Claiborne Papers, Southern Historical Collection, University of North Carolina.
42 Ames, *Chronicles from the Nineteenth Century*, I, 536.
43 U. S. Senate, 44th Cong. 1st Sess., *Senate Report No. 527*, II, part 3, 138.
44 McNeily, "Climax and Collapse of Reconstruction," 283, claims even his plantation Negroes did not support him.
45 Lynch, *The Facts of Reconstruction*, 71.
46 When Bruce, elected to the Senate to succeed Pease, appeared in the

Alcorn also expected a wider support based, without solicitation, on race and class. Years later an old friend and protagonist, Frank Montgomery, reminisced with him on this gubernatorial campaign and recalled how he, Alcorn, had "looked forward with the hope that the white people of the state, recognizing your earnest desire to come to their aid, would give you credit in advance for all you hoped and expected to do, and trust you as one of themselves without such pledges and assurances as would at that time have rendered your defeat certain and all your efforts abortive." [47] Allowing for the passage of time which, already in 1891, was causing the Reconstruction period to be viewed in black and white terms, a persistently Whiggish note lends authenticity to this remembrance. Twice before Alcorn had seen people and events in the image of a "maddened steed" which had to be run with for awhile and then led down the path it should take, being guided by an aristocratic leader capable of making decisions for, rather than as one of, the masses he would govern. There was no deliberate intent to deceive; for Alcorn this was the way to lead. But some of his would-be supporters may have sensed deception anyway.

Another factor was the doubt cast upon his "Republicanism" by his earlier speeches asserting his political independence, his bolt from the regular party convention, and his attitude in stressing personal loyalty. One white voter later declared that he had voted for Ames in preference to Alcorn because he regarded Ames "as a more consistent man." [48] Testifying before a United States Senate investigating committee two years later, Ames declared he had been induced to accept office because of "unreliable people" among the leaders of the Republican party, and Alcorn was "chief among them." [49]

The action of the Democrats in not running a candidate and in unofficially endorsing Alcorn cast further doubt on the genuine-

---

Senate Chamber to present his credentials, Alcorn refused to escort him to the President's desk to be sworn in because, as Lynch phrased it, Bruce "refused to follow him in open rebellion against his own party." Alcorn had started him on his political career by naming him county assessor in Bolivar County, and felt that Bruce was personally obliged to him. *Ibid.*, 81.

47  Montgomery, *Reminiscences of a Mississippian*, 283.
48  U. S. Senate, 44th Cong. 1st Sess., *Senate Report No. 527*, II, part 3, 1294.
49  *Ibid.*, I, 17–18.

ness of his political faith. Lynch felt that this contributed materially to his defeat.[50] It would, however, appear to be difficult to attribute Alcorn's defeat to the substantial action of any particular group of white voters, although the *Weekly Clarion* felt that "disaffected" Democrats might have changed the outcome, which suggests that Alcorn attracted only part of the Democratic vote.[51] He does not seem to have gained the support of a proportionately larger number of native Republicans than carpetbaggers. Powers, McKee, and Musgrove, as well as his principal Negro supporter, Revels, were all Northerners who came to the state following the Civil War, while prominent natives seem to have been conspicuous by their absence from the struggle—the Yergers, E. G. Peyton, H. F. Simrall, and Jason Niles.[52]

Grant's failure to support him was another factor. The following spring in a Senate speech Alcorn charged that the Grant administration had actively supported Ames with its prestige and patronage, and had wanted the colored voters to back him.[53] As an indication of the administration's stand, Grant had removed Robert Alcorn as United States Marshal for the southern district of Mississippi during the gubernatorial campaign.[54] The President's policy was that of backing the radical wing of the party wherever it seemed likely to remain in power, as in Louisiana, and abandoning it where it was failing, as he would do early in 1874 in Arkansas and Texas, and eventually in Mississippi itself.[55]

Another possibility to help explain Alcorn's defeat is that he may have seriously underestimated Ames. In the Senate debate during consideration of the extension of the Klan act, Alcorn emerged as the far better contestant, and he failed to appreciate that Ames was still an apprentice in the art of politicking. Also, he had a profound contempt for Ames which may have blinded him to his intellectual ability, polished by a good education, and his deep sense of mission which helped to carry him through the

50 Lynch, *The Facts of Reconstruction*, 76.
51 November 27, 1873; U. S. Senate, 44th Cong. 1st Sess., *Senate Report No. 527*, I, 12 (Ames's testimony).
52 Garner, *Reconstruction in Mississippi*, 292; Wharton, *The Negro in Mississippi*, 176, seem to stress Alcorn's Southern Republican support.
53 *Congressional Record*, 43rd Cong. 1st Sess. (Washington: Government Printing Office, 1874), 3591.
54 Vicksburg *Herald*, August 21, 1873.
55 William B. Hesseltine, *Ulysses S. Grant, Politician* (New York: Dodd, Mead, 1935), 347.

difficult days of learning how to campaign. Had Alcorn had a better estimation of his opponent's ability, he might not have left the fight in Powers' hands until Ames's delegates had control of the party convention, and it was too late to capture the regular organization. Alcorn, too, could have campaigned that summer under the magic label of the Republican party and made the same appeals to the Negro voters that Ames did, with the added assets of his experience and close identification with the state. Barring a personal reason, such as health, the only explanation seems to be that he believed Powers could handle the challenge presented by Ames.

For Alcorn defeat in his efforts to establish his version of Republicanism in Mississippi represented not only a personal rebuff but a failure in his duty to his region. As he wrote Frank Montgomery three years before his death, in reference to the campaign of 1873, he regretted that he had not been able to serve the people of Mississippi and the South more profitably than he had.[56] But it seems unlikely, in view of the conflict between the emotional intensity of the average Southerner's commitment to the myth of racial superiority and the Negro's legitimate aspirations, even if he had won the election that he could have long maintained the moderate stand which would have benefited his fellow Mississippians most.

His apparent success in Washington and, even more, his aristocratic concept of leadership appear to have led him into neglecting that most elementary of political tasks, keeping the political fences at home mended. Powers was simply his lieutenant and he assumed people would recognize this. When Powers faltered Alcorn evidently felt that all he had to do was grasp the reins of the "maddened steed" for a time to get it on the right path again. Bolstered by his belief in destiny and the social propriety of his leadership, he was capable of expecting the masses as well as members of his own class to recognize instinctively his qualifications and support him as their natural leader on a personal basis. But the demands of party regularity and the desire for equality that began to stir in all classes combined to thwart him. Caught between past and present, Mississippi chose Jackson rather than Clay.

---

56 Montgomery, *Reminiscences of a Mississippian,* 283.

# 10

# A Southern Republican

ON JANUARY 10, 1874, Adelbert Ames resigned as senator and Henry R. Pease was chosen to replace him for the balance of his term. Originally the plan had been for Ames to be elected as governor and then to resign to continue as senator, but when Blanche K. Bruce refused to run for lieutenant governor, and no other competent Negro could be found to take his place, it was decided that Ames would serve out his term as governor and then return to the Senate as Alcorn's successor.[1]

In the flush of victory Ames's supporters attempted to follow up Alcorn's defeat by introducing a resolution in the Mississippi house of representatives calling on him to resign as senator. This resolution was offered by M. B. Sullivan, state representative from Bolivar County, who charged that Alcorn had voted against measures of vital interest to Mississippi, particularly Sumner's supplemental civil rights bill, and that he was laboring neither "in accord or in sympathy with the administration of the United States or the State of Mississippi." Joseph E. Monroe, the sole representative from Coahoma County, voted for the resolution, as did the representatives of Issaquena, Washington, Yazoo, Warren, DeSoto, Sunflower, Leflore, and Tallahatchie counties, all entirely or partially in the Delta. W. C. Ford of Lauderdale County voted against it because, as he explained, the charges were simply of "official misconduct in reference to Mississippi Levee bonds and other matters of a more personal than political nature," and he added that there was no proof that Alcorn had not been true

1 Ames, *Chronicles from the Nineteenth Century*, I, 540.

to party principles. The senate attempted to kill the resolution by sending it back to the house "for proper engrossment," and when it was promptly returned during the same meeting "correctly engrossed," a vote to postpone it indefinitely was passed 24 to 4, through the efforts of the presiding officer, Lieutenant Governor A. K. Davis, a Negro.[2]

The hostile action in the house of representatives on the part of representatives from the Delta or "black" region suggests a large-scale defection of Negro voters from Alcorn. It could also be, as Ford's remark indicates, a reflection of another controversy which may have contributed to his defeat by alienating a portion of the Delta planters. Alcorn's views on how a unified levee system ought to be financed conflicted with those of the levee board formed by the southern portion of the Delta. He had opposed the formation of that board and no doubt used his influence to keep Coahoma County from joining it. A year after he had outlined to the legislature the kind of levee building program he wanted, it chartered a district called The Levee Board of the State of Mississippi, District No. 1, embracing the northern part of the Delta region.

Contrary to Alcorn's views the board was authorized to issue one million dollars in bonds and to repay them through an ad valorem tax of 2 percent on improved and unimproved lands within the district. Its bonds were never redeemed, the board became hopelessly bankrupt, and was abolished in 1876. Alcorn appears to have opposed it during its entire existence. In a letter to A. K. Davis as president of the Mississippi senate, he complained strongly about the board. In three years of existence it had never submitted a report as required by law, levee construction was being effected in a most unsatisfactory manner, and, further, an amendment passed by the legislature to compensate private levee builders would lead to the "plundering" of the entire state. He wanted the legislature to call for a report and he wanted to be heard in review of that report. He also asked that no further legislation be passed toward continuance of the board.[3]

2 *Journal of the Senate of the State of Mississippi* (Jackson: Kimball, Raymond, 1874), 146–60, 181.
3 James Lusk Alcorn to Honorable A. K. Davis, President of the Mississippi State Senate, December 17, 1874, in Governors' Correspondence 1870–1875, Series E, Folder No. 89, Mississippi Department of Archives and History.

In a United States Senate debate Alcorn charged the levee district with being extravagantly administered, and declared that the landowners and taxpayers were only "remotely responsible" for the situation since most of the voters were landless Negroes. Under questioning by Roscoe Conkling he admitted that his son Milton was president of the board, but implied that he had taken the position without his father's approval and had done it in order to protect the landowners.[4] State representative Sullivan made another attempt to discredit Alcorn the following year when he tried to have a bill pertaining to the Board of Levee Commissioners amended so that "said committee be, and are hereby required, also, to investigate all matters pertaining to the Liquidating Board of Levee Commissioners, of which James L. Alcorn was President." [5]

Disillusioned by past failures, Alcorn firmly believed that the only way to obtain permanent relief from floods was for the federal government to provide a unified levee system. The taxpayers, he declared in the Senate, were ready to trust the United States government to do the work. "Should the government of the United States deny this appeal, then and in that event I trust the people will make up their minds, frightful though the alternative may appear, to give up the struggle which they now make in behalf of any general system, take care of themselves as well as they can and give the rest to the unbroken and neverceasing flood of that greatest of rivers." [6] Having lost his faith in regional or state efforts, Alcorn did his best to prevent the "frightful alternative." He worked his select committee on levees overtime by requesting and usually obtaining permission to have it sit during recesses. He also introduced numerous resolutions and bills, accompanying one with an hour-long speech on the importance of cotton in the national economy and on the international scene where foreign nations were conspiring to destroy United States supremacy in cotton.[7]

In May, 1874, a bill was introduced to appropriate money and surplus army clothing for the relief of persons made destitute

4 *Congressional Record,* 43rd Cong. 1st Sess., 3586–90.
5 *Journal of the House of Representatives of the State of Mississippi* (Jackson: Kimball, Raymond, 1874), 42.
6 *Congressional Record,* 43rd Cong. 1st Sess., 3586–87.
7 James Lusk Alcorn, *Mississippi River Levees, Speech of Hon. J. L. Alcorn, Senate of the United States, Jan. 21, 1873* (Washington: Congressional Globe Office, 1873).

by an unusually severe flood on the Mississippi River. Alcorn opposed the bill on the grounds that the reports of widespread suffering were exaggerated and that the sum proposed would do little to alleviate suffering but could demoralize a community by encouraging the Negroes to refuse work and wait for a government handout. A much more economical and permanent way to provide for the relief of the region would be for the government to construct the levees and thereby provide work instead of a dole. Pease, taking a humanitarian view, pleaded for passage of the bill, but largely due to Alcorn's arguments about its effects on the labor supply, several senators, notably Conkling and Simon Cameron of Pennsylvania, changed their minds and helped send it back to committee for further investigation.[8] It was never passed.

On the closing day of the Forty-Third Congress Alcorn made a particularly strong attempt to collect a little federal largess for his region. He proposed an amendment to a river and harbor bill, calling for $3,420,000 to be spent by the Secretary of War to repair breaks in the levees. Senator John Sherman objected that it would endanger the whole bill, and the amendment lost, with such Radicals as George Boutwell, Zachariah Chandler, and Roscoe Conkling voting against it. Alcorn then attempted to get $165,000 for a survey of the Mississippi River by the Secretary of War and a report on a complete levee system, but it also was rejected. He finally had to settle for $30,000 to improve and deepen the mouth of the Pascagoula River.[9] And that had been his lucky day. All of his bills and resolutions were referred back to his own committee and dropped out of sight.

Alcorn showed little interest, for a Southerner, in petitioning for federal subsidies on behalf of another internal improvement, railroads. His interest in them was local and brief. In November, 1870, he took part in the incorporation at Friar's Point of the projected Memphis and Vicksburg Railroad Company. Among the incorporators were his son Milton and A. S. Dowd.[10] Alcorn became a director of the company but resigned his position a year later in what was reported to be a political fight with the city of Vicksburg.[11]

In July, 1870, he was listed as one of the organizers of the

---

8 *Congressional Record*, 43rd Cong. 1st Sess., 3586–96.
9 *Ibid.*, 2nd Sess., 2164, 2169, 2170, 2178–79.
10 Friar's Point (Miss.) *Weekly Delta*, November 2, 1870.
11 Vicksburg *Daily Herald*, November 14, 1871.

Southern Pacific Railroad, upon which the South pinned its hopes of an outlet to the Pacific Coast.[12] When Congress passed an act incorporating it as the Texas and Pacific Railroad, Alcorn was listed as an incorporator, along with such notables as John C. Frémont, Thomas A. Scott, Grenville M. Dodge, William S. Rose-crans, J. B. Brownlow, O. C. French, and H. C. Warmoth. But unlike Lamar in the House of Representatives, who worked actively on its behalf, Alcorn did not take any part in the company's efforts to obtain congressional help during the years he was in the Senate.[13]

A great deal of his time was taken up with his activities as a member of the Committee on Privileges and Elections which, in this period of widespread corruption in state legislatures, had more than the normal number of contested elections to investigate. Alcorn supported the claim of Radical George E. Spencer to be seated as the senator from Alabama against that of Francis W. Sykes elected by the Democratic portion of the legislature, and he voted to clear Powell Clayton, Radical senator from Arkansas, of charges pending against him. Yet he presented a resolution to expel Republican Senator Alexander Caldwell of Kansas who had been elected under questionable circumstances and who resigned under investigation,[14] and he voted with the majority against a resolution to seat Radical Senator-elect Joseph C. Abbott in his contest with conservative-backed M. W. Ransom, both of North Carolina.[15]

He went most of the way with the administration in the Senate investigation of the Louisiana election of 1872. His name appears as one of the signatories to the majority report of the Committee on Elections and Privileges that neither the administration-backed Kellogg government nor the liberal Republican John McEnery ticket had been fairly elected and that another election should be held. By accepting the findings of a federal judge whom the committee claimed had acted illegally, Grant supported the Kellogg organization. When P. B. S. Pinchback was elected to the Senate by the Louisiana radical legislature, Alcorn spoke against a resolution to admit him, basing his stand on the findings of the investi-

12 Jackson *Pilot*, July 16, 1870.
13 *Railway World* which was actively promoting the cause of the Texas & Pacific and its friends in Congress did not once mention Alcorn.
14 *Congressional Globe*, 42nd Cong. Special Sess. (Washington: Government Printing Office, 1873), 3–11, 66, 137, 164, 165–68, 192.
15 *Congressional Globe*, 42nd Cong. 2nd Sess., 2677.

gating committee and the fact that the Senate had neither overruled the report nor admitted the existence of the Kellogg government. He changed his stand at the following session after both houses of Congress recognized the radical government.[16] None of these actions can be construed as placing him in opposition to the Grant administration; rather, they only suggest he was trying to do his duty in a conscientious manner.

A prominent part of Alcorn's senatorial activity was his continuous effort to project the image of a moderate and reasonable Southerner. In a speech on behalf of a supplementary civil rights bill on May 22, 1874, he reminded his listeners that he had belonged to the slaveholding class and had been a Rebel, but that he was now an advocate of civil rights. Mississippi already had a more stringent civil rights law than the one under consideration, but his Negro constituents were anxious that the rest of the country receive similar benefits. He denied that equality before the law would be degrading to the white race because it would bring about social equality. He reasoned that "Society exists and is governed by its own laws. They are unwritten, but they are none the less determinedly maintained." That the degraded race could be brought to a level with the most exalted "is true as far as law can make it so." As so many Southerners would do after him, he denied that the South was prejudiced against the Negro, claiming that he himself had been nursed as a baby and raised by a colored nurse who was still a member of his family and was held in great affection. While he advocated nondiscrimination in theaters and hotels, he reiterated his belief in separate schools and claimed that the Negroes in Mississippi "who control the state" believed in it also.

The action of the southern people in resisting reconstruction, he asserted, was not due to prejudice "but to an inherent pride of soul. They believed that the action of the government was intended to insult and degrade them." He lashed out at "intriguing whites" who promised the Negro civil rights "and rob him at the same time." The only way for peace in the South was for the

---

16 Agnes Smith Grosz, "The Political Career of Pinckney Benton Stewart Pinchback," *The Louisiana Historical Quarterly*, XXVII (1944), 579; *Congressional Record*, 43rd Cong. 2nd Sess., 1342–44; *Congressional Record*, 44th Cong. Special Sess. (Washington: Government Printing Office, 1875), 1383–92.

southern whites to give the Negro these rights so as to remove from the demagogue his power over him.[17]

Following Alcorn's defeat in 1873 he became much more vocal as a spokesman for the South, and he attacked the Ames government and radicals in general in Mississippi whenever an opportunity presented itself. He did it to the extent that during one debate Senator Cameron of Pennsylvania objected as a matter of "good taste" to Southern senators constantly bringing up local matters, and he noted that no one was more apt to do it than the senator from Mississippi.[18]

Alcorn also showed a great knack for turning almost any subject under debate into a plea for the South. When an appropriation for the Centennial Exhibition at Philadelphia was being discussed, he announced he would vote against it because such an affair should represent the people and be supported by the wealthy, not by a tax on the "toiling millions." The rich would enjoy it, but the poor of the South would not be able to participate, and he then elaborated on the theme of southern poverty.[19]

Another time he voted against a resolution giving preference in civil service examinations to disabled United States soldiers, their widows or orphaned children on the grounds that it excluded Southerners from participation in government offices.[20] He made his strongest and most persistent efforts on behalf of Southerners holding what he felt were valid claims against the government. He believed that claims for cotton seized by the government after the cessation of hostilities should be honored without requiring the claimants to prove their loyalty,[21] and he presented numerous claims on behalf of constituents.

He urged increased endowments for land-grant colleges, including one for a "female department" for the University of Mississippi. He supported the administration's tariff bill of 1872, although he wanted the duty removed from quinine, and he was opposed to continuing the income tax because he believed it was objectional to the people and an irritant due to the venal tax collectors the government sent out.[22]

17 *Congressional Record*, 43rd Cong. 1st Sess., appendix, 303–307.
18 *Ibid.*, 3596.
19 *Congressional Record*, 44th Cong. 1st Sess. (Washington: Government Printing Office, 1876), 1031.
20 *Congressional Record*, 43rd Cong. 2nd Sess., 1523.
21 *Congressional Globe*, 42nd Cong. 2nd Sess., 2912–14, 3473–74.
22 *Ibid.*, 3763, 3637, 3921, 3991, 2042; *ibid*, 42nd Cong. 3rd Sess, 1553, 1692.

Throughout his term in the Senate, Alcorn was a very articulate member and a hard worker. He reported out many of the bills referred to the Committee on Mines and Mining although he was not chairman, and admitted that he had had to study hard to familiarize himself with the subject. He kept his select committee on levees working during congressional recesses, and apologized to his constituents in 1873 when his work on the committee investigating the Louisiana election kept him from attending Senate sessions.

He did find time to pose with the other senators for a group picture in 1874. Alcorn was by now nearly bald, and the remaining rim of hair over his ears, as well as a full mustache and short, trimmed beard, were almost white. He seemed shorter than most of his colleagues, his clothes were not as neatly arranged as in former years, and he still wore an old-fashioned standing collar.[23] Some of his fastidiousness and style consciousness seem to have disappeared under the pressure of national politics.

While Alcorn worked hard in Washington, supporting his party and the Southern viewpoint, his opponents at home made their attempt to plant the Republican party firmly on Mississippi soil. Ames began his gubernatorial term in a conciliatory manner with a plea in his inaugural address for economy, and for tolerance and understanding between the races; but by midsummer he was in trouble. The corrupt Republican regime in Vicksburg was overthrown by force, and Ames, after refusing to act on his own because he felt he had no means within his power to suppress such disturbances, appealed to Grant for Federal troops. Grant did not respond because, according to Ames, he was trying to get Democratic support for a third term. Things quieted down, but on August 25, his superintendent of education, Cardozo, was arrested and charged with fraud, and Ames wrote of the incident as "an illustration of the character of the material we have to work with." Grant finally agreed to send him troops if necessary, and forwarded assurances of support through Benjamin Butler, his father-in-law.[24]

In 1875 the pattern repeated itself, only more violently. The legislature started impeachment proceedings against Ames's lieu-

23 John Sherman, *Recollections of Forty Years in the House, Senate, and Cabinet* (Chicago: Warner 1895), II, photograph between pages 488 and 489.
24 Ames, *Chronicles from the Nineteenth Century*, I, 693, 695, 698–99; II, 14, 22–23, 78–79, 98.

tenant governor for taking a bribe in connection with a pardon; violence broke out among Negro members of his party; and the "white liners" began a wide-scale program of intimidation looking toward the fall election. Ames was frustrated in his attempts to form a militia, and his letters began to reflect more and more his disgust at the "barbarous spirit" of the whites and the cowardice of the Negroes. Early in September he asked once more for troops, and when Grant again failed to respond, he began organizing a Negro militia.

Besides violence, Ames had to contend with increasing opposition within his own party. The New York *Tribune* attacked him for his inefficiency in preserving peace, and white Republicans, both native and Northern, crossed over into the anti-Ames wing of the party. Among them were Henry R. Pease, whom he had sent to the United States Senate as his replacement; G. Wiley Wells, whom Alcorn had once accused of lack of experience when he was a federal district attorney; and Jonathan Tarbell who had originally tried to remain neutral in the Alcorn-Ames controversy. A taxpayers' convention met early in 1875 in Jackson under the leadership of a leading Democrat, W. S. Featherstone, to protest the extravagances and corruption of the Ames government. Among the Republicans who endorsed its protest were George McKee, Henry Musgrove, George C. Harris, and Robert J. Alcorn,[25] whose voice was later raised in the chorus of whites who protested that there was no violence in Mississippi.[26]

Another form which this break within the Republican party was beginning to take can be illustrated by the one incident in which Alcorn was directly involved. It appears to have been a spontaneous affair, not directly or deliberately related to similar occurrences in the state, but it arose out of the same explosive mixture of race and politics. In 1873 Coahoma County not only had voted for Ames by a substantial majority and sent a representative to the legislature hostile to Alcorn, but it had elected a pro-Ames slate of county officials.

About a month before the election of 1875 Alcorn spoke at a Republican gathering which had met to nominate a county ticket to oppose the pro-Ames one headed by the Negro sheriff John

---

25  Johnston, "Suffrage and Reconstruction in Mississippi," 192.
26  U. S. Senate, 44th Cong. 1st Sess., *Senate Report No. 527*, I, 472 (E. Barksdale's testimony).

Brown. In his speech Alcorn denounced the sheriff and charged him with "plundering" the state of several thousand dollars. Brown announced that he would answer Alcorn's charges a few days later, and Alcorn let it be known that he would be present. On the day of the Brown meeting, a rumor spread through Friar's Point that his followers were coming in armed. Alcorn, James R. Chalmers, a prewar Mississippian and Confederate general, and H. F. Reid, the insurgent candidate for sheriff, hastily organized a group of armed whites and went out to meet the Negroes who were ordered to disperse. The inevitable shot was fired, a brief battle routed Brown's supporters, and six Negroes and two or three whites were killed.[27] Brown fled from the county and wrote Ames that "J. L. Alcorn says that I shall not be sheriff any more," and that armed men were waiting to arrest and kill him if he returned.[28] A few days later the Coahoma board of supervisors declared the office of sheriff vacant.[29]

Alcorn claimed that the trouble arose out of the corrupt activities of Brown and his "ring," and particularly Brown's attempt to get a henchman elected to several county offices. He emphasized that the speakers and candidates at the protest meeting were all good Republicans, but opposed to Brown. Ames charged that Alcorn was solely responsible, that he was allied with the Democrats, and that he wanted to prevent the Negroes from meeting. The affair started with politics, but the actual clash and the brief reign of terror to which the local Negro population was subjected (Alcorn claimed it was conducted by men from other counties who should be prosecuted), show the rapidity with which it involved the race problem. Ames called it "a race war" precipitated by Alcorn to obtain white ascendancy.[30] It would appear that Alcorn, a loyal Republican, staged his own local "Revolution of 1875" to become once more *"First in Coahoma."*

With the exception of the Friar's Point riot, it is difficult to link Alcorn directly with the growing Republican opposition to Ames. In the many letters which Ames wrote during that summer

27  This version is mine, taken from Alcorn's account, *Senate Report No. 527*, I, 67–69, Ames's testimony, *ibid.*, I, 26–28, and Garner, *Reconstruction in Mississippi*, 377.
28  U. S. Senate, 44th Cong. 1st Sess., *Senate Report No. 527*, II, part 3, 20.
29  John Brown to Adelbert Ames, October 24, 1875, in Ames Papers, Mississippi Department of Archives and History.
30  Ames, *Chronicles from the Nineteenth Century*, II, 211.

and fall, with the exception of references to the Friar's Point incident, he never named Alcorn among his opponents. Nor did Blanche Ames, who spent that summer and fall with her father in Washington, mention Alcorn's name when she reported on Butler's efforts to intercede with Grant. This would seem to refute those who believe that Alcorn helped bring about Grant's decision not to intervene.[31] Lynch also claimed with considerable justification that had Alcorn used his influence to prevent troops being sent he would have known of it, and he was sure in his own mind that Alcorn had remained "reticent and refused to take sides."[32] A Radical leader and Ames supporter, Alexander Warner, named Pease, Wells, and Harris as leaders of the opposition, but was not sure about Alcorn.[33]

In spite of the fact that popular opinion focused opposition to Ames around Alcorn and the *Pilot* linked him with it,[34] he took no active part in the political affairs of his state during this period, except for the incident at Friar's Point. P. B. S. Pinchback, Negro Senator from Louisiana, sent him an inquiry concerning this affair, and he replied with a letter giving his reasons for his opposition to Brown, as well as his views on the election campaign of 1875 and the Republican party in Mississippi:

In the canvass of this year I have said not a word. I could not support the party in Miss while it was the mere mouthpiece of Ames. I could not support the democrats—and so I held my peace. . . . Ames has pretty well wound up the Republican Party in this state. The democrats have shown great political sagacity, they supported Ames two years since that he might drive every decent white man in the state out of the party, they have succeeded admirably—it is now a settled question that no state can be maintained under carpet-bag rule.

31  Dunbar Rowland, *Mississippi a Part of the Nation*, Vol. II. of *The South in the Building of the Nation*, eds. Julian Alvin Chandler, *et. al.* (Richmond: Southern Historical Publication Society, 1909), 441; and James Ford Rhodes, *History of the United States* (New York: MacMillan, 1920), VII, 132. Both Rowland and Rhodes believed that Alcorn influenced Grant.

32  John R. Lynch, "Some Historical Errors of James Ford Rhodes," *Journal of Negro History*, II (1917), 362. Garner, *Reconstruction in Mississippi*, 381–82, in naming those most active in opposition to Ames does not mention Alcorn. Nor, in his list of anti-radical Republicans in Mississippi, does Nordhoff, *The Cotton States in the Spring and Summer of 1875*, 83–84.

33  U. S. Senate, 44th Cong. 1st Sess., *Senate Report No. 527*, II, part 3, 1804.

34  Jackson *Pilot*, September 25, 1875.

He added that with good government Mississippi could have been kept in the Republican ranks, but he expected the party now to lose control of the state house of representatives. He closed with a brief summary of his political position: "I am a republican now as in the past, have done all I could to save Mississippi from democratic rule, have spent six years of my life in the cause. All my labor is lost." [35]

As the situation continued to deteriorate, Butler made another appeal to Grant, which resulted in the latter's famous opinion that the country was "tired of the annual autumnal outbreaks in the South." However, a representative from the Attorney General's office, George K. Chase, was sent to Mississippi, and he met with Ames and Democratic party leaders Ethelbert Barksdale and J. Z. George. As a compromise Ames agreed to disarm his Negro militia in return for a promise of a fair election, and the Attorney General promised to send troops if the agreement was not kept. Acts of violence continued to occur, which Barksdale and George vigorously denied.[36] They managed to keep the situation in status quo until the eve of the election, when Ames found the troops too far away and their orders too ambiguous to be of any help. He bitterly described Grant's order placing soldiers at his disposal as "a sham, and the election a fraud." [37] The Democratic party gained complete control of the state through the election of its members to local offices and the legislature, leaving Ames isolated in the governor's mansion.

This method of overthrowing Republican carpetbag rule became known as the "Mississippi plan," a program of intimidation and violence kept just short of what would provoke federal intervention. It was aided in Mississippi by the Grant administration which had begun during 1875 to withdraw its support of Ames by disregarding his requests concerning patronage.[38] This action made the administration's attitude so evident that the Republican state convention refused to endorse it, although the executive committee did do so before it went to Washington in an unsuccessful attempt

35 James Lusk Alcorn to P. B. S. Pinchback, October 29, 1875, in the Rutherford B. Hayes Library, Fremont, Ohio.
36 U. S. Senate, 44th Cong. 1st Sess., *Senate Report No. 527*, II, part 3, 1804.
37 Ames, *Chronicles from the Nineteenth Century*, II, 114, 125–26, 167, 171, 191, 195, 200, 240, 248, 250–51.
38 Garner, *Reconstruction in Mississippi*, 397–98.

to have Pease and two other Ames opponents removed from Federal office.[39] But Ames put his finger on the underlying reason for his predicament and failure when he wrote his wife: "I am fighting for the Negro; and to the whole country a white man is better than a 'Nigger.' " [40]

Early in 1876 the predominantly Democratic legislature started impeachment proceedings against Ames, who had already that preceding fall, in the midst of his disappointment and disgust, indicated that he wanted to resign. When in a letter he notified his lawyers that he would relinquish his office were the impeachment charges not pending against him, the Mississippi house of representatives quickly passed a resolution dismissing them, and he immediately resigned.[41]

In the United States Senate Oliver Morton of Indiana introduced a resolution calling for an investigation of the Mississippi election. A few weeks later he gave a long speech reviewing the pattern of violence which had occurred, and on March 30 and 31 several senators, including Blanche K. Bruce, Mississippi's junior Senator, also spoke, after which the resolution was passed. While Alcorn was absent during the initial and final debates, he was present during one of Morton's speeches, but he still had nothing to say.[42]

The investigating committee spent the summer taking testimony in Washington and Mississippi, and it heard numerous witnesses from every county in that state. The majority found that "force, fraud, and intimidation had been generally and successfully used in the canvass," but the report was presented only a week before Congress adjourned, its members were preoccupied with the coming presidential election, and the report itself appears to have been regarded more as a campaign weapon than anything else.[43]

The demoralized Mississippi Republican party met in state convention on March 31, as Morton's resolution was being passed by

39	New York *Tribune*, May 22, 1876.
40	Ames, *Chronicles from the Nineteenth Century*, II, 200. The reasons advanced by historians seem to reduce themselves to this one noted by Ames. John Hope Franklin, *From Slavery to Freedom* (New York: Knopf, 1948), 324–25; Vincent P. DeSantis, *Republicans Face the Southern Question* (Baltimore: Johns Hopkins Press, 1959), 45.
41	Ames, *Chronicles from the Nineteenth Century*, II, 217, 352–53.
42	New York *Tribune*, December 17, 1875 and April 1, 1876; *Congressional Record*, 44th Cong. 1st Sess., 901, 1298–99.
43	William Dudley Foulke, *Life of Oliver P. Morton* (Indianapolis–Kansas City: Bowen-Merrill, 1899), II, 375–76.

the Senate, and Ames was resigning his office. Defeat produced a surface conciliation, and the leaders of both factions were included in the state's delegation to the national presidential convention. The delegates at large named were Alcorn, Bruce, Powers, and Ames.[44] The state convention adopted a resolution thanking Morton for his efforts on behalf of Southern Republicans, but did not instruct the delegates. Alcorn attended the national convention at Cincinnati and was named to the Republican congressional committee.[45] One reporter in describing the Mississippi delegation at the convention noticed Alcorn and Ames seated in the same row, with Bruce, the chairman of the delegation, no doubt uneasily occupying the seat between them.[46]

As an indication of how superficial the conciliation had been, the Mississippi delegation scattered its votes among the contenders in varying patterns until the seventh and last ballot, when it joined the movement toward Hayes.[47] It is impossible to ascertain how Alcorn voted, but it is difficult to imagine him casting a ballot for Conkling, Morton, or James G. Blaine. Blanche Ames, writing to her husband at the convention, expressed surprise at Hayes's nomination, but added that "at least Alcorn's man was beaten." [48] The most likely possibility seems to have been Benjamin H. Bristow, who was a native Kentuckian.

Regardless of whom he had supported, Alcorn continued to be an active Republican. On July 15, 1876, he gave a long speech at the Friar's Point courthouse in which he reviewed again the prewar and post-Appomattox blunders of the South, and blamed them all on the leadership provided by the Democratic party. He cited Rutherford B. Hayes's conciliatory letter and promised that if the South would support the Republican party new issues would arise to take the place of war, race, and reconstruction. Political parties would again be like the Whigs and Democrats of earlier times.[49] In September the Memphis *Daily Appeal* interviewed him and found that he expected Mississippi to go Democratic that fall. He also

44 New York *Tribune*, May 6, 1876; McNeily, "Climax and Collapse of Reconstruction," 471.
45 *Official Proceedings of the National Republican Conventions of 1868, 1872, 1876, and 1880* (Minneapolis: Charles W. Johnson, 1903), 346, 372, 306–27.
46 New York *Tribune*, June 15, 1876.
47 *Ibid.*, June 17, 1876; *Official Proceedings . . .* , 306–27.
48 Ames, *Chronicles from the Nineteenth Century*, II, 395.
49 Friar's Point (Miss.) *Delta*, July 26, 1876.

said that he had refused the solicitations of "influential leading Republicans" to be candidate for governor. Carpetbaggers had ruined the Republican party in Mississippi, infesting it with thieves and rascals, and it was his desire to see them kicked out and the party placed in the hands of honest, honorable men.[50]

Nevertheless he continued to campaign in Mississippi for Hayes, speaking at one meeting on the same platform with a Judge Stafford who three years before had been an Ames supporter. The Democrat against whom they were both debating was an Alcorn opponent of twenty-years' standing, Albert Gallatin Brown.[51] Alcorn was also still enough of a regular Republican to vote against his old friend and comrade-in-arms at the Friar's Point riot, James R. Chalmers, whose political affiliations at that time were, and continued to be, highly ambiguous.[52]

It may be that Alcorn still hoped to obtain, through a favor to himself, some recognition by the party of white Southern Republicans. The appointment of Robert Alcorn in June, 1876, to be receiver of public monies at Jackson was a suggestion of rising administration regard.[53] Just before the national convention Alcorn wrote Amelia: "In the Herald of 22n you will observe . . . speculation for V [Vice] Presidency. Its speculation on my name is idle. I could not reach it, if I could would not have it." [54] Three days later Charles Nordhoff of the New York *Tribune* wrote Ohio Governor Hayes that Grant had informed "Southern men" he would like to see either Alcorn or George W. McCrary of Iowa nominated for the Vice-Presidency.[55] While the speculation on Alcorn's name was, as he so clearly saw, ephemeral, it indicates that he had established himself as a representative of the white Southern Republican wing, a proper recipient of favors to that group.

This is apparent later that year when after his nomination and apparent election, Hayes began to consider appointments to his cabinet. In line with his desire to include a Southerner, he spe-

50 Memphis *Daily Appeal*, September 17, 1876.
51 Ranck, *Albert Gallatin Brown*, 277.
52 James R. Chalmers, *An Open Letter to the New York Times* (Friar's Point, Mississippi: n.p., November 24, 1876).
53 New York *Tribune*, June 3, 1876.
54 James Lusk Alcorn to Amelia Alcorn, May 23, 1876, in Alcorn Papers.
55 Charles Nordhoff to Rutherford B. Hayes, May 26, 1876, in Rutherford B. Hayes Memorial Library, Fremont, Ohio.

cifically considered Alcorn,[56] and received numerous letters from constituents in Ohio as well as the border states and the South urging his appointment.[57] One such letter suggested Alcorn for Secretary of the Navy, and Lynch, who claimed that he, too, interceded for Alcorn, later wrote that Alcorn wanted to be Postmaster General.[58]

However, according to recent research, a meeting of Southerners was held at Alcorn's home in Washington early in February, 1877, to promote the candidacy of a Southern Democrat, David M. Key, to be Postmaster General.[59] At some point Hayes decided not to encourage the conservative white Southern wing of the party, and Alcorn may have felt this was the best way left to promote the interests of his region. In any event, he had already disengaged himself from state politics, and now he was withdrawing from partisan national politics also.

While Hayes was trying to make up his mind concerning southern representation in his cabinet, Congress faced a far more serious matter, that of the challenge by the Democrats of the validity of Hayes's election. Nor were all Republicans in Congress, where the issue would have to be decided, ready to support the President-elect. Some feared he might be under the influence of the reform wing of the party, and Southern Republican congressmen were concerned that his reconciliation policy in the South might mean lack of support for them.[60]

In December one of Haye's friends in Washington expressed uneasiness because "no one seems to know how Alcorn of Mississippi stands." [61] Early in January, just before the Electoral Commission plan was presented to Congress, Alcorn made his position known to Hayes, and when he did so it was with an emphatic

---

56   Charles Richard Williams, (ed.), *Diary and Letters of Rutherford Birchard Hayes* (Columbus, Ohio: Ohio State Archeological and Historical Society, 1924), 412; DeSantis, *Republicans Face the Southern Question*, 74.

57   Hon. Wm. D. Kelley to Rutherford B. Hayes, December 17, 1876; Blanton Duncan to Rutherford B. Hayes, December 25, 1876; R. Kennedy to Rutherford B. Hayes, January 14, 1877; Hon. Charles Foster to Rutherford B. Hayes, February 7 and 10, 1877, among many others in the Rutherford B. Hayes Memorial Library, Fremont, Ohio.

58   Lynch, *The Facts of Reconstruction*, 178–79.

59   C. Vann Woodward, *Reunion and Reaction* (Boston: Little, Brown, 1951), 184.

60   Williams, *Diary and Letters of Rutherford B. Hayes*, 515.

61   James N. Tyner to General James M. Comly, December 23, 1876, in Rutherford B. Hayes Library, Fremont, Ohio.

statement of support. He declared that it was his belief that Hayes had been honestly elected, that Samuel Tilden could not have carried Louisiana in an honest election, and that Mississippi should not be counted for either side since the Democrats were in "armed occupation" and the election had been a fraud and a farce.[62]

It has not been possible to ascertain whether or not he had reason to believe he was still being considered for a position in Hayes's cabinet when he made this statement. On September 17, 1876, in an interview with a reporter from the Memphis *Daily Appeal* he had expressed concern that if Tilden were elected by a slim majority "we may have a revolution in which the stability of our form of government will become involved." Even if the possibility of political reward were still present, a factor which may have inspired his silence in December, Alcorn's realistic appraisal of the situation in the South and a sincere concern with the preservation of his country's institutions no doubt also prompted him to take this stand.

In the Senate he translated his views into a course of moderation. Consistently supporting Grant's position, Alcorn voted for the establishment of the Electoral Commission, in opposition to Democrats who feared Republican domination of it and Republicans who felt it would compromise the validity of Hayes's claim. He also spoke on behalf of the commission and helped defeat hampering amendments which would have empowered it to go behind the findings in each state and would have permitted it to sit "with open doors." As the findings of the commission on the election in each state under investigation were presented, Alcorn voted with the majority to accept them.[63] His position during these two crucial months as Congress struggled to resolve the election dispute did not waver, although at one point during the period he learned that he was no longer being considered for a cabinet post. This meant the end of his political career since the Democratic Mississippi legislature had already selected Lamar to succeed him as Senator.

After casting the last of his votes on behalf of the findings of the Electoral Commission and witnessing the peaceful inaugura-

62 R. B. Avery to Rutherford B. Hayes, January 18, 1877, in Rutherford B. Hayes Library, Fremont, Ohio.
63 Congressional Record, 44th Cong. 2nd Sess., 904, 912–13, 1683; Hesseltine, *Ulysses S. Grant*, 419.

tion of Hayes, he returned to Coahoma County and retirement from state and national politics. His political career had been buried in the collapse of the Republican party in Mississippi and at the age of sixty-one he had no desire for new adventures of that nature, even had he been able to overcome his deep dislike of the Democrats. The hopes with which he had gone to Washington had failed to materialize. He obtained only sporadic backing from the Grant administration in spite of the support which he gave it; he received none when he needed it most; and the Hayes administration appeared even more unpromising. He had brought home no Federal money for the Delta, and seemingly he made little lasting impression with his speeches on behalf of the South.

At home he had been unable to lead his organization to victory over Ames in 1873, and in 1875, as Ames headed for certain defeat, he refused to assume the leadership of the opposition. Men and events had moved along in time further than Alcorn realized, thus destroying the rapport between him and other white Republican leaders. While Alcorn thought in terms of a neo-Whig party, ex-Whigs, such as Simrall, Peyton, and the Yergers became indistinguishable from latter-day native and Northern Republicans, such as Powers, McKee, Pease, Wells, Musgrove, and Vasser. Alcorn was unable to adapt to this new era the Whig political framework from the past within which he had hoped to build his organization. Whiggery, the only viable political opposition to the Democrats which had ever existed in the state, could not be revived, and with the failure of the Republican party political impoverishment settled over Mississippi.

# 11

# Retirement and a Last Contribution

AFTER THE ADJOURNMENT of Congress in March, 1877, Alcorn returned home to Friar's Point and began to devote most of his time to developing his plantations. Even under his part-time supervision they had been prospering. In the fall of 1870 after a tour of inspection of his Jonestown plantation, he professed satisfaction with the amount of cotton picked.[1] Early in 1871 a tornado seriously damaged most of the buildings at that plantation and a fire at the gin-house on his Friar's Point place caused another heavy loss.[2] Yet by midsummer he felt he had recovered from both disasters. His corn crop was good, and he was sanguine about his stand of cotton: "A good crop this year will pay all my debts and recover from my sight the disasters of last spring, disasters in which I lost $100,000 in cash, not a dozen men in all the South could have lost so much and again risen under that loss." [3]

At no time does Alcorn appear to have had to go into debt. He carried on his operations on a cash basis and prospered generally in the lean years as well as the fat ones. After the war he began to buy lands farther away from the river, and gradually to sell those he had held previously. His diaries and letters indicate he was no longer concerned with floods, as he had been in the days when he lived on the Yazoo Pass.

1 Friar's Point (Miss.) *Weekly Delta*, November 30, 1870.
2 Robert Somers, *The Southern States since the War, 1870–1871* (New York: Macmillan, 1871), 249; James Lusk Alcorn to Amelia Alcorn, February 22, 1871, in possession of Mrs. V. A. Hain.
3 James Lusk Alcorn to Amelia Alcorn, July 16, 1871, copy in Box 3, Folder 38, Rainwater Collection.

By 1876 he owned approximately twenty thousand acres in the vicinity of Jonestown and paid one-ninth of all the taxes of Coahoma County. He grumbled in his diary about being "land poor" one year when his tax bill was $5,101, but he had no trouble paying it.[4] Poor whites from the uplands came down to pick his cotton at a fixed rate, while the Negroes who lived in groups of cabins scattered throughout his lands were credited with one-third of the profits from the crops, against which they drew rations at the plantation store.[5] This one-third arrangement appears to have been somewhat less than regular sharecropping, since the Negro tenants were not expected to share in the losses of the spring of 1871, and their profits were carried on the plantation books as "wages." [6]

Alcorn recruited his tenants by building clusters of cabins in areas he wished to clear. Wandering bands of Negroes would take up residence in them, and since they needed supplies, they would soon appear at the plantation store where work contracts would be arranged. As a contemporary described the process: "A contract is soon made, the negroes are paid for their labor in food or money, trees are 'deadened,' and the dense undergrowth is swept away, and within a brief period cotton and corn grow luxuriantly about the congeries of white cottages not long before hidden in the foliage of the matted vines and among great towering oak and cypress trees." [7]

The proprietor of these lands continued to be a very busy man. In his diaries he recorded business trips to Washington, Memphis, St. Louis, and Jackson, personal supervision of much of the work done on his plantations, and concern that things were not being done as well or swiftly as they might. Christmas worried him: "So much idleness and senseless dissipation." When a shipment of goods arrived for the plantation store the whole family helped mark and shelve the items, and often Alcorn or other members of the family worked behind the counter, taking orders and selling goods.[8]

In spite of this middle-class concern with personal hard work, Alcorn achieved in his domain a reasonable facsimile of the old antebellum dream of a lordly plantation and an aristocratic way

4  James Lusk Alcorn diary, in Alcorn Papers, January 29, 1879.
5  Jackson *Clarion*, May 24, 1876; Somers, *The Southern States*, 249.
6  Somers, *The Southern States*, 249.
7  Jackson *Clarion*, May 24, 1876.
8  James Lusk Alcorn diary, in Alcorn Papers, August 12, 1879, in particular.

of life. His enterprise became in many ways a self-contained unit, with manorial overtones. It had its own post office, eventually a railroad station, blacksmith shop, lumber mill, and gin-house. The store supplied all of the tenants' needs, including liquor, and there court was held to dispose of petty offenders. On the shore of Swan Lake, which lay within the boundaries of his plantation, Alcorn presided over political rallies and barbecues for his tenants at which both Negro and white candidates spoke, and his white neighbors came to watch, seated in their carriages. Besides cotton as his principal cash crop, he raised corn, shipped out lumber, kept a herd of cattle, and bred fine horses.[9]

On his lands near Jonestown, Alcorn built a twenty-two room mansion in 1879. Erected in the prevalent Victorian style, it was three stories high, with tall bay windows, a sloping roof and dormer windows, and a small square observatory. Reminiscent of antebellum architecture with its precautions against fire, it had an outside entrance to the second story, a "breezeway" connecting the house to the kitchen and storerooms, and an enclosed interior staircase. Inside were wide halls, high-ceilinged rooms, inlaid walnut floors, imported Italian marble mantels, and ornate crystal chandeliers.[10]

The home faced Swan Lake, which lay along the northern boundary of the plantation, and its angular shape was softened by the planting around it of oak trees and extensive gardens of flowers and tropical plants. Nearby Alcorn planted a fruit orchard and, in imitation of English lords, maintained a deer park. Behind the grounds a cedar brake cut a crooked line east and west across the cotton fields, with tenant cabins clustered here and there on its banks.

In patriarchal fashion Alcorn selected a nearby Indian mound for a family cemetery. Here he brought the bodies of his parents and that of his son Henry. After his death a statue of him was placed on the center of the mound—one which, with the innocent vanity of the age, he had had sculptured and erected on the grounds

9 James Lusk Alcorn diaries (Mrs. V. A. Hain), entries for the years 1877, 1880, and 1882; and Alcorn diary (Alcorn Papers), for the year 1879. Amelia Alcorn diaries (MSS in possession of Mrs. V. A. Hain), entries for years 1883, 1884, 1885, 1888, 1891, and 1894; Amelia Alcorn diary (MS in possession of Mrs. M. G. Heins, Memphis, Tenn.), for year 1889.

10 Mrs. N. D. Deupree, "Some Historic Homes of Mississippi," *Mississippi Historical Society Publications*, VI (1902), 249–50; Somers, *The Southern States*, 249.

of his new home—"a first class Italian Marble Statue on a seven foot base for 2200$ a good likeness." [11] It is a good likeness of extant photographs and paintings of him, and depicts him standing, faultlessly dressed, with one foot slightly in front of the other, his right hand tucked into his vest in imitation of Napoleon whom he admired, and his left hand slightly extended, holding a sheaf of papers.

Eagle's Nest, as the home and plantation were now known, became a Delta showplace. In it Alcorn played to the hilt the role of Southern aristocrat as he had envisioned it. He set his table with fine china, heavy ornate silver, and cut crystal, and presided over it in a manner befitting a country gentleman and a host in the Southern tradition; he was described as genial and having "a charm about his conversation that few possess." [12] He entertained friends, political opponents and supporters, associates of his children, and the numerous writers and reporters who came to see how a cotton plantation in the Delta was operated, and went home to write articles praising his husbandry, home, and hospitality. Visitors included James Chalmers, Henry Musgrove, J. F. H. Claiborne, M. C. Gallaway, editor of the Memphis *Appeal* and vigorous opponent of Alcorn, E. M. Rector (son of Arkansas' first Confederate governor) who married one of Alcorn's daughters, and A. H. Longino who later became governor of the state. With three of his daughters, Rosebud, Gertrude, and Justina, coming home periodically from a convent school in Georgetown or later from college in the East, and another daughter, Angeline, and two young sons, Glover and James, at home, Eagle's Nest was the setting for many social affairs.

As the years passed, it became in the memory of the residents of Coahoma County a symbol of the lavishness of the late nineteenth century, and also an echo of what the South liked to think the earlier period had been. "It was the gathering place of belles and beaux of that period of history when romance, culture and lavish entertaining were the ruling elements in the lives of the idle rich. Servants were at the beck and call of the masters and mistresses." [13]

Thus Eagle's Nest and all it symbolized contributed to the

11  James Lusk Alcorn diary (Alcorn Papers), June 26, 1879.
12  Hot Springs (Ark.) *Republican*, March 2, 1906.
13  Friar's Point (Miss.) *Coahomian*, November 27, 1931.

Southern myth, while for Alcorn it marked the achievement of all he had striven for on a personal basis. But he was in some ways a sensitive man, and his diaries indicate a subtle awareness of the limitations and unsatisfying nature of this affluence, a discontent with the demands of the role he had chosen. Aging no doubt had something to do with this. He became more and more the victim of deep depressions, particularly when Amelia was away from home, and he complained of recurring fevers and attacks of lumbago. The death by suicide of his oldest son Milton saddened the move in 1879 from Friar's Point to his new home at Eagle's Nest. Yet, Alcorn did his best for his children. He sent them away to school and encouraged both his sons and daughters to go on to college. His three oldest daughters did so, but his sons were not as responsive. Glover was not interested in attending college and James attended only one session at the University of Mississippi, after which his father sent him on a European tour. To each of his children who married while he was alive—Milton, Rosebud, Justina, Gertrude, and James—he gave a plantation, and he still left a sizable estate to his widow.

Any inclination Alcorn may have had to turn his attention to political activities outside Coahoma County was effectively squelched by the Republican administration. Early in 1878 Alcorn wrote to a friend who had asked him for an endorsement to his application for a judgeship:

I regret to decline the letter you ask at my hand. I decline all and every application for endorsement to the President. The President cares nothing for the endorsement of Southern Republicans, for he has thrown himself bodily into the embraces of the democratic party of the South. I would feel no more humiliated in requesting an appointment at the hands of Jeff Davis, if he were President, than I would at the hands of President Hays [sic]—would have as much to hope in one, as in the other case.[14]

Nevertheless, in May of 1879, in a discussion on changes in cabinet appointments, particularly that of Attorney General, President Hayes suggested Alcorn as a possible candidate, but objections were raised on the grounds that the Midwest should be favored

14 James Lusk Alcorn to Kenneth Rayner, February 6, 1878, in Kenneth Rayner Papers, Southern Historical Collection, University of North Carolina.

since it was the center of Republican strength.[15] Apparently Alcorn was still remembered, even if the Republican party in Mississippi was not.

In July, 1877, radical Republican leaders had gone to the extent of expressing their feeling of abandonment at Hayes's southern policy by adopting resolutions at the Republican state committee meeting formally to dissolve the party in the state.[16] Negro leaders continued to support Hayes because although he did not extend patronage to them as a political group, he did reward individuals with appointments,[17] but the party itself became moribund.

However, as the presidential election year of 1880 approached, the Republican party in Mississippi began to revive, stirred into life by John Sherman's efforts to enlist presidential delegates pledged to himself. When the party reanimated, it did so in two factions, one composed largely of white Republicans, both native and carpetbaggers, and the other mostly of Negro Republicans. The white faction was headed by George C. McKee, and included Jason Niles, his son Henry C. Niles, Greenfield C. Chandler, George W. Gayles, Eliza Jeffords, Luke Lea, Harvey R. Ware, and Robert Alcorn. Leaders of the Negro wing were James Hill, Blanche K. Bruce, and John R. Lynch.

A movement to reorganize the Republican party was reported in 1878,[18] and by 1880 it had developed enough to allow for subtle degrees of infighting. The faction pledged to Sherman as presidential candidate dominated the state convention held in May, and the Grant adherents led by McKee threatened to bolt. At the national convention the Mississippi delegation split three ways, supporting Sherman, Blaine, and Grant.[19] During the one ballot for Vice-President, four members of the Mississippi delegation refused to go along with the party favorite, Chester A. Arthur, and cast their ballots for Alcorn.[20] Since his name had not been mentioned in any of the nominating or seconding speeches, the action suggests that it was still a symbol of protest within the party.

15  Anonymous, Griggs House, Washington, D. C., "Personal Memoranda," May 25, 1879, in Rutherford B. Hayes Memorial Library, Fremont, Ohio.
16  DeSantis, *Republicans Face the Southern Question*, 116.
17  *Ibid.*, 131–32.
18  New York *Tribune*, August 22, 1878.
19  *Ibid.*, May 6, 1880, and May 7, 1880.
20  *Official Proceedings of National Republican Conventions of 1868, 1872, 1876, and 1880*, pp. 632–44.

In the spring of 1881 the McKee wing began to hope for favors. Chandler wrote Claiborne about his hopes of getting an appointment from Garfield as circuit judge, saying that J. L. Morphis, McKee, and Alcorn would support him, adding that "these men were in Congress with Garfield, & will have more influence with him than any other Mississippians." He was sure it would be Garfield's policy to conciliate Southern men.[21] Garfield did so to some extent by giving McKee the position he requested as postmaster at Jackson, but in spite of Chandler's prediction, he completely ignored several letters of recommendation written by Alcorn, who finally again refused to write such a letter, explaining: "I am therefore by the very proprieties of the situation restrained from again offering to the President any letters in the form of suggestion."[22] Republican administrations seemed to go out of their way to insure his retirement.

Alcorn's political horizons may have shrunk drastically, but he was not completely ignored in his own state. In 1881, a gubernatorial election year, Alcorn was again considered as a candidate. An admirer in Coahoma County regarded him as the only independent statesman in Mississippi, and as the only man who could lead a Republican ticket to victory.[23] The following month a "Peoples Committee," headed by McKee and John Lynch, and supported by the Greenbackers, offered Alcorn the nomination for governor. He refused, writing a friend that he had "ceased to care for the fortunes of the Republican Party," and had resolved to tend to his own affairs.[24]

He may also have been backing away from the confusion of allegiances behind the invitation. McKee, Lynch, and the Greenbackers indicate a broad spectrum of support; but another faction of the Republican party, headed by James Hill, the local collector of internal revenue, and his "Revenue Ring" which had been and would again support John Sherman, absolutely refused to back Alcorn under any conditions, and they indicated they would

21 G. C. Chandler to H. F. J. Claiborne, February 25, 1881, in Box 1, Folder 15, Claiborne Papers, Southern Historical Collection, University of North Carolina.
22 James Lusk Alcorn to Kenneth Rayner, June 26, 1881, in Kenneth Rayner Papers, Southern Historical Collection, University of North Carolina.
23 Friar's Point (Miss.) *Gazette*, May 27, 1881.
24 James Lusk Alcorn to Kenneth Rayner, June 26, 1881, in Kenneth Rayner Papers, Southern Historical Collection, University of North Carolina.

support Benjamin King, "an old Democrat." [25] After Alcorn's refusal the Republican executive committee decided not to make any nominations, and the Greenback party nominated its own candidate.

In Coahoma County W. A. Alcorn became regular Republican party candidate for sheriff against R. E. Bobo for the People's Party, and Robert J. Alcorn was among the "influential Republicans" who denounced the idea of a fusion ticket and who supported the Democratic ticket on the state level. That fall Alcorn spoke from the same platform as Eliza Jeffords, John R. Lynch, W. A. Alcorn, "other prominent Republicans," and two members of the People's Party. [26] He apparently was also wary of fusion attempts.

The fusion which those influential Republicans denounced was that of an alliance with the Greenbackers, but they were practicing their own version of fusion or coalition politics. The "Revolution of 1875" had been a Democratic victory on the state level, but in several of the Delta counties, as well as on the national level, a compromise had been worked out with the Republicans. In Washington the Democratic Mississippi delegation, with Lamar leading, supported the efforts of the leaders of the Negro wing of the Republican party in Mississippi to obtain Federal patronage, thus keeping the party in the state identified with them and discouraging sizable white defections to it. For their part, Negro Republican leaders avoided strong opposition to Democratic control within the state. [27]

In Washington, Adams, Issaquena, Bolivar, Sharkey, and Coahoma counties, where Negro labor was essential, the political leaders worked out another form of Republican-Democratic compromise. As an election drew near, a mixed ticket would be drawn up, dividing the local offices between white and Negro candidates, with the whites taking the more important offices. Theoretically the ticket had to be approved by leaders of both parties, but the whites, mostly Democrats, usually controlled the choices, [28] and

---

25  George C. McKee to President Garfield, June 24, 1881, in Letters Received, Vol. 144, No. 197, Garfield Papers, Library of Congress.

26  Friar's Point (Miss.) *Gazette*, July 1, Aug. 19, Sept. 2, Sept. 9, and October 28, 1881.

27  Willie D. Halsell, (ed.), "Republican Factionalism in Mississippi, 1882–1884," *Journal of Southern History*, VII (1941); DeSantis, *Republicans Face the Southern Question*, 185.

28  Wharton, *The Negro in Mississippi*, 202–203; New York *Tribune*, August 14, 1890.

in Coahoma County at least, the whites of both parties worked together to select the ticket. This arrangement allowed a certain degree of political action to Negro voters, and some of the Delta counties continued to poll Republican majorities during the eighties and as late as 1890 sent Negro representatives to the state legislature.[29]

In 1881 the Hill group opposed Alcorn probably because he might have been strong enough to upset the state-national compromise, while on the local level fears that an insurgent coalition would upset county compromises may have inspired the Coahoma Republicans in their denunciations and contributed to Alcorn's refusal to be a candidate.

Futile protests against these arrangements were made from time to time by various groups, but only one serious threat arose and this was in the person of James R. Chalmers. Chalmers had had a varied career. He had been a member of the secession convention, became a Confederate general and was held responsible for the Fort Pillow massacre. In 1872 he campaigned as a candidate for presidential elector pledged to Greeley, and the following year he became an Ames supporter. But during the Friar's Point riot he helped Alcorn drive out the Ames officials, and by 1878 he had joined the Democratic party. Under its auspices he ran for Congress in 1880 against John Lynch. Presumably he won, but Lynch successfully contested the election, and Chalmers claimed that he had not been sufficiently backed by his own party because of its agreement with the Republican Negro leaders. In an effort to strike back at Lamar, whom he mainly blamed for his loss, he moved from the Sixth District where Lynch had opposed him, to Lamar's home district in northern Mississippi. There in 1882 he became a candidate for Congress as an Independent Democrat in opposition to the regular candidate Vannoy H. Manning.

Chalmers' stand during these years should have endeared him to the old planter group and to aspiring industrialists, Democrat or Republican. He denounced the free coinage of silver as a tax on the people for the benefit of the silver producers and urged that the federal government promote internal improvements, particularly railroads.[30] In an interview in 1880 he declared himself in agree-

---

29 Wharton, *The Negro in Mississippi*, 203; Wallace, *A History of the Negroes of Mississippi*, 152.
30 James R. Chalmers, *The Tariff—The Use of United States Troops in*

ment with the belief that "the intelligence and property which pay the taxes shall draw all the drafts upon the public treasury," and defended Mississippi's "Revolution of 1875" and the use of "every means short of violence to preserve to the intelligent white people of Mississippi supreme control of political affairs in that state." [31]

In an attempt to break the control of the Democratic party in Mississippi, President Arthur supported Chalmers, who attracted a variety of discontented groups within the state. Alcorn endorsed Chalmers[32] possibly because the latter's platform advocated a high tariff to protect southern manufacturers and promised to seek Federal help for the Texas and Pacific railroad and for levee rebuilding.[33]

The Democratic governor of Mississippi J. M. Stone, certified that Manning won the election, but after another long contest in which he had administration backing, Chalmers was finally seated. His coalition was unable to establish itself in the struggle against white Democrats and black Republicans, and it failed to provide enough appeal for the growing number of disaffected small farmers. In 1884 Chalmers' support was so weak he did not attempt to succeed himself, and although he ran two years later, he again saw his opponent declared the winner, and lost in his attempt to contest the election. He then retired from politics except for an attempt several years later to obtain an appointment as a Federal judge, for which Alcorn wrote him a recommendation.[34]

There is no indication that Alcorn took an active part in Chalmers' struggles. The two men were good personal friends, and if Alcorn's allegiance to the Republican party had cooled as he indicated, the Whiggish flavor of Chalmers' platform and attitude may have had enough appeal to induce him to lend at least his

---

Elections—A Defense of "The Mississippi Plan"—Military Academy—Coinage of Silver Dollars (n.p., 1878); Chalmers, The Opinions of the Fathers upon the Power and Duty of the General Government to Make Internal Improvements. Collated by Hon. J. R. Chalmers, of Mississippi, to Encourage Aid for the Mississippi Levees and the Texas & Pacific Railroad (n.p., 1878).

31 New York *Tribune,* December 17, 1880.
32 Albert D. Kirwan, *Revolt of the Rednecks. Mississippi Politics: 1876–1925* (Lexington: University of Kentucky Press, 1951), 10.
33 Willie D. Halsell, "James R. Chalmers and 'Mahoneism' in Mississippi," *Journal of Southern History,* X (1944), 43.
34 James R. Chalmers to James Lusk Alcorn, February 23, 1891, in possession of Mrs. V. A. Hain.

name to the effort. Also, unusually heavy floods in the spring of 1882 made vivid once more the reluctance of the Democratic state government to aid in building levees. Governor Robert Lowry's desk was deluged with protests, and veiled threats to seek political redress elsewhere.[35] The economy-minded legislature passed a resolution empowering the governor to appoint three commissioners to go to Washington to seek federal aid, but failed to provide for their expenses. The governor appointed W. A. Percy, Frank A. Montgomery, and James Alcorn. Alcorn did not go, and the efforts of the other two were, like earlier attempts, unsuccessful.[36] Dissatisfaction with the attitude of their Democratic allies on this question of levees might have tempted Alcorn and other Republican leaders in the Delta to turn to Chalmers.

From 1876 to 1884 the upper Delta region did not have even nominal aid of its defunct levee board. Many of the wealthier planters constructed private levees, and a series of low-water years contributed to the general apathy which lasted until the spring flood of 1882.[37] This disaster prompted the Board of Mississippi Levee Commissioners, which represented the lower Delta, to invite the upper counties to a convention at Greenville on June 19, 1882, to consider the formation of a unified district. The convention ended that same day in failure because of local differences, and Alcorn, who had evidently been named a delegate and arrived too late for the meeting, opposed unification and gave a speech that evening. Percy, a member of the Board of Levee Commissioners and a proponent of a unified system, replied to him, resulting in what Alcorn dryly called an "interesting debate."[38]

The flood brought the first direct government aid when a federal agency, the Mississippi River Commission, made funds available for closing some of the larger crevasses in the levees.[39] At another levee convention, in Vicksburg in 1883, Alcorn belittled its efforts, claiming that the construction was done "in a gingerly manner," and that the commission was afraid to have its efforts become known.[40]

He also declared that Congress formerly had not been afraid

35 Kirwan, *Revolt of the Rednecks,* 42–43.
36 Montgomery, *Reminiscences of a Mississippian,* 294.
37 Harrison, *Levee Districts and Levee Building,* 59.
38 James Lusk Alcorn diary (Mrs. V. A. Hain), June 19, 1882.
39 Harrison, *Levee Districts and Levee Building,* 71.
40 Friar's Point (Miss.) *Gazette,* October 12, 1883.

to appropriate money (he meant land) for levees and charged that the members were now afraid of harming "political parties in other sections of the country." He told the delegates they had a right to the proceeds of the cotton tax in the treasury for levees and should demand "enough to build the levees torn down by the hand of war." He did not believe in the system of building levees by contract, and felt that if Congress would not help, state convicts should be used directly under state supervision.[41]

Instead, early in 1884 the state legislature chartered a new levee district for the northern part of the Delta region, to be known as the Yazoo-Mississippi Delta Levee District. It provided for the sale of $500,000 in bonds and an ad valorem tax on real and personal property, including railroad property. The Memphis and Vicksburg Railroad, then under construction through the Delta, naturally preferred a cotton tax, and offered to float the bond issue if the Board would urge the legislature to permit such a tax.[42] Alcorn opposed both the cotton tax proposal and the issuance of bonds, and argued for a "pay as you go" policy.[43] His antebellum financial struggles as president of the Board of Levee Commissioners and the postwar Liquidating Levee Board's involved transactions to quiet claims had created in him a very conservative attitude on levee financing. Also, the relatively safe position of his lands probably removed some of the urgency which the problem had had for him in former years.

Although the Yazoo-Mississippi Delta Levee District was more successful in matters of solvency and construction than its counterpart in the southern Delta, real insurance against flooding was not achieved until the federal government assumed responsibility with the Flood Control Acts of 1917, 1923, and 1927, long after Alcorn's death.

Other local issues also continued to interest him. In the fall of 1883 he was elected without opposition to the Coahoma County board of supervisors. The following year it was rumored that he would run for Congress in opposition to Jeffords, a member of the white Republican wing, specificially to obtain an appropriation to construct a "perfect levee system," [44] but there is no indication

41  *Ibid.*
42  Harrison, *Levee Districts and Levee Building*, 75–79.
43  Friar's Point (Miss.) *Gazette*, October 2, 1885.
44  Memphis *Commercial-Appeal*, August 9, 1884.

he even considered the idea. He drifted further away from regular party affiliation that fall when he voted for Grover Cleveland for President.[45]

As one of Coahoma's leading citizens, and in accord with the fusion politics of the time, he endorsed the candidacy of both its representatives in the state legislature: J. W. Cutrer, white Conservative Democrat, and William H. Allen, Negro Republican. He also published a letter to the latter noting with approval his stand against a cotton tax to support levee construction, pointing out that such a tax was a burden on the laboring class of which he was the particular representative. The local paper credited Allen with rescuing Alcorn University "from decay," helping to pass the levee bill which gave them an independent levee district, and being "largely instrumental" in bringing about an investigation of abuses in the convict leasing system. Cutrer's platform was almost identical to Allen's, and both were reelected.[46] That October, Alcorn was scheduled to speak on levees and the cotton tax at five different points in Coahoma County, occupying the platform with Cutrer, Allen, E. M. Yerger, and other local celebrities.[47]

Alcorn also endorsed a lecture given by Negro ex-state senator Robert Gleed on "Earnest Workers," after which Societies of Earnest Workers were established at Jonestown and Eagle's Nest.[48] He worked on and off for the abolition of Quitman County which, in one of the many confusing gerrymanders of the period, had been formed out of the eastern portion of Coahoma County, and for years he tried to induce the voters of his county to locate the county seat at Jonestown. Once he offered to give enough land to accommodate a courthouse and sheriff's office, and to donate $5,000 which, together with the proceeds from the sale of the old buildings at Friar's Point, he felt ought to be enough "for a substantial, and sufficiently ornamental, Jail." [49] His offer was not accepted, and eventually the county seat moved to Clarksdale.

He continued to travel and to maintain many social contacts. Visits to his daughters' school were also occasions to meet with

45  *Ibid.*, May 10, 1885; Swift, "James Lusk Alcorn," 30.
46  Friar's Point (Miss.) *Gazette*, June 19, August 7, and November 6, 1885.
47  *Ibid.*, October 2, 1885.
48  *Ibid.*, June 12, 1885.
49  James Lusk Alcorn, *To the Voters of Coahoma* (Denver: n.p., July 9, 1887).

ex-colleagues in the Senate,[50] and journeys to Memphis on business or shopping expeditions always included calls on M. C. Gallaway and his wife. When in Jackson he made the social rounds, calling at Musgrove's home and visiting McKee and Robert Alcorn. He was entertained by Governor Robert Lowry at the executive mansion, and after one such affair wrote his daughter that the furniture and food there were poor. He did not think much of the economy-minded legislature which was discussing an appropriation of $2,000 to refit the mansion. "Such are democratic ideas of making things elegant," he added. "I should dislike to have those old, long eared grangers fit up rooms for me." [51]

In the fall of 1886 Alcorn suffered the first of a series of strokes and was partially disabled. The following summer he and two of his daughters took a trip for his health to the west coast and Alaska. In San Francisco where he was interviewed by a reporter for the *Alta California*, he praised John C. Frémont for his engineering feats in crossing the Rocky Mountains and described his state of Mississippi as a prosperous, peaceful and happy one.[52] By fall he had recovered sufficiently to attend a western waterways convention at Memphis and to give an interview on his favorite theme of federal aid for levees.[53] But a year later although he was appointed by the governor as a delegate to the Southern Inter-State Immigration Convention at Montgomery, Alabama, he did not attend.[54]

In the spring of 1889, on his way to New York to see his son embark on a visit to Europe, Alcorn stopped off in Washington where he called on President Benjamin Harrison and arranged for a letter of introduction for his son to the various consuls from Secretary of State James G. Blaine. He was described by a reporter as a conservative Republican, and the adjective at least was appropriate. Alcorn declared that he did not believe Harrison could build up a white Republican party in the South because that region was "born and bred essentially Democratic and cannot be changed

50 James Lusk Alcorn diary (Alcorn Papers), June 26, 1879.
51 James Lusk Alcorn to Gertrude Alcorn, February 3, 1882, in Alcorn File.
52 San Francisco *Alta California*, July 26, 1887.
53 Memphis *Appeal*, October 23, 1887.
54 Governor Robert Lowry, certificate of notification, to James Lusk Alcorn, November 21, 1888, in possession of Mrs. V. A. Hain; entries of December 12 and 13, 1888, Amelia Alcorn diary, in possession of Mrs. V. A. Hain.

from without." The Republican party had missed its opportunity after the war when it could have divided the South, and specifically he felt that had Grant backed him in 1873 there would now be a white Republican party in his state.

He also stated his views on the race issue:

The Southern people will not have negro rule. The negro is not a white man with a black skin. He is a different race. He is a barbarian, and barbarians cannot rule civilized people. His head is covered with wool; he is a sheep. The white man has straight hair like a lion. The negro is an infant. He has the flat nose, the retreating chin, the protruding lips of an infant. It will take centuries of development to thoroughly fit him for civilization.[55]

The following winter in another interview he further described the Negroes in the South as wanting to be left alone and as being docile, willing, not dangerous, and the natural labor supply for the cotton fields. The southern states had made a great mistake in setting them free without obtaining compensation, and he added: "The United States had no power to liberate the slaves; it required the indorsement of sovereign States [and it was] an everlasting shame to the Legislature [sic], which convened after the war, that it passed a bill sanctioning the liberation of the slaves."

It had been too anxious to show submission and had deprived widows and orphans of their only support. The question of freeing the slaves might have been used to prevent passage of the Fourteenth and Fifteenth amendments.[56]

In spite of this retreat to the right, and forgetfulness of the situation as it really had been, there was a basic consistency in Alcorn's views. Although he had once in a Senate speech characterized slavary as "a cancer upon the body of the nation," [57] he had not intended the analogy as a moral one, and he saw no reason why its removal could not be exploited for the benefit of his region. During the Reconstruction period he undoubtedly trimmed his sails to the prevalent political winds, a controversial means to an end which he never tried to conceal and was seen only too clearly by many of his opponents, Negro and white. Racial inequality was an unspoken but basic assumption in the postwar society he wanted to build, as it was in most of late nineteenth-

55 Washington *Post*, April 30, 1889.
56 Memphis *Daily Commercial*, January 5, 1890.
57 *Congressional Globe*, 42nd Cong. 2nd Sess., 3424.

century American society. Now that political pressures had been removed and his social and economic prominence was secure, he could give voice to these more extreme statements—simply a sharper and harsher version of his fundamental belief which contacts with such men as John R. Lynch and Blanche K. Bruce had not shaken.

In the activities of his autumn years Alcorn came close to personifying in microcosm the leader he had wanted to be on a larger scale. He was generous, civic-minded, and held himself above the squabbles of partisan politics. He voiced his distrust of incurring debts and, with an older generation of conservatives, did not fear government participation in internal improvements. As master of Eagle's Nest he established a relationship with his tenants like that he had hoped to achieve with the Negro voters of his state. He took care of them, scolded them, bailed them out of jail, carefully supervised their political activities, and encouraged them to be "earnest workers." As befit their inferiority, his attitude was strongly paternalistic, but he took his duty (as he saw it) toward them as seriously as he did his duty to his family, region, and country.

To those outside his circle of influence he appeared to take on the coloring of an elder statesman. A Democratic newspaper in 1889 spoke of him as an able and conscientious Republican, and called him the "Sage of 'Eagle's Nest.'" [58] Historians took a brief interest in him. Soon after his retirement he entered into correspondence with Claiborne, who was then writing the second volume of his *History of Mississippi*, and in 1879 sent him the bulk of his papers.[59] Claiborne devoted several chapters of this projected second volume to a review and vindication of Alcorn's postwar public life, but the project ended tragically when manuscript and papers were lost in a fire, and Claiborne died shortly thereafter. Frederic Bancroft also corresponded with Alcorn, and called him "a contribution to history." [60]

58  Jackson *Clarion-Ledger*, January 16, 1889.
59  James Lusk Alcorn to J. F. H. Claiborne, March 28, 1879, in Box 1, Folder 8, Claiborne Papers, Southern Historical Collection, University of North Carolina.
60  Frederic Bancroft to James Lusk Alcorn, October 13, 1888, in possession of Mrs. V. A. Hain; Jacob E. Cooke, *Frederic Bancroft, Historian* (Norman: University of Oklahoma Press, 1957), p. 38, claims that Bancroft interviewed Alcorn in 1888. However, Bancroft's notebook shows he spoke with a *Judge* Alcorn in Yazoo City, Mississippi, probably either Robert J. or William A. Alcorn.

Alcorn's views and reputation placed him in the mainstream of Southern reaction, a position which he had always occupied to a much greater extent than his Republican label seemed to his contemporaries to indicate. By 1890 this reaction had reached the point where Southerners would attempt to erase the last vestiges of reconstruction from their governments by rewriting the constitutions drawn up in the years following the war.

For several years there had been periodic demands for a new constitution in Mississippi. Many felt that the Negro should be legally disfranchised so as to eliminate the fraud and intimidation which had been degrading Mississippi elections ever since 1875. Also, Democratic politicians were not happy with the fusion tickets of some Delta counties which permitted Negroes a share, albeit small, in local government and continued to result in some Negro representation in the state legislature.[61] Through these fusion tickets, or by intimidation, the minority group of white voters in the black counties had come to exercise a disproportionate amount of power, so that to a large extent it was not Negro domination but white domination from one region that was being protested. Because of this preponderance of power, it was felt the Delta was not paying its full share of taxes.[62]

The struggle for political control of the state between the hill counties and the Delta was an old story. It had shown itself in the rise of the Democratic party to power after the broadening of the franchise in 1832, had had a part in the secession struggle, and had been ever present in hostility to state-supported levee programs. Besides this rivalry, insurgent farm groups in the white counties had stimulated an interest in reforms such as an elective judiciary, elimination of convict leasing, and the restrictions of the powers of corporations.[63] The Chalmers revolt had delayed action on this issue, but now with "Chalmerism" almost dead and the wanderers back in the Democratic fold, the hill counties had sufficient strength to force the issue over objections within the Democratic party. Governor Lowry, L. Q. C. Lamar, and Edward C. Walthall consistently opposed calling a convention, sensing in the movement a threat to their conservative position.

61 Wharton, *The Negro in Mississippi*, 202–203.
62 C. Vann Woodward, *Origins of the New South, 1877–1913* (Baton Rouge: Louisiana State University Press, 1951), 329.
63 Kirwan, *Revolt of the Rednecks*, 60.

Alcorn also opposed a constitutional convention. He felt that it would be useless as it would not cure the real or imaginary ills of the state, and might prove more mischievous than beneficial. Tinkering with the franchise would be likely to disturb existing conditions without benefit to Negro or white voters.[64] Another issue which Alcorn felt might come like Banquo's ghost to haunt the convention was that of the repudiated Planters' and Union bank bonds. Before the Civil War, like all good Whigs, he had favored payment of those bonds, but later he had been instrumental in having passed an amendment to the constitution forbidding their payment. His reasoning was that the war had so radically changed the character and value of the property (land) upon which the obligation to pay had been based, that this obligation was no longer binding. He seemed to feel that if the convention were held the bondholders would attempt to have the amendment repealed.[65]

In the spring of 1890 pressure forced Lowry to issue a call for a constitutional convention to assemble on August 12. On June 10 the Coahoma County Democratic convention unanimously nominated Alcorn to be a delegate, writing in their letter of notification that the members were "mindful of the fact that in two important crises your prominent services have been of inestimable value to the commonwealth. We have an abiding faith in your ability to meet this third important crisis." [66] A month later local Democrats and Republicans invited him as a nominee to the convention to deliver a speech at Friar's Point,[67] and shortly thereafter he and Cutrer were elected to represent Coahoma County at the convention. Since their county was one of those which had achieved political peace and white supremacy through the fusion system, Alcorn and Cutrer probably went to the convention pledged to preserve as much as possible the status quo, with strong backing from all groups, white and Negro, Democrat and Republican.

The convention register listed Alcorn as being seventy-four years old, a planter by occupation, and under "Political Preference," it described him as a "Conservative." The register also included one Republican, Isaiah T. Montgomery, a Negro planter and business-

64 Memphis *Commercial*, clipping, no date. Internal evidence indicates summer of 1890.
65 Memphis *Daily Commercial*, January 5, 1890.
66 Robinson, "A Sketch of James Lusk Alcorn," 43.
67 J. B. Chism, *et. al.*, to James Lusk Alcorn, July 3, 1890, in possession of Mrs. V. A. Hain.

man, one "National Republican," H. F. Simrall, who had been Chief Justice during Republican rule, one Greenbacker, and 130 Democrats.

Alcorn and Simrall were received with unusual deference and consideration by the Democratic majority. They were quoted as not being afraid of Negro supremacy, and while they were deeply concerned that neither the law nor the spirit of the Constitution be violated, they were in complete sympathy with the prevailing wish of the white people of Mississippi "to have a better condition of things at the ballot box." The *Weekly Appeal*, a Democratic newspaper, believed that "in all their careers, they have never been so favorably situated for a fair and considerate hearing of their views." [68] As a further gesture to their age and standing, they, together with four others similarly honored, were allowed to choose their seats in the hall ahead of the other delegates[69]—quite a concession for a group of men meeting in the August heat of a Mississippi summer before the age of air-conditioning.

Alcorn was surprisingly active in spite of his age and the disabling nature of the strokes he had suffered, which had partially paralyzed his facial muscles. He was present at every session except the first one, and had something to say about most of the subjects debated. He was a member of the committees dealing with the militia and penitentiary reforms, and the all-important one dealing with elections and franchise. During the opening discussion on rules he delivered a plea for "a full and free opportunity for the minority to be heard in debate," and such a rule was adopted.[70]

Perhaps remembering some of his own difficulties as governor, he defended a proposed clause for the new constitution which would provide permanent funds for a militia, rather than leave the matter to the legislature. When asked if he was afraid to trust the legislature in this matter, he replied bluntly that he was.[71] However, the change was not adopted and the legislature retained its control.[72]

68 Memphis *Weekly Appeal*, August 20, 1890.
69 *Journal of the Proceedings of the Constitutional Convention of the State of Mississippi* (Jackson: E. L. Martin, 1890), 17.
70 Memphis *Weekly Appeal*, August 20, 1890.
71 *Ibid.*, September 10, 1890.
72 Francis Newton Thorpe, (ed.), *The Federal and State Constitutions, Organic Charters, and Other Organic Laws* (Washington: Government Printing Office, 1909), VI, 2116.

During a discussion on temperance Alcorn became involved in some particularly obtuse reasoning in support of his stand against additional regulations of the sale of liquor. The people of Mississippi, he argued, obviously wanted saloons or they would not exist. If these saloons were not dignified by being licensed, and if everyone had the privilege of selling liquor, they would soon become disreputable places. Penalizing something merely increased the people's fondness for it.[73] He may have been thinking of the bothersome petition he had to make to the Coahoma County Board of Supervisors each year for a license to sell liquor at his plantation store.

Members of the more radical farm groups and incipient Populists urged adoption of a clause to provide for an elected judiciary, pointing out that the constitution of 1832 had included such a provision. Alcorn opposed them, replying that the people were not as well informed now as they had been then, and that he doubted the proposed franchise plan would justify a change. He was part of the majority who voted to table the proposed clause. He also voted with the majority against dropping the office of lieutenant governor.[74] A strong government was still attractive to him, if it were not too democratic.

The Committee on Rules reported unfavorably on the creation of a Special Committee on Rivers and Harbors, Levees, Waterways and Navigation. With Alcorn's help the committee's report was rejected and the proposed special committee established, but Alcorn was not named to it.[75] He was active, however, on the Penitentiary Committee and supported a plan of his fellow Coahoma delegate, Cutrer, to work the convicts on the levees under state supervision. He noted that before the war (he referred to it as "the flood") slave owners had treated their slaves kindly and found humane overseers for them. The state could do likewise with the convicts, and he added that not until the Democrats had come into power did abuses begin in the convict leasing system. The *Weekly Appeal* felt that the two delegates from

---

73  Memphis *Weekly Appeal*, October 1, 1890.
74  *Ibid.*, October 15, 1890.
75  *Ibid.*, August 27, 1890; however, Cutrer, almost 40 years later, claimed that Alcorn had been a member. *Proceedings of a Reunion of the Survivors of the Constitutional Convention of 1890* (Jackson, Mississippi: published by the Department of Archives and History, n.d.), (meeting held November 1, 1927), 21.

Coahoma County, through their speeches, succeeded in divesting the idea of its horror,[76] and the convention responded to the extent of adopting a section permitting the use of convicts on public works as part of Article X.

Through his efforts on behalf of this article Alcorn contributed toward a reform he had unsuccessfully advocated as governor. It forbade the leasing of convicts to private contractors after December 31, 1894, authorized the legislature to establish a state farm, and restricted the practice of also leasing county prisoners.[77] For a time the prohibition on convict leasing was successfully circumvented, but by 1906 the state had regained control of all its prisoners.[78]

The most important object of the convention was the elimination of the Negro vote, and for this purpose the Committee for Elective Franchise, Apportionment and Election was created. Almost one-fourth of the delegates at the convention were on it, including Alcorn, and out of it came the "understanding clause," [79] the first of the many subterfuges the South would use to disfranchise the Negro without violating the letter of the Fifteenth Amendment.

Its adoption did not come about without a struggle. The Delta delegates preferred property and educational restrictions; as H. F. Simrall expressed it, all that was necessary could be accomplished by giving the vote "to virtue and intelligence (and that means the white people)." [80] J. Z. George and Edward L. Mayes (Lamar's son-in-law) speaking for the white counties, favored reducing representation in the black counties through reapportionment. Some Delta delegates responded by threatening to vote for a public ballot on the constitution, then attempting to defeat it at the polls.[81] Alcorn was part of the minority of the committee which made an

76  Memphis *Weekly Appeal*, September 10, 1890.
77  *Journal . . . of the Constitutional Convention*, 1890, pp. 671–72; Thorpe, *Federal and State Constitutions*, 2117; J. H. Jones, "Penitentiary Reform in Mississippi," *Mississippi Historical Society Publications*, VI (1902), 118–19.
78  Kirwan, *Revolt of the Rednecks*, 169; Woodward, *Origins of New South*, 424.
79  *Journal . . . of the Constitutional Convention*, 1890, p. 676. "To qualify every elector shall . . . be able to read any section of the constitution of this State; or he shall be able to understand the same when read to him, or give a reasonable interpretation thereof. . . ," which left to the discretion of the registrar of voters who was eligible to vote.
80  Memphis *Weekly Appeal*, September 24, 1890.
81  *Ibid.*, August 20 and September 17, 1890.

attempt on the floor of the convention to have the words: ". . . or he shall be able to understand the same when read to him or give a reasonable interpretation thereof," stricken from the clause.[82] This would have reduced it to a simple literacy test, thereby eliminating ignorant white voters also. The convention adopted the "understanding clause" as presented, a reapportionment plan, and, perhaps as a concession to the Delta, retained the poll tax, but with the proviso that collection could not be enforced by criminal proceedings.[83]

The hill counties would appear to have won their real victory in the reapportionment plan, although historians disagree on the effectiveness of the changes.[84] The constitution of 1890, which is still in effect, rearranged representation by creating new counties so that a clear majority in the state house of representatives would be from counties having white majorities. It also stipulated that to be elected to any state office a candidate must receive a majority of the votes cast as well as a majority of the 140 electoral votes, which corresponded, county by county, to the number of representatives in the house. If a candidate should not get both, the election would be thrown into the house where the white counties had a majority.[85] Most of the delegates from the Delta opposed the plan, and Alcorn was among the many who spoke against it, but apparently he did not doubt its efficacy once passed, since he was later quoted as saying that under it white supremacy would be guaranteed even though all Negroes were allowed to vote.[86]

In view of rising opposition throughout the state, the convention decided not to submit its new constitution to the voters, but instead it declared it the law of the land itself. After listening to a closing speech extolling white supremacy, the convention

---

82 *Journal . . . of the Constitutional Convention,* 1890, p. 542.
83 *Ibid.,* 676.
84 Woodward, *Origins of New South,* 340–41; Albert D. Kirwan, "Apportionment in the Mississippi Constitution of 1890," *Journal of Southern History,* XIV (1948), 245; Alfred H. Stone, "The Basis of White Political Control in Mississippi," *Journal of Mississippi History,* VI (1944), 225; William Alexander Mabry, "Negro Disfranchisement in Mississippi," *Journal of Southern History,* IV (1938), 326; Edward Henry Hobbs, *Legislative Apportionment in Mississippi* (Oxford, Miss.: University of Mississippi, 1956), 13–14.
85 Stone, "Basis of White Political Control," 225.
86 Kirwan, *Revolt of the Rednecks,* 81–83.

adjourned and Alcorn returned home, expressing himself satisfied with the results.

He probably had in mind the points he successfully supported; an end to convict leasing, use of convicts on public works, retention of the clause prohibiting payment of the Planters' and Union bank bonds, and a clause specifically authorizing the state to accept federal aid for levees. But what he did not see in his endorsement of its guarantee of white supremacy was that this did not turn the state back from the threat of "ignorant black rule" to an age of enlightened Whig administration. Rather, it returned the state to a position roughly analogous to that of the immediate prewar Democratic rule, when "fire-eating" Southern nationalists had overruled conservative planters to lead the state into a disastrous war. Under the new constitution the "Bourbon" rule of Lamar, Walthall, and George gave way to the rise of the "rednecks" under James K. Vardaman and Theodore G. Bilbo. Mississippi turned its face to the past, but not the past as Alcorn envisioned it.

His part in the constitutional convention was his last public activity, and it was proper that, as he had taken part in the start of Reconstruction and was active during the period, he should have participated in the removal of the last evidences of it from his state. His role throughout this era has been subjected to harsh criticism, but while it needs to be evaluated critically, his opponents on the whole, have chosen to attack the wrong aspects and have overlooked his real weakness.

His vanity and boastfulness, in the idiom of the nineteenth century, were not inordinate, and the degree to which he appears opportunistic was also well within the ethical limits of his period. His drive for power was tempered, by a desire to serve and a love of country (as he comprehended that concept). Personal desire was also restrained by a strong sense of personal right and wrong, moral values which were implanted by his religious upbringing. Such politicians, as America knows, are not always right or wise, but they are seldom vicious and have contributed more to, than they have detracted from, the welfare of their country. Alcorn belongs well within the limits of this group.

His apparent willingness to associate with and make concessions to Negroes has been roundly condemned by race-conscious historians. Secure in his own sense of class identification, he saw no danger to his status because he worked with and for his Negro constituents, nor did he feel the need for the barriers and regulations in race relations which his less socially secure critics were demanding. It was not a belief in equality that he demonstrated, but rather a much stronger faith in the immutable nature of an unequal society than that of his opponents who were proclaiming this doctrine so noisily.

Nor can his efforts to provide a share of Mississippi's political life to the Negroes be regarded as demagoguery. As was evident during his term as governor and his support of fusion politics in the Delta, the role assigned the Negroes would always be a minor one. Had he really been willing to use the race issue to forward his own political fortunes he had two excellent opportunities in 1873 and again in 1875, when he could have joined either group of extremists and exploited his own abilities and prestige. However such an appeal to the emotions of the mob, which would serve later politicians so well, was alien to his concept of the gentleman in politics. One might run with the mob for a time in order to guide it down a road which reason and morality approved, but one did not deliberately arouse or pander to such passions.

The failure of his public career can indeed be explained by his weaknesses, but they were not those pointed out by his enemies. Briefly put, he lacked the breadth of vision necessary to grasp some of the implications underlying the changes with which he tried to deal. He recognized that it was Jacksonian democracy which was thwarting him, but he did not understand how it was doing this; namely, by destroying class lines and thereby bringing about a naked confrontation of the two races. Alcorn's solution was an attempt to return to the past, the pre-Jacksonian past, and he hoped to cage the lion of race adjustment within the confines of social classes. He did not realize that the novelty of the challenge he faced required responses transcending previous experience. Alcorn was a practical rather than an imaginative man, but it must be remembered that no one else effectively answered the challenge.

In 1890 a reporter described Alcorn as having been a "Whig among Whigs," and as being more Whig than Republican.[87] The proud young man who had navigated a houseboat down the Ohio and Mississippi rivers in search of his fortune never changed the form in which he would accept that fortune. Upon a basic and

87 Memphis *Commercial*, clipping, summer of 1890.

consistent Federalist-Whig doctrine he erected a pragmatic super-structure of practical actions which seemed to guide him on a tortuous course across Mississippi history. At the end of the rainbow lay the prize he had sought all along—lands and the duties and privileges of an aristocratic way of life which they supported. Ambition and a deep sense of duty and destiny drove him on, and his frontier background and practical bent of mind led him down unusual paths. But as he achieved his goal, performed his duty to the best of his ability, and fulfilled his destiny, he returned to the orthodox ways of the past. Alcorn began and ended his career as a Whig.

His health failed steadily after 1890, and by 1894 he was in a wheelchair. On Thursday, December 20, 1894, at 12:55 A.M. he died quietly at Eagle's Nest. As befit the patriarch of the family, he was buried at the center of the Indian mound he had selected for the family cemetery. Directly over his grave stands his statue: the stocky, erect figure in a Prince Albert coat, one hand tucked into his vest and the other holding the speeches he loved to make. His hair flows down onto his shoulders and his face is hidden behind drooping mustaches and a full goatee, but under bushy eyebrows the piercing eyes gaze west toward the Mississippi River and across the cotton fields that symbolized so much to him.

# Critical Essay on Authorities

COLLECTING DATA ON Alcorn presents a challenge to the researcher. The surviving Alcorn letters are primarily personal and are, in rather even proportions, in the Southern Historical Collection, of the University of North Carolina, the Mississippi Department of Archives and History, and in the possession of Alcorn's granddaughters living in Hot Springs, Arkansas. Several diaries written by Alcorn, as well as some kept by his wife Amelia, are extant and, with the exception of one at the University of North Carolina, are owned by descendants of Alcorn. These diaries contain mostly agricultural and household information, but the one kept by Alcorn in 1863 was valuable for its observations on the war in the Delta, and the ones covering the later years of his life aided in sketching the scope of his social life.

The Rainwater Collection in the Mississippi Department of Archives and History includes a small but valuable collection of copies of Alcorn letters, the originals of some of which have disappeared. A few additional letters have been found among the Lamar and Mayes papers in the Mississippi Department of Archives and History, in the J. F. H. Claiborne collections at the University of North Carolina and in the Library of Congress, in the Hamilton Fish Letter Books at the Library of Congress, in the Rutherford B. Hayes Library, Fremont, Ohio, and in the William Alexander Graham, William Leroy Broun, and Kenneth Rayner collections at the University of North Carolina. The Mississippi Department of Archives and History has an Alcorn File containing the manuscript biography by his son-in-law, Charles Swift, Jr. and some personal letters, among which are the letters he wrote while he was courting Amelia; and additional letters were found in the Governors' Correspondence files. The Mississippi Department of Archives and History, the National Archives, and the *Official Records* together contain a nearly complete collection of messages he wrote and received relative to his war experience. All the above, numbering fewer than 150 pieces, would seem to compromise the Alcorn papers, exclusive of pamphlets and official messages.

Since Alcorn was particularly articulate in the Senate, the *Congressional Globe* and *Congressional Record* for the Forty-Second, Forty-Third, and Forty-Fourth Congress are very helpful in showing his views on a number of subjects; in fact, he had something to say about almost every issue that came up for consideration when he was present. Also rewarding to the careful user are the pertinent sections in the two voluminous congressional reports on violence in the South: House Reports, 42nd Congress, 2nd Session, No. 22 (1872) and Senate Reports, 44th Congress, 1st Session, No. 527 (1875). The *Journals* of the House of Representatives and the Senate of the State of Mississippi for the years when Alcorn was a member provide some information, although necessarily sketchy, except for some excellent reports on levee construction he submitted in 1858, 1859, and 1861, and, of course, his Inaugural and Annual messages. Although they left a great deal unsaid, the *Journals of the State Conventions* of 1861, 1865, and 1890 were helpful, as were the *Reports of the Auditor of Public Accounts to the Legislature of Mississippi* for the years 1870, 1871, 1875, 1878–79, and 1880–81 for a comparison of expenditures in those periods. One unofficial report which turned out to be inaccurate but interesting for its sidelights was the *Proceedings of a Reunion of the Survivors of the Constitutional Convention of 1890* (Jackson, n.d.; [meeting held November 1, 1927]). Another, which contributed to knowledge of the Republican Party in Mississippi after 1875, was the *Official Proceedings of the National Republican Convention of 1868, 1872, 1876 and 1880* (Minneapolis, 1903).

Alcorn's views as expressed in pamphlets he had published appear to be well covered in the following: *Address of J. L. Alcorn, (Republican Candidate for Governor) to the People of Mississippi* (n.p., 1869); *An Address to the People of Coahoma County, Mississippi, Upon the Subject of Levees* (Memphis, 1858); *An Address to His Excellency, William McWillie, Governor of the State of*

*Mississippi, upon the Subject of Levees, and The Reforms in Legislations; and Administration Necessary to Success* (Memphis, 1858); *The Case of Mississippi Stated (Governor Alcorn to the Editor of the New York Tribune)* (Jackson, 1871); *Letter of Gov. Jas. L. flow Lands on the Mississippi River* (Jackson, 1870); *Memorial flow Lands on the Mississippi River* (Jackson, 1870); *Memorial by J. L. Alcorn to both Houses of Congress* (Washington, 1866); *Mississippi River Levees, Speech of Hon. J. L. Alcorn. Senate of the United States. Jan. 21, 1873* (Washington, 1873); *Special Message of Gov. James L. Alcorn on the Subject of the Establishment of a University for the Colored People, Etc.* (Jackson, 1871); *To the Voters of Coahoma* (Denver, 1887); *Views of the Hon. J. L. Alcorn on the Political Situation of Mississippi* (Friar's Point, Mississippi, 1867). Other pamphlets directly cited for their pertinency were two by James R. Chalmers, *The Opinions of the Fathers upon the Power and Duty of the General Government to make Internal Improvements. Collated by Hon. J. R. Chalmers, of Mississippi, to Encourage Aid for the Mississippi Levees and the Texas & Pacific Railroad* (n.p., 1878); and *The Tariff—The Use of United States Troops in Elections—A Defense of "The Mississippi Plan"—Military Academy—Coinage of Silver Dollars* (n.p., 1878); also Amos R. Johnston, *Speech of Hon. Amos R. Johnston at Sardis, Mississippi, October 13, 1869, on Alcorn's Record* (n.p., 1869), and John W. Wood's defense of his actions in *Union and Secession in Mississippi* (Memphis, 1863).

Newspaper coverage of Alcorn's activities was sporadic, and research was hampered by incomplete files and the fact that he belonged to minority political groups whose organs of publication, particularly the Republican ones, were not as widespread or as vocal as those of the Democrats. The best continuous source of information throughout his career was the Memphis *Commercial-Appeal* under its various names. Other pre-Civil War newspapers which were helpful were the Grenada, Mississippi, *Harry of the West*, the Jackson *Southern* and *Flag of the Union*, the Natchez *Courier*, the Vicksburg *Southern Herald*, and the New Orleans *Daily Picayune*. The only newspaper during the war found to have mentioned Alcorn was the *Mississippian* of Jackson. For the postwar period, the single most valuable discovery was an almost complete file of Robert J. Alcorn's short-lived newspaper, *The Leader*, in the Carnegie Library at Clarksdale, Mississippi. Other newspapers used were the Friar's Point, Mississippi, *Coahomian, Delta,* and *Gazette,* the Oxford, *Falcon,* the Bonneville, Mississippi, *Prentice Recorder,* the Vicksburg *Herald,* the Jackson *Clarion,* under its various name combinations, and the *Pilot.* The New York *Tribune* provided consistent coverage of the highlights of Alcorn's Reconstruction career. Individual items were gleaned from the San Francisco *Alta California* and the Hot Springs, Arkansas, *Republican.*

For additional insight and information one has to turn to contemporary writings. The richest of these is Blanche Butler Ames's two-volumed *Chronicles from the Nineteenth Century* (1957) which contains priceless material on the situation both in Mississippi and in Washington during the Reconstruction period. Other contemporary views of Alcorn can be found in Reuben Davis, *Recollections of Mississippi and Mississippians* (New York, 1891), H. S. Fulkerson, *A Civilian's Recollections of the War Between the States* (Vicksburg, 1886), Frank A. Montgomery, *Reminiscences of a Mississippian in Peace and War* (Cincinnati, 1901), and Robert Somers, *The Southern States Since the War* (New York, 1871).

No full-length study of Alcorn has been written for publication, and of the available biographical sketches the best one is that by Mrs. Mary Fisher Robinson, "A Sketch of James Lusk Alcorn," in *The Journal of Mississippi History,* XII (1950). The others tend to be factual but not always completely accurate, and when they venture a judgment, they seem, with varying degrees of enthusiasm, to portray him as probably sincere but misguided in his efforts, trying to stand between the people of Mississippi and the rapacity of the carpetbaggers. Interestingly, the sketches closer in time to the events of his life were the more sympathetic and accurate ones. The unpublished manuscript study in the Mississippi Archives by Alcorn's son-in-law, Charles Swift, Jr., appears to be based on reminiscences by Alcorn and members of the family, collected years later. It contains sections taken completely from Robert Lowry and William McCardle, *A History of Mississippi* (Jackson, Miss., 1891), and corroborating evidence for many of its statements and conclusions has been impossible to find.

Except for sidelights and some purely factual information, little reliance was placed on secondary accounts of Alcorn's life. The sketch of the opening years of Alcorn's career contained in John Livingston, (ed.), *American Portrait Gallery, Containing Portraits of Men Now Living* (New York, 1854), especially conveyed a valuable sense of immediacy. Also of direct help were Henry S. Foote, *The Bench and Bar of the South and Southwest* (St. Louis, 1876), which contained a contemporary's reaction to Alcorn's rise to prominence, and Dunbar Rowland, (ed.), *Mississippi*, four vols. (Atlanta, 1907), the secondary account of his career upon which most subsequent sketches have been based. In addition, Rowland's *History of Mississippi* (Chicago-Jackson, 1925) was used, as were Clayton Rand, *Men of Spine in Mississippi* (Gulfport, 1940), and William B. Hesseltine, *Confederate Leaders in the New South* (Baton Rouge, 1950).

Works which particularly aided in placing Alcorn within the general complex pattern of his times before the Civil War were Gerald M. Capers, Jr., *The Biography of a River Town. Memphis: Its Heroic Age* (Chapel Hill, 1939); Carl Russell Fish, *The Rise of the Common Man, 1830–1850* (New York, 1927); Avery O. Craven, *The Growth of Southern Nationalism, 1848–1861* (Baton Rouge, 1949); Edward Arthur Miles, *Jacksonian Democracy in Mississippi* (Chapel Hill, 1960); Charles S. Sydnor, *The Development of Southern Sectionalism, 1819–1848* (Baton Rouge, 1948); Vernon Louis Parrington, *1800–1860, The Romantic Revolution in America*, Vol. I of *Main Currents in American Thought* (New York, 1927); and Walker D. Wyman and Clifton B. Kroeber, *The Frontier in Perspective* (Madison, 1957). The Whigs are treated in a manner both pertinent and helpful to this study in Arthur C. Cole, *The Whig Party in the South* (Washington, 1913); R. McKinley Ormsby, *A History of the Whig Party or Some of Its Main Features* (Boston, 1859); Ulrich B. Phillips, "The Southern Whigs, 1834–1854," in *Essays in American History* (New York, 1910), a collection of essays dedicated to Frederick Jackson Turner; Daniel M. Robison, "Whigs and the Politics of the Confederacy," *East Tennessee Historical Society Publications*, XI (1939), 3–10; and Charles Grier Sellers, Jr., "Who Were the Southern Whigs?" *American Historical Review*, LIX (1953–54), 335–46.

Material on Mississippi politics and particularly the underlying issue of slavery was obtained from Henry S. Foote's *Casket of Reminiscences* (Washington, 1874); James Wilford Garner, "The First Struggle over Secession in Mississippi," *Mississippi Historical Society Publications*, IV (1901), 89–104, (a much less helpful work than his book on Reconstruction); Jack W. Gunn, "Mississippi in

1860 as Reflected in the Activities of the Governor's Office," *Journal of Mississippi History*, XXII (1960), 179–91; Cleo Hearon, "Mississippi and the Compromise of 1850," *Publications of the Mississippi Historical Society*, XIV (1914), 7–230; and most helpful of all, Percy L. Rainwater, "An Analysis of the Secession Controversy in Mississippi, 1854–61," *Mississippi Valley Historical Review*, XXIV (1937–1938), 35–42, and *Mississippi Storm Center of Secession, 1856–1861* (Baton Rouge, 1938). Background for this section was provided by Allan Nevins, *Ordeal of the Union*, 2 vols. (New York, 1947), and Walter Lynwood Fleming, *The Sequel of Appomattox* (New Haven, 1919). Excellent for agricultural conditions in Mississippi was Herbert Weaver, *Mississippi Farmers, 1850–1860* (Nashville, 1947).

Most of the information for the chapter on the Civil War came from letters, Alcorn's diary of 1863, and the *Official Records*, but some further light was shed by Ralph Wooster, "The Membership of the Mississippi Secession Convention of 1861," *Journal of Mississippi History*, XVI (1954), 242–57; Dunbar Rowland, ed., *Jefferson Davis Constitutionalist, His Letters, Papers and Speeches*, 10 vols. (Jackson, 1923); Andrew Brown, "Sol Street, Confederate Partisan Leader," *Journal of Mississippi History*, XXI (1959), 493–513. Background of a more general nature was obtained from E. Merton Coulter, *The Confederate States of America, 1861–1865* (Baton Rouge, 1950); Clemont Eaton, *A History of the Southern Confederacy* (New York, 1954); and Charles P. Roland, *The Confederacy* (Chicago, 1960). Only the article by Wooster contained any direct reference to Alcorn, but the others aided in placing him in perspective with regard to the Delta and the South during this period.

Among the many quasi-contemporary accounts of Reconstruction which appeared between 1890 and about 1905, only a few were cited, and these were used because of the revealing nature of their references to Alcorn or because of mention of pertinent incidents. Because these writers were caught up in the reaction to Reconstruction, their works have to be read judiciously. In spite of a most outspoken hostility to everything and everyone connected with Reconstruction, J. S. McNeily proved unexpectedly helpful in providing details in his series of overlapping articles: "From Organization to Overthrow of Mississippi's Provisional Government. 1865–1868," *Publications of the Mississippi Historical Society*,

*Centenary Series* I (1916), 9–413; "The Enforcement Act of 1871 and the Ku Klux Klan in Mississippi," *Mississippi Historical Society Publications*, IX (1906), 109–71; "Climax and Collapse of Reconstruction in Mississippi, 1863–1890," *Publications of the Mississippi Historical Society, Centenary Series*, II (1918), 165–535. Others close to the period whose works were of help were Frank Johnston, "Suffrage and Reconstruction in Mississippi," *Mississippi Historical Society Publications*, VI (1902), 141–243; W. H. Hardy, "Recollections of Reconstruction in East and Southeast Mississippi," *Mississippi Historical Society Publications*, IV (1901), 105–32, VII (1903), 124–199, and VIII (1904), 137–51; and Edward Mayes, *Lucius Q. C. Lamar: His Life, Times and Speeches* (Nashville, 1896). John R. Lynch, *The Facts of Reconstruction* (New York, 1913) must be considered an important contemporary account since its author was Mississippi's foremost Negro political leader, but while the sincerity of its tone impresses the reader, the number of things left unsaid due to Lynch's loyalty to the Republican party exasperates even more.

Although not containing direct mention of Alcorn, Charles Nordhoff, *The Cotton States in the Spring and Summer of 1875* (New York, 1876) was valuable for specific information on Mississippi at that time, although, in evaluating his judgments, one has to keep in mind the policy of the New York *Tribune*. Also somewhat helpful for background information was A. T. Morgan, *Yazoo, or, On the Picket Line of Freedom in the South* (Washington, 1884).

Two book-length studies of the Negro in Mississippi have been made: Jesse Thomas Wallace, *A History of the Negroes of Mississippi from 1865 to 1890* (Clinton, Mississippi, 1927), and Vernon Lane Wharton, *The Negro in Mississippi* (Chapel Hill, 1947). Wharton's book proved more helpful both with regard to factual material and interpretation. Education in Mississippi is discussed in Edward Mayes, *History of Education in Mississippi* (Washington, 1899) and Stuart G. Noble, *Forty Years of the Public Schools in Mississippi with Special Reference to the Education of Negroes* (New York, 1918), with Noble's work providing the broader view of education and including, as the title indicates, a worthwhile evaluation of the efforts toward educating the Negro.

For the purposes of judging Alcorn's efforts during reconstruction, the following works dealing with the neighboring state of Louisiana were helpful: Agnes Smith Grosz, "The Political Career of

Pinckney Benton Stewart Pinchback," *Louisiana Historical Quarterly*, XXVII (1944), 527–623; Francis Byers Harris, "Henry Clay Warmoth, Reconstruction Governor of Louisiana," *Louisiana Historical Quarterly*, XXV (1947), 523–649; and Donald Bridgeman Sanger and Thomas Robson Hay, *James Longstreet* (Baton Rouge, 1952).

Secondary works which contained specific references to Alcorn and were of help in tracing his activities during Reconstruction were David H. Donald, "The Scalawag in Mississippi Reconstruction," *Journal of Southern History*, X (1944), 447–60; Winbourne Magruder Drake, (ed.), "A Mississippian's Appraisal of Andrew Johnson: Letters of James T. Harrison, December, 1865," *Journal of Mississippi History*, XVII (1955), 43–48; William D. McCain, *The Story of Jackson. A History of the Capital of Mississippi, 1821–1951*, 2 vols., (Jackson, 1953); James Byrne Ranck, *Albert Gallatin Brown, Radical Southern Nationalist* (New York, 1937); Charles Richard Williams, (ed.), *Diary and Letters of Rutherford Birchard Hayes*, 5 vols. (Columbus, Ohio, 1924); C. Vann Woodward, *Reunion and Reaction* (New York, 1951; and John R. Lynch, "Some Historical Errors of James Ford Rhodes," *Journal of Negro History*, II (1917), 345–68, who also warned, with considerable prescience, against Democratic party propaganda's being accepted as history.

Other books which were helpful in providing information and interpretation with regard to the Grant administration were William Dudley Foulke, *Life of Oliver P. Morton*, 2 vols. (Indianapolis-Kansas City, 1899); William B. Hesseltine, *Ulysses S. Grant, Politician* (New York, 1935); Allan Nevins, *Hamilton Fish. The Inner History of the Grant Administration* (New York, 1936); and John Sherman, *Recollections of Forty Years in the House, Senate and Cabinet*, 2 vols. (Chicago, 1895).

Besides photographs and family reminiscences (particularly those provided by Mrs. V. A. Hain), aid in describing Alcorn's Victorian mansion at Eagle's Nest was provided in Mrs. N. D. Deupree's article, "Some Historic Homes of Mississippi," *Mississippi Historical Society Publications*, VI (1902), 245–64. Jacob E. Cooke, *Frederic Bancroft Historian* (Norman, Okla., 1957) indicates the brief interest Alcorn held for historians during his lifetime. Information on post-Reconstruction Mississippi politics, where they touched, however obliquely, on Alcorn in retirement, was provided by Albert D. Kirwan, *Revolt of the Rednecks. Mississippi Politics:*

*1876–1925* (Lexington, 1951); Vincent P. DeSantis, "President Arthur and the Independent Movements in the South in 1882," *Journal of Southern History*, XIX (1953), 245–363, and *Republicans Face the Southern Question—The New Departure Years, 1877–1897* (Baltimore, 1959). Miss Willie E. Halsell helped greatly in disentangling the party factions of the period with "Republican Factionalism in Mississippi, 1882–1884," *Journal of Southern History*, VII (1941), 84–101, and "James R. Chalmers and 'Mahoneism' in Mississippi," *Journal of Southern History*, X (1944), 37–58.

Background for the Constitutional Convention of 1890 was obtained from C. Vann Woodward, *Origins of the New South, 1877–1913* (Baton Rouge, 1951). Works which were helpful because they discussed issues considered by the convention were Edward Henry Hobbs, *Legislative Apportionment in Mississippi* (Oxford, 1956); J. H. Jones, "Penitentiary Reform in Mississippi," *Mississippi Historical Society Publications*, VI (1902), 111–28, Albert D. Kirwan, "Apportionment in the Mississippi Constitution of 1890," *Journal of Southern History*, XIV (1948), 234–46; William Alexander Mabry, "Negro Disfranchisement in Mississippi," *Journal of Southern History*, IV (1938), 318–33; and Alfred H. Stone, "The Basis of White Political Control in Mississippi," *Journal of Mississippi History*, VI (1944), 225–36.

For information on levee construction and the attitudes and reactions of the local population, Robert W. Harrison, "Levee Building in Mississippi before the Civil War," *Journal of Mississippi History*, XII (1950), and *Levee Districts and Levee Building in Mississippi. A Study of State and Local Efforts to Control Mississippi River Floods* (Washington, 1951) were invaluable; and John William Wade, "Lands of the Liquidating Levee Board Through Litigation and Legislation," *Publications of the Mississippi Historical Society*, IX (1906), 273–310, unraveled some of the intricacies of disputed land titles resulting from the actions of the levee boards.

The two reference works cited were Francis Newton Thorpe, (ed.), *The Federal and State Constitutions, Organic Charters, and other Organic Laws*, 7 vols. (Washington, 1909), and John Livingston, *Livingston's United States Law Register and Official Directory* (New York, 1859).

# Index